FOREWORD

Every piece of writing should have a name. I could think of nothing for this one that was not trite, or inane or boring, so I have titled it thus. It's a "No Drums, No Trumpets" thing (you can research that one for yourself).

When my granddaughter was about nine years old, she discovered that I was a good source of information on numerous subjects and would telephone for help with her homework. Unfortunately she spoke very rapidly with little regard for intelligibility and it would take several guesses and clues for me to interpret her needs. One evening the phone rang, and Katie asked if I knew anything about demons and sprockets. I repeated what I had heard to make sure that I was on the right track and she confirmed that I had got it right. Once again, I said "Demons and sprockets?" and once more she said yes.

I was stumped. "What else can you tell me about it" I asked, not wanting to say that I couldn't understand a word she said.

"Well, I think it is in Darlington Railway Museum" she replied, with perfect clarity.

The fog of misunderstanding lifted. "Ah, Stephenson's Rocket" I suggested.

"That's what I said, " she told me, since which time the expression has become part of the family lore, and the byword for anything unintelligible. It seems as good a title as any for my monumental literary work. However, my friendly neighbourhood publisher thought that the title "Demons and Sprockets" may well suggest that these words could lead the potential reader to infer that the subject matter was more suitable for children and involve some witchcraft. I beg you to take warning and do not let a juvenile read it.

The object of the exercise of writing this book is two-fold. I wanted to put on record the housing and living conditions as they were when I was a child, since so many aspects of life have changed since then. We take for granted now, things that were not even thought of in the first half of the twentieth century. My early experience of technology was winding up the gramophone. My second reason is rather sadder. Before too long, I shall be an old woman sitting in a chair, dribbling, and wetting myself. When that time comes, when I am even more tiresome than I am now, maybe you can read these pages and realise that I was once a child with childish fears and dreams. That I was a young woman, full of hope and looking for love. If you now experience passions and emotions, I trod those lanes long before you. I, too have shed bitter tears. Been there, done that, got the tee-shirt!

May your God go with you.

THE FROG STORY

Once upon about seventy years ago, there was a big little girl with freckles and brown mousy-coloured hair, which was uncompromisingly un-curly. Everyone else thought she was a little girl called Shirley, but she knew that in reality she was a frog. However, her father seemed to know the truth because he used to call her 'Funny Face', at the same time pushing at her nose with the palm of his hand and laughing. He wouldn't let the little girl call him 'Daddy' - maybe because he was ashamed of her, so she called him Johnnie instead, because that was his name. She used to tell people, if they asked, that she didn't have a Daddy. She only had a Johnnie, who seemed to be younger and more fun than a daddy. Nevertheless, she was sad that she didn't have a daddy, like the other girls and boys.

She knew she was different to the other little girls because anyone could see the difference. They were smaller, thinner, and prettier. They had daintier hands and nicer feet, curly hair and, very often, pink and white cheeks. Before she was six years old, the little girl knew that all the others would probably turn into beautiful princesses one day. She knew, even then, that she would just grow into an even bigger frog. With bigger hands and bigger feet. And straighter, mousier, hair, and absolutely no chance of a Handsome Prince ever wanting to kiss her and turn her into a Beautiful Princess.

One day she sat looking at herself in her bedroom mirror and she thought "Mirror, mirror on the wall, who is the fairest of them all?" (because she had seen the film "Snow White and the Seven Dwarfs"). The mirror looked back and seemed to say, "Not you, you ugly little frog. The best thing you can do is to be very good and well behaved. To work hard at school and be considerate and kind. Then, perhaps, people will love you even though you are a frog."

The Frog sat there looking at herself and she cried because she really wanted to be pretty and look like the little girls on the front of boxes of chocolates or in story books. She wanted to be lovable.

So the Frog spent all her spare time reading and doing quizzes -even learning the answers. She asked for extra homework, and tried to be one of the cleverest in the class. She tried to please the teachers at school, and her Mummy at home. Not that she was at all sure that her Mummy was her Mummy because sometimes she was told that she wasn't their real little girl at all. Sometimes they said that they had found her in a basket on the doorstep.

Well, if grown-ups expect children to believe that storks deliver babies, that Santa Claus delivers presents, that the Tooth Fairy compensates you for losing teeth and all the other rubbish they tell you when you are trusting and young, then why not believe every-thing? So, the Frog never really knew who she was, or if she really belonged anywhere.

At night in bed, the Frog used to lie awake for hours playing 'Let's Pretend' games instead of going to sleep. She would pretend that she had golden hair, all curls, and blue eyes and pink cheeks, just like the pictures in storybooks. Instead, she had rather yellow skin, which turned brown in the summer and got covered in little brown spots called freckles, and brown hair that one of her grandmothers called rats-tails. It was really rewarding to feel that she had rat-tails hanging from her head and this knowledge did nothing for her self-esteem at all. Sometimes she used to pretend that she had found a little girl with no Mummy and Daddy, who was dirty and hungry and poor, but who had fair hair and blue eyes. Then she could turn that girl into a Beautiful Princess - and that would be almost as good as being one herself. But, of course, that never happened.

There seemed to be very little chance that a Handsome Prince would ever even look at her, much less kiss her. However, because she went to the cinema rather a lot (there was no such thing as television in those days), she noticed that it wasn't always the prettiest girl who had the most appeal. Look at Bette Davies: not a thing of beauty! Sometimes a nice, quiet, kind but not particularly pretty, girl ended up with the Handsome Prince. Sometimes it was the clever, scheming one, who was not pretty but seemed to have an interesting way of moving and sitting. So the Frog decided to learn to walk like a Beautiful Princess, and move her arms and hands like one, and sit gracefully. This was quite hard for someone with big hands and feet, and who knew she was a frog with a funny face. Then disaster struck, and put an end to all her plans to become beautiful, mysterious, and alluring.

When she was nine years old, the School Doctor said she must have spectacles. Nasty round brown ones. There was a war on you see, and there weren't any pretty ones, and they made her even uglier. Only her big cousin, Joy, who was very nice looking, didn't seem to mind that the Frog was ugly. When they were together, playing pretend games, Joy always let her be the Princess, or Red Riding Hood, or Cinderella. She never noticed the turned-up nose with the bumps on the end, or called her Keyhole Kate like a character in the Beano (or was it the Dandy?).

The Frog did look like Keyhole Kate, and her schoolmates loved to tell her so. All except her friend Pat, who was even taller and whose feet were probably bigger, and who probably felt that she was in no position to laugh. Maybe she had no ambition to be a Beautiful Princess, or maybe she was just too kind to laugh at the Frog.

The years went on. The Frog worked hard at her lessons, and did lots of homework and was very popular with all her teachers and just a few of the other little girls. Then something happened that changed everything. Her Mummy took her to a place where a lady taught people to do ballroom dancing, and the Frog thought to herself "If I become a really, really good dancer, maybe no one will notice that I am a frog". So she decided to have private lessons, in the hope that she might get a chance, one day, to dance with a prince who might even kiss her and turn her into a Beautiful Princess. So for years and years she worked very hard and became a very good dancer; even teaching other frogs and some ordinary people too. She kissed a lot of frogs along the way, thinking that one of them would turn out to be a prince. Some of them looked like princes but they were not handsome inside. Then one day everything changed.

The Frog was sitting reading a book at a hotel in Spain, feeling very alone because everyone else was drinking and dancing and talking and generally enjoying themselves. Suddenly, a pale and rather insignificant young Frog came to talk to her because he thought she was lonely and might like some company. Of course, she would like someone to keep her company but a Handsome Prince was more the sort of thing she had in mind.

However, she didn't want to be too unkind so she let him join her and talk for a while. The next evening after dinner he came along in all his best clothes and asked if she would like to dance with him. She wanted to say no and nearly did, but he seemed kind and she did not want him to feel any more of a frog than he did already. So, fearing the worst, she went on to the dance floor with him. The moment he began to dance, as if a magic spell had been cast, he was transformed into a Handsome Prince. He thought the Frog was a Beautiful Princess, for some strange reason, but the amazing thing was that the moment he kissed her she turned into one. So they hopped off and were married and lived happily ever after, because no matter what anyone else might believe, they always remembered that together, they had been touched by magic.

CHAPTER 1
ALL THE MEN AND WOMEN MERELY PLAYERS

In 'The Gathering Storm', the first volume of Winston Churchill's monumental literary work, he stated in the House of Commons in November 1933, that extraordinary imports of scrap iron, nickel and war metals were entering Germany. He said that a military spirit was rife in that country and a philosophy of bloodlust was being nurtured in their youth. Seeing these forces on the move, and remembering that this was the same mighty Germany that fought and almost beat the world, there was alarm throughout the whole circle of its surrounding nations. Incredibly, the Prime Minister, of this country, Ramsey Macdonald worked for the disarmament of France and equalisation of arms for Germany.

Into this uncertain world, on January 13th 1934, I was born. I have lived in an uncertain and often dangerous global environment ever since and seem to have been fearful from the start. Perhaps the psychologists would find an explanation for this, not in world affairs but in my own debut. Bowlby, with his theory of maternal deprivation would certainly have a contribution to make. The one life experience my mother never shared with me was the pain and triumph of childbirth and the thrill of holding an angry squirming new life in your arms. Before I had the opportunity to make that momentous first trip, my mother was dangerously ill with an eye infection, hospitalised and in urgent need of surgery. I have been told that at one stage, my grandfather, who was on hand at the time, was informed that a choice might have to be made between saving the life of either the mother or the child. He quite naturally cast his vote in favour of his own offspring. In consequence, my mother floated through childbirth under a haze of anaesthetic, neither one of us was expected to survive. We both did.

However, because of the virulence of the infection, we did not meet again until I was ten days old and then only fleetingly. Who knows which of the nurses who fed, bathed and tended me, might have cuddled me, or held me in her arms. Did any play the role of surrogate mother or was I fed, bathed, and rapidly returned to my crib where my cries would be unanswered. I only know that for most of my life I searched for someone to hold me close and keep me safe.

On February 3rd we were finally allowed to return to the back-to-back terraced house that was home. It was my mother's 23rd birthday, a fact remembered by my Uncle Clifford, a prolific gambler and womaniser, but not by his brother, the husband who was never to be forgiven this or any other trespass. He denied fatherhood by refusing to be called anything but his known name, Johnnie, and he was Johnnie to everyone: Granddad Johnnie to his grandchildren and great-grandchildren, until the end of his days at 91. Many years later, he and I did have a revealing conversation one afternoon, as we sat across the kitchen table. I have no idea what prompted it; maybe we were speaking of the early days of his marriage to my mother. She always loved dancing, but he didn't dance, so it appears that she used to go alone to the local Palais de Danse, which I personally find a little odd, especially in 1933. One night, he followed her and saw her come out with a man, get into his car and disappear for an hour or more. "So, I don't know if I'm your father or not" he said.

"Are you serious?" I asked, not surprised at the thought of it. After all, both my parents were small of stature, I was 5 feet 9 inches when I was sixteen. All the same, I was astonished at the doubt being expressed now, after 65 years. Ten seconds of thinking time passed, then he said, "No, of course not " I never pursued it with him again, but it would explain a lot about his denial and apparent lack of interest in me when I was a small child. Two years after he died, I queried my mother, thinking that she might like to unload some long held secrets before she too went the way of all flesh, (she had been married to someone else for fifty one years) but she was adamant. She would be, I never knew her to admit to weakness or being wrong about anything, she was perfect and expected me to be a perfect replica of her perfect self. I must have been quite a disappointment!

However, let us move on to set the stage for my formative years. The house that was my home until the summer of 1938 was a back-to-back terraced house, number 27 Darfield Crescent, in the district of Harehills, Leeds. To my surprise, I have discovered that this particular type of housing is unknown to folk from less industrialised regions. Street after street of these humble dwellings was constructed in the later eighteen-hundreds and early nineteen-hundreds to provide basic housing for miners, mill workers and those employed in the steelworks and dockyards of the increasingly industrialised towns and cities around the country. Whole families would live in the same street or the one at the back and this provided a tight family unit in which the children grew up with a friendly knee never too far away and an aunt or grandparent who was readily available for minding the young ones and telling nursery rhymes and fairy tales. Today, grandparents may live hundreds of miles away and a television set, a computer or a childminder fills their places.

Our house was typical and is still standing today, in 2003. I suppose it was comparatively modern, certainly in comparison to the home of my maternal grandparents a few streets away. There was a yard at the front, entered through a gate, and at one side of the door, some steps led down to the cellar that was quite bright and airy as it had a large window through which the daylight entered. My mother, a frustrated dancer, later took tap-dancing lessons and used to practise on the concrete floor, wearing grey shorts and red tap shoes that made a wonderful noise. I never had the least desire to follow her example, but I loved watching her and listening to the sound of her fairly ample thighs slapping together as she danced.

On the ground floor there was a tiny kitchen, with a brick construction about three feet high, maybe the same square, in one corner. This had a little arched opening at floor level and a small fire was lighted under the archway, on Mondays. This was known as 'the copper', and was the washing machine of those days. Unfortunately it had no moving parts except for the housewife who leaned over and stirred the steaming brew heated by the fire underneath the arch. Where the smoke went to I do not know. The eventual evacuation of the water was also is a mystery. And, why it was called a copper when it was obviously made of brick was not made clear to me until I was in my forties. Only then did I discover that the huge brick structure housed a lining like a large stew pot, the sort in which cannibals supposedly boil up their man sized Sunday lunch, which was made of … copper.

The only living room was about twelve feet square, and was entered directly from the yard, so there was a curtain made of heavy fabric hanging over the door to keep out the draught. An open fireplace of grand proportions accommodated an oven with a water heater behind it, though I have no recollection of a bath, or even a bathroom. I am fairly sure there was a lavatory outside near the cellar door. There was no hall or passage so the stairs led directly from the living room. This necessitated another door and another blanket-like curtain behind which coats hung, giving the impression that someone was hiding underneath. That's what I was afraid of, anyway.

Upstairs there were two bedrooms and probably an attic although I don't remember that, but most houses of the period had an attic and a cellar. I could really enjoy a cellar now, all the junk could go in there, but of course I would have to have an armed guard to escort me down in case the bogeyman came to get me. Why do adults enjoy scaring small children? I've been frightened of the bogeyman all my life because stupid adults were wont to tell me that he would come and get me if I didn't watch out. The Bogey Man was my first demon. If ever I have to live alone again I hope I can afford to employ a minder.

Preferably six feet tall or more, very handsome and intelligent, amusing and useful around the house, who will protect me from all the bogey-men. The one I have at present is a little on the shorter side but his other talents compensate. He is known as 'my lovely David'.

I was fortunate to have a complete set of grandparents, plus one pair of great-grand parents, and for thirteen and a half years I was the only one of my ilk. For my maternal grandparents, Fred, and Ada Foster, I was the only one regardless of ilk. Fred was a brass-founder by trade, though quite what that means I do not know. I still have a brass fire rake, toasting fork and poker made by him long before I was born, all antiques now like their present owner. He was a silent hardworking man, a renowned judge at dog shows, and a writer for 'Our Dogs' magazine. Otherwise, he was totally unambitious. He preferred to hand over opportunities to his brother-in-law, Ada's

Grandad Fred Foster and the Author, 1936

7

sibling, Sam, who made a great success of his life, in economic terms at least.

Ada herself was a tiny martinet who, after a difficult confinement, was advised not to make a habit of procreating, and no doubt put her own interpretation on this, which could have been why Fred was so wrapped up in his dogs. He used to breed Yorkshire Terriers in the attic! My grandmother was fond of recounting the tale of her confinement, an experience that left a profound scar on her psyche. I understand, because she explained in graphic detail, that the labour was prolonged and the infant pronounced almost dead on arrival. The midwife wrapped up the tiny scrap and placed it near the fireplace and the Doctor said that further children would be inadvisable. I am in no doubt that this was interpreted as a stern warning not to indulge in any activity that may result in a pregnancy.

These two had started courting in their teens. She was two years his senior, and, because she told me she had been a shoemaker, I think that both families had emigrated from

Grannie Ada Foster

Northampton. Fred certainly started life there. Their house was similar to ours, but the access to the cellar was from the kitchen. There was no 'copper', but there was a bath, covered by a wooden top that provided a large and spacious shelf on which stood groceries, dishes, bowls, and basins. The removal of these would have taken some considerable time and involved finding an alternative home for the goods.

My only bathing experience in that house, either as a participant or as a spectator, was in an enamelled tin bath in the living room. Hygiene was not a priority. The lavatories were up the street, several houses to each of the two in the 'the yard' which also housed the dustbins, known as 'the middens'. To save the need to go trotting up to the yard at all hours, a pail with a lid was kept under the table in the kitchen and this was the indoor toilet, emptied every day by the long suffering Fred. No wonder the working classes were prone to disease: imagine cooking the family meals a yard away from a bucket full of effluent.

Each house had a key to their particular convenience, which had a scrubbed wooden seat and a hook behind the door from which hung sheets of newspaper cut into squares. If you wanted anything less hard on the private parts, you took your own supply on each visit. This more sensitive toilet tissue was salvaged from the material used to wrap loaves of bread after purchasing these at the bakery. Even washing was a beastly ordeal. The kitchen sink was about four inches deep, three feet long and made of stone, with a washbowl to allow for a little more depth of water but which unfortunately made the most horrible grating noise that set ones teeth on edge, when moved. The towel, made to last a week, hung behind the door, always wet and reeking of stale soap and water and usually threadbare. New towels were a luxury, and laundering a major operation, which involved stringing a line from one side of the street to the other in order to dry the sheets.

Following her dreadful experience in producing my mother, Ada was a determined invalid for the rest of her days, practising her deathbed scene until she was eighty-seven. At this time she must have practised it once too often and subsequently died, having worn down poor old Fred years earlier. She did not succumb to any of the ailments from which she had been dying: it was just old age and awkwardness.

However, these two were both devoted to me, in their undemonstrative way, especially my Granddad Fred. I well remember sitting at the dining table helping him rub and blend the tobacco for his pipe. Their living room housed a three-piece suite, a square table and four large dining chairs, a sideboard of gargantuan proportions, a floor-standing radio, a bookcase and writing desk, another cabinet and a birdcage. Moving from one part of the room to another had to be plotted on a plan otherwise a tragic accident could have disabled someone. This, of course did have a bonus aspect for Ada, because it was easier all round if she sat in her chair and let everybody else move about.

Meet the Great Grandparents and the Gibbon Family

Because of her mother's frailty, my own mother enjoyed a less than joyous childhood, spending most of it on her knees, scrubbing floors. In addition, she ran miles on errands to get milk, still warm from the cow, fish as soon as it was in the shop, then more milk in the afternoon. This entailed long absences from school from the time Dorothy was five years old - only her remarkable ability enabled her to emerge at fourteen years of age with a reasonable standard of literacy and numeracy.

By the time that I came on the scene, Grannie Ada must have come to the stage in her life when she could tolerate simple cow's milk that was delivered to the door. Maybe this was due to the fact that there was little alternative since the long suffering daughter had left for pastures new. This delivery of milk came courtesy of Tom, the milkman, who brought it round the streets in huge churns which were carried on a cart pulled by a tired looking horse. When he was heard to be approaching, the housewife would take a jug which was kept especially for the purpose, and meet him at the door where Tom poured the required amount from an aluminium measure. I understand that this was a down-market metal, some folks got their pint in a copper vessel. I have no memory of milk arriving at my own house in anything other than a glass bottle but Tom carried on with his horse and cart until at least 1946.

At one point early in of her working life, my mother was invited to join an accountancy firm, to be trained in that discipline and become a rare female accountant, but the drop in immediate earnings in favour of greater returns later was not acceptable to her unemployed father. I doubt whether she ever experienced mother-love and at twenty-one, she was probably grateful to escape into marriage, and retirement. In those days married women rarely went out to work but after a few months of marriage, she did, probably to earn the money to get out and put a foot on the middle-class ladder of home ownership. Her story was that my father did not take kindly to the expense of keeping a wife.

My father came from a very different environment. This was not because his family was superior. My paternal grandfather was a well-known drunk and wife-beater. He was a man of enormous charm on occasions and a magical character for a child, this particular child at least. However, because of his predilection for the demon drink and abuse of his wife, my father, the eldest child, whose imminent arrival had precipitated the nuptials in the first place, was farmed-out to be raised by his maternal grandparents.

These two, known to everyone, children, grandchildren and friends and neighbours alike, as Ma and Dada, lived in a very different world to their eldest daughter, who, at eighteen, was already pregnant with her second child. Dada, to the best of my knowledge, came from Flamborough, where there are still Gibbons who are probably relatives. One of these, George, is commemorated on the monument in the village square, which pays tribute to a lifeboat crew who perished in the line of duty. My great grandfather was John William Gibbon and his mother, Ethel Watson, hailed from Wold Newton. Ma and Dada Gibbon were on their way to achieving middle-class status via the locality in which they lived, though Dada himself had started his working life as an apprentice in the printing trade and climbed the promotion ladder in the same works until his retirement. By the time I was born, they lived in a much more salubrious area than their offspring, in a four-bedroomed, semi- detached house in a residential district in North Leeds, close to a huge park and relatively open country. Subsequently, my father went to a local school in a 'nice' area and followed in his grandfather's footsteps as far as work was concerned. He became a skilled printer, the first colour lithograph printer in Leeds. As soon as he became a wage-earner his parents reclaimed him.

In the meantime my grandparent's fortunes had taken an upward turn, Grandad's brother having died and left to him his house, his shop in Leeds market, and a considerable collection of jewellery and some silver. Later on Granddad became known throughout the family as 'the Old Man' though he was in fact only in his early forties when the name took hold. Having named his second son in his own image, he was also referred to as Big Clifford, as opposed to Little Clifford. After the move to a more respectable property, having formerly lived in the squalor of Brown's Yard, a true relic of the industrial revolution, he may have tried to mend his ways, as befitted his elevated position.

He still drank, but reduced the violence a little, although I did once witness him pulling off the tablecloth in his rage. Unfortunately, the Sunday dinner was on the table at the time but not for long. He then struck Granny Taylor and tried to push her down the cellar steps. Stories about him when under the influence abound but I only saw him unpleasant to that extent the one time. He was very capable of verbal unpleasantness, sober or not, and had a most volatile temper. The trait was inherited by my father, (and some would include me,) though in the case of Johnnie, it was over in an instant and he was all smiles again. Unfortunately, Grandad's actions under the influence of booze were not limited to the confines of his home.

One day, after a lunchtime drinking session, while driving home in his green and cream Wolseley saloon, along Chapeltown Road, Leeds, he hit a large old stone horse trough, killing his passenger and breaking his own legs. He never walked without a stick after that, but it didn't stop him drinking. I never saw him outside the house dressed in anything other than an immaculate three-piece suit, a bow tie, black shiny lace up boots and a Homburg hat. He might not be wearing his false teeth and he was often inebriated. In spite of this, he always looked like a gentleman. He once went missing for many hours but later telephoned from Scarborough to say the fancy had taken him, when slightly the worse-for-wear, to go to the seaside with a friend. He was dressed as usual except that he was wearing his slippers.

The house in which they lived, at 175 Harehills Lane, was a big step-up from my first home. Theirs was considerably more affluent and was my first introduction to the scent of money. There were two living rooms and quite a big kitchen. The cellar steps led from the back room which was next to the kitchen, and both of these looked out on to a walled yard and the back door of the next door neighbours house. From this living room, a passage led to the 'front room', the posh one. This had a bay window, fitted carpet, an enormous fireplace and a green velour three-piece suite. Unlike the best room at many houses, which only came into use at Christmas and for funerals, this one was under regular occupation.

The room had dark brown velvet curtains and an all-pervading smell of cigars. The Old Man only smoked cigars or Woodbines, a very small cheap cigarette, although he used to buy a better brand for me when he considered me old enough to smoke. I was five years old when I tried my first 'Passing Cloud' and he always kept some in the house for me. In view of this, the wife-beating, the drink-driving and the manslaughter that once resulted, he would possibly be doing time nowadays, and gambling with the prison officers. But I digress.

The one great and glorious thing about 179 Harehills Lane, which is unforgettable, was the bathroom. It was a real room, with a toilet that had a mahogany seat, white and navy blue tiles, and seagulls flying round the walls. I loved it, and used to bathe there at every possible opportunity. In fact until we moved in 1938 it was the only place I recall bathing at all!

The most wonderful thing in the house however, was Reba, a large crossbred wire-haired fox terrier. We were devoted to one another, and I desperately wanted a dog of my own. There were just two bedrooms in the house and when I stayed, which was every weekend until I was five years old and school intervened, Reba shared mine at least until I was asleep. Where my father and his brother slept when they both lived at home I do not know, presumably the attics were used as bedrooms then, though I understand that Clifford rarely occupied his own bed if a place in some willing lady's boudoir was available.

By the time I was old enough to venture alone up to the attics, they were used only as storerooms. They housed treasure, especially two old theatrical trunks full of sequinned and spangled costumes, a joy for a plain little girl who wanted to be a fairy princess. I used to spend hours up there pretending to be a star though when I was once presented with the chance to make the dream come true, I chickened out and flatly refused.

There was a strong theatrical tradition in the Taylor family. Granddad had enjoyed a spell treading the boards or so I was given to understand. He might have been a mere stagehand for all I know but one of his sisters, Evvie, was a song-and-dance girl, known at the time as a soubrette. Legend has it that her early marriage to a much older man was, in some way, 'arranged' and that she sat up in a chair all night rather than share her new husband's bed. The following morning, she absconded with Uncle Willie Henshall, a Jewish gentleman of German origin who was also in 'the business'. They lived in sin for the next forty years until Evvie's husband died, when she was made an honest woman at last. Uncle Willie, who I only met very infrequently since his business was London based, was a theatrical agent and used to put together second-rate shows which toured the music halls.

Along the way, Willie and Evvie produced two little girls, out of wedlock, and by the time the younger of these was in her teens, Evelyn Junior, known only as 'Baby' to the family and as the 'Blonde Bombshell' to the theatre going public, was Uncle Willie's star turn. However, he had another potential star under watertight contract. Playing second fiddle to 'Baby' in the billing, there was a comedian who deserved better than he got. His name was Sid Field, and he was spotted for stardom and offered lucrative contracts, which would have brought him, fame and acclaim. Uncle Willie said "No" and refused to release Sid from his ten-year contract.

I met him many times when the company was appearing at the Leeds Empire or Bradford Alhambra and it was he who wanted me to play the part of a little girl stolen by the gypsies in one scene from the show. What me! Dress up like a fairy and go on the stage. No way. Sadly, for Sid, his career had just taken off when he died, but he is still remembered today by the older generation and is a legend in the profession. His famous golfing sketch has been reprised by several of his fellow performers. Sid also starred as Elwood.P. Dowd in the London production of a play called 'Harvey', all about a man who had an imaginary friend who was six feet tall, named Harvey. Nothing odd about that you may well think. Elwood always carried his friend's coat and hat. The latter had two holes in it so that its owner could poke his ears through. Harvey was a giant white rabbit!

However, back to the family. Baby was a platinum blonde of minimal talent but great glamour who eventually became an agent herself and achieved some fame as the manager of Adam Faith and Sandie Shaw, among others, in the sixties and seventies. She had many glamorous friends in show business, one of them a speciality act, a contortionist and tap-dancer of considerable talent who eventually married Uncle Clifford, quite unexpectedly. At least, the family were surprised: Granny received a telegram from him in London saying "Send clean shirt Stop Getting married Wednesday".

The lady who became my Auntie Nan, was as thin as a rail and at one stage performed an acrobatic routine clothed only in a G-string and silver paint. She introduced 'toe-tap dancing' to this country in a short film, and had a small role in another film. It was very exciting to see a relative on the screen and even better to have the actual costumes to play in to my hearts content. It was a 'different' sort of childhood but very much stabilised by my mother, who was determined that I was not to be 'spoilt' and compensated for any indulgences of my paternal grandparents with her rigid discipline. For the rest of her life, she delighted in telling me that it took her all week to put right the damage done to my impeccable behaviour over the weekend by the pair to whom she only referred as 'the Taylors'.

I understand that Dada, my great grandfather, was an inveterate fumbler under the skirt of any woman unwise enough to be left alone with him and tales of the females in the family going around in pairs to provide a show of force are legion. Many years later, on the return journey from his funeral, Ma exhibited no grief but commented that his time had definitely come because he was getting very slow with the washing up. Her widowhood showed her to have some interesting facets to her character. She had grown up in a hard school in a period when it was common for ones children to fall foul of sundry infections such as Diphtheria and Scarlet Fever. I know that she had seven children in all, but two of her children must have been amongst the casualties because all photographs of the family portray only five, presumably, the ones who survived to adulthood.

Ma herself was hardy and tough and, when I visited Flamborough to spend holidays there, she went paddling with me in the icy waters of the North Sea and she was in her seventies at that time. The climb back up from the beach alone was enough to induce a heart attack!

My father had a cousin, George, who went to visit her when she was in her ninety fourth year and she failed to recognise him, telling him that he could not stay long because she was expecting her grandson. It seemed impossible to convince her that George was indeed the gentleman in question so he walked half a mile to another cousin and grandchild, Joy, who accompanied him and at last Ma welcomed him in. I will tell the rest of the tale in his words, passed on to me about two years before he died at the age of eighty-two.

"I took her to the Deer Park for a drink and when we got back to the house, she showed me to my room. It was February. There was no double-glazing and the room was icy cold. I slept in my socks and gloves. Next morning when I awoke, I couldn't see out of the windows due to the ice on the inside, so I got up and went downstairs to find her. There was no sign of her in the house but I could hear a banging coming from outside. I followed the sound and discovered Ma in the garage wearing only her nightgown, chopping sticks for lighting the fire, regardless of the cold. My God, she was hard. Do you know, they used to billet commandos with her during the war so she could toughen them up before they were sent to the front."

There were other examples of this. One night walking back from that same pub, again in her nineties, she took her handkerchief out of her pocket to blow her nose having forgotten that she had wrapped her false teeth in that very same hankie. When she arrived chez Ma, the teeth were not there! Fortunately it was summer so she set the alarm for four a.m. and she retraced her steps in daylight. There in the gutter were the missing dentures. On another occasion the weather was less favourable, she arrived back at her door and dropped her keys in the thick snow where they were impossible to locate. Undaunted, she curled up on the covered porch, open on two sides and spent the freezing winter night there until the milkman arrived at six o'clock armed with a torch. How she survived the icy night is a mystery but she was born before the days of central heating and maybe she had been well toughened in her youth.

My father used to call every Friday with green-groceries for her and one day was alarmed to find her in a sorry state in her armchair. She was incoherent but kept telling him that she was feeling no pain, so in view of her age he phoned the family who came to be with her when she passed on to pastures new and summoned the doctor. They were all sitting solemnly awaiting his verdict, but when the family medical expert descended the stairs he announced that the reason that she was feeling no pain was that she was blind drunk. Apparently she had ordered a half-bottle of Scotch with her groceries from the local shop and off-licence and consumed the lot, presumably so that it wouldn't go off once it was opened. After the second similar incident it was decided to put her out of harm's way and she lived her last two years in a residential home, eventually dying at ninety-seven. Her sister Maggie survived to a similar age. Her daughter Ethel, my grandmother, only lasted into her late eighties but the latter's sister Dolly nearly made the century. However the only man in the family to make really old bones was my father, Johnnie, who died two months before he was ninety-one.

Now dear readers, the stage is set, the players are cast, apart from a few bit parts, sundry so called aunts and uncles and the odd second cousin or friends. The main event is about to commence.

CHAPTER 2
MY LIFE ALREADY

According to the Baby Book kept by my mother, I was the perfect child. Naturally. Anyone who knew her would have been amazed at anything less. I weighed in at 7 lbs and 5 ounces, a good weight for a girl at that time and was baptised a month later, cut my first tooth on September 11th, and made a good walk on December 5th. See, perfect. The baby book says: "Shirley could dance as soon as she could walk and loved to sit on the floor lifting up her legs and touching her head." I probably liked flashing my panties, it took forty years to get out of the habit. Any innate dancing ability was in the eye of the beholder, I'm sure. My own recollection of my expertise was well below my mother's interpretation of my early efforts. In fact, I was regarded as clumsy and certainly saw myself as big, plain, and ungainly.

Happily for me, my mother was not alone in her approval of my skills and beauty; all my grandparents were equally besotted. They had to be, I was all they had, so I reaped the benefits. In the case of the Taylor family, these included the best that money could provide in the way of clothes, dolls, other toys, dolls houses, and staying at the best hotels in Blackpool, Morecambe or Bridlington. These benefits also encompassed occupying the best seats in whatever theatre we were attending. I had a magical childhood from one point of view, and probably the most magical part of it was Grandad Taylor, who made it quite clear that he, at least, considered me to be a Beautiful Princess. Unfortunately, my father nicknamed me 'Funny-Face' so I knew that I was really a frog.

When I was still very young, one of the most famous film stars was a small girl named Shirley Temple. She was all singing and all dancing, she had big brown eyes, like me, and a mop of golden brown curls, unlike me. I wanted to be Shirley Temple. I expect every little girl did. As a comfort, I was told that I was Shirley Pimple and that was the first nickname I ever had. Unfortunately, I heard that because of the risk of kidnapping, she had a bodyguard. I didn't.

I spent most of my childhood terrified that I was going to be kidnapped and the rest of my life expecting a bogeyman to appear from behind every door or corner. I don't like being alone at night.

Grandad Taylor had the ability to make me feel that I was good at everything. He would let me comb and cut his white wavy hair and laugh happily when I practically balded him, showing off to his drinking pals the next day. He would apparently share secrets with me, pretending that Granny was to be kept in the dark about sixpences slipped into my hand or chocolate or later on, five-pound notes. It was years before I learned that she had known all along. When we went away for weekends or even weeks in Blackpool, our favourite haunt, we used to stay at the Imperial Hotel, the best in town then, as it is now, and the room always had two beds, a double and a single. The single was for Granny and I can clearly remember tying Grandad's leg to mine with his pyjama cord to stop him leaving in the night. What a furore there would be these days if a four-year old were to share a bed with a gentleman in his fifties.

Sometimes, just the two of us went off together at half term, when I was eight or nine years old and I was free to roam around Blackpool on my own while he sat in the bar at the hotel with his cronies. Due to the war, The Imperial was closed to visitors at that time so we had to make do with The Palatine, now long gone. I rode on the open topped trams and in the horse-drawn cabs free as a bird and without fear of being abducted, that sort of thing didn't seem to happen then, or were we too busy with news of the war to notice such reports in the newspapers? At night we would go to shows, the best entertainers in the country used to appear in Blackpool but there were no illuminations. Unfortunately, they were turned off on the night of September 2nd 1939 for the duration of the war.

Due to my mother's drive to achieve middle-class status and give me the advantages of growing up in a middle-class environment we had moved from our back to back house in 1938, and now lived in a three bedroomed semi-detached house far from the smoke and grime of the town. The houses had been built on farmland and one access was via a dirt road past a field with real cows in it. The farm sold milk and eggs and apart from our street and the one that was at the back of us, three rows of houses in all, there were no other homes close by. The streets were surrounded by fields and a wood, and it was a lovely place to grow up. I could play in fairly open countryside yet still catch a tram and be in the centre of Leeds within half-an-hour of leaving our house. We had a large garden at the back of the house, which consisted of a lawn with borders all around, neither of my parents were very keen on gardening. We also had a smaller front garden that consisted of a lawn with borders round each side. You can deduct from this that not only did they lack enthusiasm but also vision, imagination and expertise. Then again, my mother had never had a garden before and my father, not since he had left his grandparent's house when he was fifteen.

I enjoyed being out in the fresh air though I used to spend lengthy periods looking under bushes to see if I could find a baby there. After all, I had been assured that this was where they came from. I presumed that I too had been discovered under one such bush although I was often assured that I had been found in a laundry basket, on the doorstep. Maybe this was merely a ruse to stop my annoying habit of kneeling down to peer below the branches of the vegetation whenever we went out. There was a period when I imagined that I had been dropped down the chimney by a weary stork that was sick of flying around with me in tow. There seemed to be supporting evidence for the case against me being the natural child of my so-called parents. I could not call my male parent 'Daddy' and according to them, I had appeared from nowhere. I was pretty certain that if I was naughty or grubby in any way, I may be returned whence I came, but in a much bigger basket. Eventually, some knowledgeable little friend informed me that, generally speaking, babies came from their mummies tummies. Fortunately, I learned to read at a fairly early stage and found a book describing the full horror of childbirth in some detail, so the truth was out. However, this did not reassure me that I had arrived in my parent's household by the method described in the previously mentioned manual.

My big friend at the time was the only boy in the street, Barry Caress, who was quite happy to do my bidding, and play any role I chose for him, although he was older than I, and very well informed. He seemed to know all about the rules for Cowboys and Indians, and Cops and Robbers, so we played far more interesting games than the other kids on the block. They were all female, older than we were, by at least three months, which is a long time when one is only four or five. I loathed them all, they seemed to think that I should do what they told me to do, and I was not used to being bossed about by other kids.

So, it was Barry and Shirley against the rest. Like me, he was not a thing of beauty, big-eared, freckled, and not too tall. Of course, I was freckled and very tall, but size-wise I was to meet my Waterloo in the very long shape of Pat Whitman, a little girl at school, who made me feel positively normal in terms of height. She was my Barry replacement. We never had a disagreement that I can recall: we were the best of friends until our choice of school sent us down different routes and soon after, we lost contact for more than fifty years.

I loathed school from the start. I objected to being one of a crowd, having to conform, to sit on a hard chair. And most of all, I loathed the all-pervading reek of wet knickers. Not mine you understand. The whole exercise of going to school seemed to be a waste of time, I didn't want to play silly games or play out in the playground with all the others. I thought school was about learning to read and do sums.

We all had our photographs taken, only once; the outbreak of war saved me from that indignity again. I looked plain and unattractive and certainly did not want a permanent record of that fact. It was only when I turned out to be brighter than the average bear, that school suddenly developed a little appeal. The one thing I dreaded was being required to read out loud, though it presented no technical difficulty. Nowadays, I do it at every available opportunity! Mainly because I like the sound of my own voice and partly because people tell me I am an expert at it. If I may quote the late Sammy Davis Jnr., "Gee, I wouldn't do it if I wasn't good at it".

I found going to school fraught with all manner of embarrassments and indignities. For instance, I loathed going to the ghastly toilets that smelt as though most children never made it to the actual lavatories. I particularly objected to the necessity of raising my hand during a lesson to request permission to visit the ablutions and the worst of all the horrors was having to strip down to my navy blue knickers, vest and liberty bodice for P.T. (Physical Training). This was another thing I grew out of but by the time I was happily flashing my underwear, it was not navy blue with a pocket. Sex discrimination was rife. I certainly do not remember any little boys running round in their underpants, which in those bygone days were distinctly unlovely.

I recall most clearly during one jolly, soppy gym class that the boys were standing waving their arms being trees, while the girls were curled up at their feet, maybe pretending to be fairies asleep (or in my case, a frog).

My problem was that I always had trouble getting to sleep, even in bed, so I looked upwards, right up the trouser leg of Michael T, my tree. Floppy underpants in no way restricted my view so I had the privilege of seeing his, without having to bargain and promise to show mine. I never told a soul, especially not Michael, but years later he had his innocent revenge by unintentionally ramming me in the solar plexus during a solo playground game and felling me. The resulting concussion laid me low for weeks, much of the time spent in a darkened room with vinegar poultices on my head. I wonder if there is any scientific basis for this remedy?

Perhaps before we leave this period, I should explain the meaning of the words 'liberty bodice'. This was a fleecy sort of sleeveless vest with vertical strips of reinforcing cotton adorned with rubber buttons in order that girls could in some way anchor their stockings. More I do not know because I never wore stockings but I do know that some children were sewn into their liberty bodices in October and released in May. I jest not! The rest of us used to change our clothes every week but remember we did not have washing machines, so the "wear once and throw it in the linen basket", rule did not apply.

The other subjects that I loathed were sewing and art. In Miss Ratcliffe's class I made a nightie, by hand, out of yellow winceyette. Why we were required to do this, I never knew since my mother was a needle-woman of some considerable talent, and I never wore a nightdress anyhow. I wore pyjamas. I think my mother had wanted a boy and so anything feminine was not for me. I did have two party dresses however, probably bought by my grandparents, the first one fitted me for two years and the second one the same. Number one was pink, the only pink thing I ever had apart from pyjamas, (remember, pink is what pretty girls wear) with a layer of net and frills over a taffeta base and small flowers and ribbons at the waist. The second one was the same only turquoise.

Number three never materialised. I was told that I looked better in plain things - well, you can't make a silk purse out of a sow's ear, can you? Or was it just because there weren't enough clothing coupons to spare for luxuries like party dresses? Not that something like the lack of a few coupons would have stopped Grandad Taylor: he would have bought some on the Black Market. For me it was a clear message: "You are a plain child, therefore you should wear plain clothes." Watch your mouths, Mothers, some kid might be listening and take what you say seriously. I took some comfort from the story of The Ugly Duckling and always kept hoping that one day I would turn out to be a swan.

One day, when I was about six years old, I stood looking at my plain brown little face in the mirror and weeping hot tears of despair, I was acutely aware that I was plain and so wanted to be pretty and loveable. I still do but I think it is too late now, I grow more like a frog and less like a beautiful princess every day.

My hairstyle was another source of aggravation to me. It was dead straight, mid-brown, referred to as mousy, and cut short in a bob of sorts, the back of my neck shaved by my mother or a hairdresser wielding handheld clippers with a resulting shower of fine hair down the inside of my clothes. A thick clump was dragged back away from my face with an incongruous chocolate box bow. It was a popular style but not with me. Many years later, my ex-husband took our daughter out and brought her home with the same style. I went ballistic, unfortunately not with him. He had beaten a hasty retreat so my precious girl got the full blast of my anger. I have asked for forgiveness but she tells me that the whole episode was of no significance to her. There you go, and I have been agonising over it for years.

All the other children's parents seemed old to me and I could not possibly imagine them ever rolling around on the floor playing silly games or doing balancing stunts, playing aeroplanes, we called it. My children and some of my grandchildren will know what I mean, ought I to explain? The larger, usually adult player lies on the floor flat on their back with both feet in the air at right angles to the body. Next they bend the knees while the second player leans forward to interlock fingers with the prone partner, while simultaneously establishing a good contact between the feet of the first party and the stomach of the second party. At this point the legs of the floor bound person are straightened, the other participant being elevated, at the same time lifting their legs and straightening their arms. It is possible to balance like this for several seconds and equally likely that there will be a collapse of one or both parties. For a child of any age it is a game of magical quality and I have played it as both aeroplane and lifting device certainly into my sixties.

The girl who lived across the road from us, also named Taylor, was my bête noir. She too was an only child and also of apparently more middle aged parents. Her name was Adele Taylor, I disliked her more than I disliked any other girl though quite why, I know not. Maybe it was because she was prettier and had long wavy golden hair, or maybe it was due to the fact that her parents treated her like a princess and she thought that she really was one. When Adele went to a party, she wore silver or gold shoes and her person and her party dress were protected by one of two ankle length hooded cloaks, one red, one blue, crocheted in wool and lined with some silky fabric. I hated her even more at parties. In addition to looking like a storybook heroine, I thought she was bossy, vain, and self-opinionated, though her parents were pleasant enough.

I came back to live with my father when I was nearly eighteen but had very little to do with Adele. However on the very cold morning of my 21st birthday, at eight o clock, Mrs Taylor knocked on the door bearing a gift. She felt sorry that I seemed to have no one to make my special day memorable. She was right. My mother had sent six pairs of nylon stockings, very practical but not the sort of gift to keep as a memento of a very special day. My only aunt, Nan, the reformed contortionist, gave me a truly horrid dark brown jumper and nobody was going to take me to the ball. Especially not if I was wearing that jumper. Adele's mother had brought me a lovely dress scarf in vivid colours. I wore it until it had faded to a rag. Thank you, Mrs Taylor: I never forgot your kindness, not to say your memory for dates. I think Adele married well, she was unlikely to have fallen in love with a poverty-stricken peasant or a penniless gnome. The last time I saw her, on a tram, she looked well groomed and elegant, thus silently assuring me that I was still a frog and that she was still a beautiful princess.

The only neighbourly relationship I enjoyed was with Jean Cotton, who came to live next door to us. The resident occupiers had done a bunk at the start of the war and rented their house for the duration to a family from Ilford in Essex. Mr. Cotton worked for a company called The Ragasine Oil Company and was certainly an older parent. He had fought in the First World War and as a result was a little deficient in the foot department. To the tune of two, in fact. He seemed to manage very well with the prostheses and could go for stomps in the country, I always wondered if he slept in the false ones in case an air raid necessitated a speedy exit from the house.

Jean, the only child, was four years older than I, but this never presented us with a problem. We had matching 'Siren Suits,' a fashion started by our wartime Prime Minister, Winston Churchill, intended to be donned when the siren warned of approaching enemy aircraft, and worn to keep us warm when we were sitting in the air raid shelter waiting for the 'All Clear' to sound. For some reason Jean was quite happy to entertain a younger friend, though she was small for her age and very thin. I was tall and more sturdily put together so we didn't look too incongruous when we were out in each other's company. We used to sleep the night at each other's houses and one year we went on holiday to Llandudno, the first two weeks with her parents in charge. They went home as mine arrived so we were very privileged to have three weeks holiday in wartime. Wow!

My amazing academic career continued as I learned to read write and do sums, at all of which I was an expert. I was also very, very, good and quiet and well-behaved because I had learned early in my life that I would only be loved if I were a good girl. At home, my mother met any misbehaviour with withdrawal of affection and an implied threat that if I failed to change my ways, she might leave me. In fact, she kept this up my whole life. I eventually grew up (i.e. after I was sixty) and I stopped caring.

One morning, when dressing me, my mother sussed out that I had spent some of the bedtime hours awake and engaged in a voyage of discovery around my more intimate body parts. To say that this knowledge incurred her disapproval is to put it very lightly. For the first time in my life I was told that I was wicked not to mention disgusting. And dirty. I knew that already, having once, aged three, filled my britches while playing outside. By the time I was four or five years old I had been indoctrinated in the belief that anything that went on below the belt was unspeakable grubby and unacceptable.

This was not an uncommon way to raise children, particularly the female variety. No doubt this served to keep them pure and virginal until their wedding night. At this time, the untouched and terrified bride was supposed to fling her knickers into the shrubbery along with her deep seated inhibitions and revel in the joys of sex.

I was never smacked. I was un-chastised on the outside, and irreparably damaged on the inside. Once when my teenage behaviour had displeased her, my mother displayed a classic demonstration of martyrdom involving total withdrawal of communication for several days. This was designed to show how much I had disappointed her and bring me to my knees in submission. Frankly my dear, I didn't give a damn and found the whole performance a tiresome piece of playacting, but I lacked the courage to say so and thus I sat it out and let her do her long suffering thing if it gave her some pleasure.

This was not the first or the last episode of this nature, so I spent my life afraid of losing approval and affection, growing up intimidated by authority figures. I did the complete opposite and beat the hell out of my children on a regular basis, trying to show that they were still loved even if their behaviour had temporarily been less than was tolerable. I hope it worked.

One day, my friend Pat announced that she was going to dancing classes at the Pamile School of Dancing. She had a special dress for the occasion, like a party frock only black. It had a white lacy collar and a red sash so I joined too, much to the delight of Mummy dearest who had made previous attempts to interest me in Terpsichorean delights, without success. This foray into tap dancing was equally doomed, neither Pat nor I seemed to be the right size, shape or have the right number of feet for tripping the light fantastic. In addition, we had joined after everyone else, it was hopeless trying to catch up. I never even got as far as getting tap shoes but because of my mothers' sewing skills, I did have the dress, it was almost like having a party frock again. A very much earlier attempt to interest me in dancing classes had failed miserably when I was about four. The sight of girls prancing about in ballet dresses horrified me: I was never going to do that!

My association with the Brownies fared only a little better. I'm not into group activities or games: I think I'm a loner and I will only play if I am the star of the show. Nowadays, the door of the fridge opens, the light inside comes on and I am ready to jump up and do my act. What a shame that my desire for stardom came too late, long after the opportunity had passed.

In addition to sewing and painting, making models, PE, games, and playtime, I loathed poetry at school, especially if asked to stand up and read aloud. I think most people will agree that this is a truly horrific experience, but along with the dancing, the sound of my own voice has become fascinating to me, and fortunately to some others as well. I was honoured to be asked to deliver a reading at both of my son's weddings and also did the honours at my mother's funeral. On this last occasion, the young funeral director came to me as I stepped down. "Lovely reading," he said wearing a synthetic but suitably sad and sympathetic expression, which collapsed around his jaw when I replied brightly: "Thank you, I do weddings and Bar Mitzvahs as well". This was something of an exaggeration, since I've never even been to a Bar Mitzvah.

However while I am on the subject of Jewish rites and rituals, I did have the misfortune to hear the circumcision of a week-old Jewish baby in St. James Hospital in Leeds. This was, for me, also the week-old mother of a baby boy, not Jewish, but bound for the same fate, unnerving. I did not do a reading on that occasion, though, a couple of years later, I did let out a small scream after the two doctors had left my house following the at-home snipping of my younger son when I found the unwanted piece of foreskin, on a saucer, which had been used in the bedroom designated for surgery.

In a way it was lucky that I was a loner because by the time I was six years old my mother was working four days a week at the fruit and vegetable stall in Leeds market. Previously, the business was owned by my great uncle but for many years now, had been the property of my magic grandfather. My grandparents ran the huge greengrocery and fruit shop with the assistance of a young man who did the heavy lifting and the occasional presence of my father's younger brother. Grannie Taylor made her contribution to the smooth running of the shop by sitting on a wooden crate in which the imported oranges arrived from foreign parts, keeping her eye on everyone else. She always wore a white cotton coat over her clothes to keep them clean. On her fingers a variety of rings sparkled and she invariably wore a fabulous pair of diamond earrings, inherited from her late sister in law and promised to me from the time I was old enough to admire them.

Unfortunately the business had been left severely in debt due to the gambling and womanising habits of my uncle Clifford and the drinking habits of my grandfather. The younger Clifford escaped the consequences by enlisting in the army shortly after the declaration of war on Germany. Both of them had used the till as a bottomless pit of funds. The difficulty came to light only when there was no more credit, they had reached the bottom. My mother could never resist a challenge and so once again, Dorothy to the rescue! She borrowed the money, using the diamond ring that presently sits on my finger and Granny's much greater treasure chest of inherited gems as security in order to pay off the creditors and then arranged to pay on delivery for all future supplies.

Quite why my mother undertook this task, for people she disliked, I will never know. It made no difference to our lifestyle since my father was not involved in the family business. However, her commitment to it meant that there was no one at home when I left for school, nor at lunchtime nor when I came home again at four o clock, in fact from eight in the morning until six-thirty at night. Not every day, just Tuesday, Thursday and Friday although I did go to my great-grandmother's house, not too far from school, on that last day for my lunch. She always made rice pudding and provided blackcurrant jam to put in it, which turned it an appealing mauve colour.

Also a working day for my mother, Saturday was the day when I dressed myself and caught the tram down to the home of my maternal grandparents for the day and spent my time in a dark living room, heated winter and summer alike by a coal fire. During the school holidays I used to fend for myself during the week and play with my dolls or my friend Pat or Jean next door. It was just as well that I learned to read at an early age because in the absence of company, I spent my time to reading. I devoured anything and everything, including general knowledge tests and adult novels. When I had measles and later on, chickenpox, I was left in bed with only periodic visits from Mrs Cotton next door to ensure that I was still breathing. Schooldays are the happiest days of your life. Get real!

There was one great advantage to my somewhat lonely life of reading and entertaining myself, one of the forms of entertainment came in the form of a polished wooden box with knobs and dials, from which came a variety of noises and sounds, according to the degree of twiddle given to said knobs and dials. This was called a radio and it became my friend. I knew all the radio actors and comedians by voice, faces were often imagined, but an annual publication, around Christmas time each year, "Radio Fun" by name, put faces to the funny men in sketch or cartoon form. I was delighted when the Americans came into the war because I could then listen to AFN (American Forces Network) early in the morning and hear The Jack Benny Show and The Bob Hope Show. These were the BIG American radio stars and the latter had a long career in films.

In addition to the fun bits, I used to listen to plays, the news programs, quizzes and classical music, and so I got on the right track for a pretty wide general knowledge. I learned how to light a fire, in the fireplace, and clear it out the next day ready for the relighting. There was no such thing as central heating and I had a fairly chilly existence. Even having a bath was a luxury; only five inches of water were allowed, though I never heard of an Inspector of Baths, or anyone being prosecuted for over-indulging. But, it may have been where the expression "Save water, bath with a friend" originated. By this time, there was a war on, you know.

CHAPTER 3
THE WAR YEARS

In the Daily Mail on Saturday, November 10th 1934, there was an article entitled "Germany Piling Up Guns" followed by a comprehensive report on the situation in that country. I discovered the yellowed newspaper in the bottom of an old trunk several years ago and kept it because the date was close to the date of my birth. I was about ten months old when the article was written. The persecution of Jews, gypsies, even the mentally-retarded was already under way in The Rheinland. Did nobody understand what was happening?

The correspondent reported that the artillery stocks were superior to those possessed during the World War, at which time the huge guns, nicknamed Big Bertha were able to shell Paris from a distance of thirty five miles. The Bussing and Daimler works were turning out not limousines but tanks and armoured cars. The former arsenal at Spandau which had been transformed into a furniture factory in 1919, was now manufacturing gun tubes and other munitions under the very noses of foreign military attachés. It was stated that the only industry to thrive in Germany at that time was in fact the war industry. Even railway coach works were turning out tanks and other factories made bombs and torpedoes. The workforce was subject to military rule and subject to the death penalty if secrets were revealed.

The Hitler regime was also organising coastal defences. At Swinemunde, long-range guns capable of a wide arc of fire lay in wait for any attack, the jetty had been repaired, and hidden shelters held huge stocks of machine guns. Fortifications, condemned and destroyed under The Treaty of Versailles, were now being rebuilt or strengthened and armed. The Scharnhorst, a battle cruiser of almost 35,000 tons was launched at Wilhelmshaven on September 3rd 1936 followed by her sister ship, the Gneisenau, only two months later. It is astonishing that the rest of the world turned a blind eye to all this for so long.

I clearly remember, in September 1938, Mr Neville Chamberlain flying back from meeting Adolf Hitler in Munich. I heard his triumphant return on the radio at my Grannie Ada's house and his now well known words "I have here, a piece of paper ...... peace in our time". His scrawny neck stood up from his wing collar looking more like a chicken's about to be wrung than a Prime Minister's. In a way, it was! The price of this so-called peace was an agreement not to interfere in Hitler's plans to occupy the Sudetenland area of Czechoslovakia. Only six months after the Munich agreement, German troops marched in and took over the remainder of that country.

By the time another half year had passed, Hitler's armies were jack-booting across Europe and our ineffective Prime Minister and his supporters could do little to stop Hitler's domination. Lord Halifax and numerous members of the aristocracy supported appeasement. "Let Mr Hitler have his way in exchange for Britain's safety from invasion"

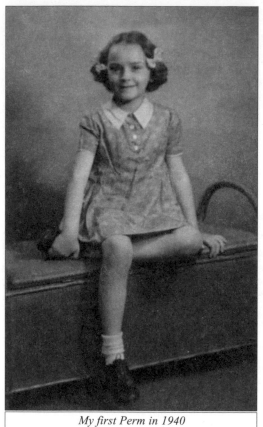

My first Perm in 1940

was their plea. Eventually, after the armies of the Reich marched into Poland, the British government issued an ultimatum to Hitler, demanding their withdrawal. There was no response from the Fuhrer to the British demands and at 11:00 a.m. on September 3rd 1939 war on Germany was declared and announced to the nation on the radio.

In fact, I was on holiday in Blackpool when that particular piece of unpleasantness began but not in residence at The Imperial. My mother, my father's cousin Joy (another magical character), and I were staying at a more modest accommodation. On the Saturday night, the 2nd, we had been to the early performance of the Ice Show on the Pleasure Beach. When we came out, the lights along the Golden Mile had been blacked out, not to come on again for nearly six years. The following day the shops were selling blackout material, cars poured in to collect holidaymakers and the world would never be the same again.

I suppose that there were many of the better-off British who were taking their holidays in Europe that summer and they undoubtedly bolted for home. These days there would be millions. Foreign travel was not as affordable to the masses in those days, nor did it figure in the lifestyle and expectations of the working and lower-middle-class families. Wages were often negotiated on an individual basis and employers paid as little as possible, at a time when the Unions did not have a stranglehold. Men working as bricklayers, plumbers, joiners, and decorators may have enjoyed a slightly better income than their brothers, the farmhands, the unskilled factory workers, and shop assistants. Few were house-owners and holidays, other than a week in a boarding house in Blackpool, Southport, or Hastings, were not even dreamed about. Equal pay for the fair sex was unheard of.

I could be wrong but I am sure that my school, Talbot Road Infants, the same school that my father had attended while he lived with his grandparents but now rather more modern and upmarket, did not reopen for some time. This was because many teachers had been "called up" to serve in the armed forces or the factories. This was the time of the

Phoney War, so called because nothing seemed to happen. The sandbags were filled and air raid sirens were installed.

The Home Guard was formed, though they were originally known as the L.D.V. (Local Defence Volunteers.) The theatres and cinemas certainly closed for two weeks by order of the Lord Chamberlain but reopened when the Government realised that the British people needed the distraction that entertainment offered.

Before too long, an organisation was cobbled together with the express purpose of providing shows in all manner of unlikely venues, aircraft hangars, factories, tents, and in the open air. Some of the performers were not very good and the acronym ENSA (Entertainment National Services Association) became the byword for substandard entertainment, quite

Grandad Taylor,
The Author and her Mother, Dorothy

unjustly in many cases. The popular interpretation of these initials was "Every Night Something Awful". My new Aunt Nan gave her services; I believe it was the only way to keep out of the factory or the armed forces apart from getting pregnant. This was not exactly appropriate for the male population.

Many big stars of the music hall and variety theatre, as well as the lesser players, risked their lives travelling to the war zones. This was their way of trying to lift the spirits of the fighting men and also the factory workers who worked long hours to turn out the tanks, trucks, aeroplanes, ships and ammunition that were in such short supply. Temporary dance halls were erected under canvas during the summer months, on the outskirts of some cities. These were called The Big Tops because from the outside they resembled circus tents. They continued to operate throughout the war years and many of the dancers were clad in khaki, navy, or blue: men and women alike. As far as I know, it was an offence for a service person to be out of uniform.

Everybody expected the bombs to start falling on September 4th and we obediently carried our gas masks in cardboard boxes with a carrying strap to go over the shoulder, wherever we went. Gas mask practice was a regular feature of the school day. It was truly awful sitting at our desks wearing the awful black monstrosities which gave off a ghastly smell of rubber and always reminded me of the even more dreadful anaesthetic mask at the dentists. We all took aluminium pans and cooking utensils to school for the scrap metal collection firmly believing that these were going to be melted down and transformed

Dads Army. Johnnie, 1940

into aeroplanes which would fly to Germany and bomb Hitler. In the First World War, the authorities cut off all the lovely decorative iron railings on the same pretext: I don't think any of it was ever used. Maybe they kept our pans for the unfortunate families who had lost their homes during the bombing raids.

"There's a war on, you know," was an almost comic phrase during those long years between 1940 and 1945, but the words were meant to express an explanation of why conditions were less than good. There was a limited amount of imported food, and ration books were issued in October 1939 though the restrictions did not come into force until January 8th 1940. Clothing coupons first appeared in June 1941, and petrol became unobtainable unless you had a special reason for needing it. Only home-grown fruit was available: there was none imported. Yes, we have no bananas, no oranges, no coconuts, dates, figs, grapes, or lychees. There were no nuts, and only homegrown tomatoes, so that meant that these were unavailable except in the summer months. Tesco would have closed down. In fact the big supermarkets could not have existed. We had no fridges and no freezers and if we had, there was little to put in them. There was a method of pre-serving some foodstuffs, such as fruit and vegetables, in jars, which dated back to a much earlier time in history.

The fruit was packed tightly into either special jars known as Kilner jars or into jam jars with special lids, which were then placed in a large pan of hot water and simmered for a lengthy period. I think this was to expel all air and bacteria. When cool, the lids were fastened down tightly and there you were, tinned food in a bottle. Yes, tinned food was rationed too, and sweets, the allowance of which varied and diminished. By 1944 probably, the ration of sweets was down to half-a-pound a month and cigarettes were mainly 'under the counter', meaning out-of-sight and saved for regular customers only. There were queues everywhere: for meat, for fish (the only thing not on ration), for beer, spirits, and fruit. In fact if you saw a line of people you joined them and asked later what it was that you were queuing for. Not until 1953 did sweets 'come off the ration'.

In our house, there was no great problem; Grandad Taylor had fruit and vegetables, so he would do a deal for extra butter, sugar, tea, and margarine or clothing coupons We even had chocolate biscuits and cheese. My mother would make cakes using one egg to about half-a-pound of flour. I didn't know there was any other way until my daughter was in cookery classes at senior school. No wonder my baking was not too popular. I was never allowed to bake when I was a child: presumably because my efforts may have been a failure and all that precious margarine, sugar and egg would have been wasted. I made my first cake when I was sixteen!

Clothes rationing came into force in June 1941. The allotted amount of coupons was supposed to provide for one outfit a year and the phrase "make-do-and-mend" came into our language. Skirts became shorter, no longer than knee length. Trousers had no turn-ups. Stockings were replaced by ankle socks, or dye was applied to female legs with a dark line carefully drawn up the back to simulate the seam on conventional hose. It was at this time that women in trousers became the norm. Quite apart from the practicality, it made some statement about the role of the female sex in society. Shirts could have new collars and cuffs made from the parts normally hidden from view which were cut off and replaced with another fabric, maybe rescued from a different piece of clothing far beyond saving. Sheets which were worn in the centre would be cut in half, the edges stitched together to make a new middle and the worn parts turned into the sides.

I still did this during the early days of my marriage. I have also turned collars and once, a whole skirt of a suit, which extended it's life. A Health Visitor admired the grey Chanel type outfit and I told her that I had just turned the skirt, taking it completely apart and re-making it on the other side. "You are funny," she said, "You are wearing a mink coat one day and a turned skirt the next". It stopped me for a moment, then I said " That is how I can afford the mink coat." I was still economising in this way until a few years ago: old habits die hard.

One of the lasting developments of these hard times during the war was the concept of 'Utility' goods, made to approved government standards and bearing a distinctive mark 'CC41'. A bit like the kite-mark we know today. Utility goods were well made but of strictly utilitarian design: no frills or fancy bits. Newly-weds received a special allowance to help them set up home.

We did have substitutes for some of the rationed items. There was powdered egg, still used today in catering, and powdered milk, now available in supermarkets. And always in my larder, just in case. Christmas trees became smaller: there isn't a lot of room in a shelter or a cellar. But, the one we had at home was ceiling height as usual. Substitute coffee became the norm, and Camp coffee, a mixture of coffee and chicory, was very popular. I don't think that in Britain we ever had the 'ersatz' coffee made of acorns, like the people of occupied Europe, but what would a child know? My war-years were more comfortable than most. I was never hungry, never wore cast-offs, never spent the night in an air raid shelter, or saw a victim of the bombing in my home-town.

We did not have to worry too much about my father being wounded in action although he had made serious attempts to enlist but was rejected. He had tried the Air Force first, because it was a nicer coloured uniform. Then the Army, but they all refused to take him away. I think the fact that he suffered a hearing loss may have had something to do with it but I gather that printing was a 'reserved occupation'. Someone had to print the newspapers and the propaganda which kept up the bulldog spirit. My father was not abroad fighting the foe, although eventually, he was in munitions production in Walsall and Darleston in The Black Country of the Midlands. He was fortunate to be living in the rather upper-crust home of his youngest aunt. However, the Midlands suffered from more than a passing interest by the Luftwaffe, so there was no place to hide that was totally safe.

I did not see too much of him, though he did get home sometimes and one Christmas my mother and I went on the train to spend the festive season with him at Auntie Dolly's. Eventually he was posted back to Leeds and enjoyed the title of Inspector of Tanks. This meant that he would take a Cromwell tank off the production line and proceed to Harewood estate, a distance of several miles. Once there, he drove it at a great rate of knots around the grounds of this stately home destroying anything that got in his way. It must have taken years to return the estate to its former glory. One day, toward the end of the hostilities, I was walking on the shopping parade at Moortown, on the Harrogate Road, in Leeds, when a tank loomed up, drew alongside, and my father jumped out. I felt very important, I knew nobody else whose father could drive a tank, although my friend Pat's step-dad was in the RAF so maybe he could fly an aeroplane?

One very early morning in May 1940, I was standing in the front bedroom looking out of the window, when I saw a figure walking down the farm road. It was a man wearing a Naval greatcoat and boots, no trousers, and it emerged later, no anything else. As he came closer, I recognised him as Ronnie, one of the two young men who lived next door. Later on that day I discovered that he had been at the evacuation from Dunkirk, and had escaped with his life and nothing else.

Single women and the married ones with no children, were required to register and might be 'called up' to join the ATS (the Women's army) the WAAF (Women's Auxiliary Air Force) or the WRNS (Women's Royal Navy Service). Nurses were in great demand and there were special service units for them. Alternatively, one might be summoned to work in the munitions factories, producing aeroplanes, bullets, guns or any of the parts thereof, or it might be your choice to join the Land Army as my lovely half cousin Joy did, and work as a very low paid farm-hand. Another option was to get married, get pregnant, and get out of working outside the home at all. This period was responsible for ending forever the notion that girls did not need a career or that they should think in terms of a job only to pass the time until marriage rescued them from the workplace. Although initially, there was a marked reluctance to employ the fair sex in any role which might put them in harms way, they were allowed to prove themselves.

By the end of the war, women had become used to their independence, both personal and financial and many marriages paid the price. Some women had not seen their husbands for nearly six years when they finally came home. Many were unsure if their men, to whom they had waved goodbye, were even alive or whether they had died in the jungles and prison camps. There were thousands of wartime romances. Everyone was scared, lonely, and clinging on to any comfort and warmth they could find. If you could not be with the man or woman you loved then it was not unreasonable to love the one you were with. The separation also highlighted the weak links in many relationships and the rifts were in some cases un-healable. My own parents parted company some months before VJ Day (Victory in Japan) probably because my mother had grown accustomed to doing as she pleased and of course had never forgiven Johnnie for his lack of interest in her at the time of my birth.

Strangely, the only casualties of the almost six years of war that were known to me, were members of my own extended family. None of my schoolmates' dads or brothers failed to return. In fact, they did not seem to have been involved. Maybe they were all printers or hard of hearing. The two who were not to survive were the brothers Nelson, cousins of my father, whose family had lived near Wolverhampton in peacetime. Kenneth was handsome and kind, I adored him, and I thought Jack was handsome and creepy. My judgement proved to be correct.

One night he was at our house with others, playing cards and I, a six-year old, was asleep in bed. I awoke to find that Jack was seriously interfering with my personal bits, not a happy experience for a small girl. Fortunately, someone had taken it into their heads that he had been missing for longer than it takes to use the toilet and called up to him. I never told anyone: none of us do, until it is too late. Anyway, he got his comeuppance, having led a charmed life on board many famous warships, and always being transferred just before their final ill-fated voyages, he fell overboard off the liberty boat returning to his ship in Portsmouth harbour after a night ashore and was never found. It was Trafalgar Day, the anniversary of his name-sake's death at the Battle of Trafalgar. Strange?

Kenneth Nelson was in the army and was posted to Singapore, which everyone knew was invincible because of the mighty defences guarding it against a sea-borne attack from the Japanese forces. The invaders must have known about these defences, because they didn't even bother to try to tackle them. They simply came in from the landward side, some on their bicycles, and occupied the island, taking prisoners, men, women, and children as they went. Some civilians had already left, but many rotted in prisoner of war camps for years. Ken was taken prisoner and sent to Malaya, Auntie Dolly used to get printed cards, like multiple choice question papers every so often. One came to say he was moving, then no more. We heard later that a prisoner of war transport ship had been inadvertently bombed and sunk by American 'planes. Friendly fire, we call it now. Nothing changes, does it?

My father had many cousins, of whom George, and his sister Joan, had followed Johnnie and gone to live with their common grandma, the redoubtable Ma, when the death of their mother left them orphaned. George, like my father, followed Dada into printing, but when the war started he joined the Navy as soon as he was old enough. Only a few years ago, he told me that his only brush with the enemy had been a close shave in the Mediterranean when the Luftwaffe managed to drop a bomb right down the funnel of the vessel, but it failed to explode.

During those years there were many homeless families whose houses had fallen foul of the bombs, by the winter of 1944 half a million homes were uninhabitable due to bomb damage, and anyone with spare rooms was expected to give the survivors a home. We had two lots of tenants. The first of these was, a young lady and her baby, the husband was in the army, and although her family lived close by in some luxury, she preferred to be independent. Later they moved on and were replaced by a very stuffy older couple from the South of England. However, they were very valuable to me because they taught me to play Lexicon, a card game using letters and words which no doubt increased my vocabulary considerably. These lodgers would occupy a bedroom and one of our two living-rooms, with shared use of the kitchen and bathroom. It was a system that continued for many years after the war had ended, often for reasons of economy and to create temporary homes for the victims of the bombing.

The other homes of a makeshift nature were the 'prefabs': ready-made houses which came flat and were erected within hours, all on one level. These provided basic accommodation for a small family. Some sectional wooden buildings were imported from Canada and, sixty years on, this is a style of building that is now gaining popularity. Some of these war-time homes stayed usable for fifty years or more. Some are still in use today.

The general public took measures to protect themselves in case of an air raid and many homes had an air raid shelter, though how much use they would have been in the event of a direct hit is debatable. These shelters came in two varieties for domestic use. There was the Anderson shelter, which came in packs of corrugated metal, to be erected by the householder in the garden, and the Morrison shelter, named after a cabinet minister in the coalition government (and future Labour minister under Clement Atlee). The last was an enormous cage with a steel top, about eight feet long by three or four feet wide that occupied most of whatever room it was in. Heavens only knows what people did with them after the war, there were no recycling sites in those days. They would have been good for keeping the odd leopard in, though just a shade small for a tiger.

In those days the indoor shelter was treated as a piece of furniture and covered with a large cloth. A bedspread was about the right size and, as a hidey-hole, it had great charm for children. We need not have worried in Leeds: Hitler and his mob failed to realise that there was an aircraft factory, Blackburn's, only two miles away from where I lived. It was hidden in a wood, where it had operated since the First World War. In fact, Leeds got away almost Scot-free, in spite of being situated right in the heart of industrial West Yorkshire. Sheffield was not so lucky.

Back on the home front, in case of a bomb dropping and fire breaking out, every house was equipped with a bucket of sand and another holding water and a stirrup pump. It was laughable to think that these measures would prevent serious damage. The whole effect would be akin to the London Fire Brigade lining up and urinating on to a factory fire. Throughout the war years there were no bonfire night celebrations in case we gave the enemy clues to where we were, all windows and doors had to be made light-proof, a glimmer would bring the Air Raid Warden knocking on your door.

In Leeds we didn't have native air raid refugees: just the ones from places less fortunate. However, I did get to see a little more of the problem in an unlikely setting. My great-grandfather hailed from Flamborough, a wild and rocky spot of great natural beauty, to which he and Ma liked to return every summer. They would rent a wooden chalet-type bungalow from May until October, war, or no war, and various members of the family went along from time to time to enjoy the peace and tranquillity. There was barbed wire all around the cliff tops, in case Hitler and his merry men tried to invade, and there were soldiers encamped in the ruins of the former glory of the North Star Hotel, which is now fully restored to its pre-war condition.

The café, now a rather splendid place, at the top of North Landing, was the army cookhouse, and the owners of the many wooden holiday bungalows had closed them up for the duration of the war. I spent many solitary holidays there, a lone child with only my elderly great-grandparents for company. The pebbly beach was mine and I could wander over the rocks and in the caves, undisturbed. I wonder if anyone ever considered my safety? I used to walk about barefoot and often go down to the beach in the early morning to see the crabs and lobsters being landed and the boats being hauled up the slip-way.

One such morning, something different was happening on the shingled beach. The boats brought in a different catch. One cobble was towing a dinghy, the sort used by the RAF when their pilot had to ditch in the sea. Its passenger had not survived and was brought ashore on a stretcher, too late for human help. They carried him up the slip-way and then left the stretcher in the lifeboat housing half way up the steep pathway to the beach. As I went home for breakfast, I saw it, the imprint of his body clearly defined in sea water on the canvas. It was an image that has never left me.

Sometimes, late at night, when I was in Flamborough, I have looked out to the south and seen the sky red with fire, the flames of destruction as a result of the air raids on Hull. The following morning the homeless victims arrived in coach-loads, and were housed in the empty holiday chalets, owning nothing but the clothes they stood in. They were given blankets and food by the soldiers, and got on with the job of rebuilding their lives. My Aunt Dolly described Flamborough as "the last place God made", but I imagine it must have seemed like a little bit of heaven to the homeless of Hull. I got the impression that Flamborough was not Dolly's favourite place but I loved it and still do.

One night, back home in Leeds I was sleeping over at Jean's, next door, when we heard the planes going over. She told me that it was easy to tell whether it was a "Jerry" or a British plane by the engine noise: the British ones had a steady drone and the enemy ones made a pulsating sound. I was impressed by her knowledge and put it down to living in London for the early part of the hostilities but I was not entirely convinced that she was right. However, only a short time ago in 2001 I heard a radio programme confirming this information to be correct.

Pat and I continued to be friends and frequently used to spend the night at each other's houses. At her home, Grampa Giles was in charge but, after the untimely death of Pat's mother, a housekeeper, Mrs Greaves took over the mothering. She had a son, Tony, who I thought quite horrid, all red hair and freckles. I don't think he was any more horrid than any other boy but I resented him interfering with our long standing twosome. Sometimes when Pat slept at my house, my mother would go dancing to the Mansion in Roundhay Park and leave us on our own in the house with only Mrs Cotton next-door to keep an eye out. I thought nothing about it because it was a regular occurrence. Sixty years later, Pat remembered it and said that if Grampa Giles had known he would have had a fit. Justifiably, in my adult opinion, in fact these days it would be an offence. I don't suppose my father ever knew about it.

During the first two years of the war Britain stood alone against the might of Germany and her allies. The rest of Europe, with the exception of neutral countries Sweden, Switzerland, Portugal, and Spain, were over-run and occupied by the aggressors. Our friends, the Americans had little enthusiasm for getting involved in a conflict so far from home and they were not threatened by a close proximity to the enemy. All this changed on the morning of December 7th 1941.

Japan had been engaged in a long war with China during the course of which her troops had gained valuable fighting experience. Her aircraft had become more sophisticated and reliable and Japan realised that, audaciously applied, a combination of brute force and some skill, could achieve rewards. The country was lacking in natural resources and there was a greed and a need for the wealth and power of the western nations. Unfortunately, the United States of America stood in the way of Emperor Hirohito's ambitions to over run the whole of South East Asia. America had a giant naval base in the Hawaiian Islands. Aircraft were parked wing-to-wing on the airfields there. Although there had been warnings that the American air and naval bases might be vulnerable, no precautions had been taken.

Just before eight a.m. on that Sunday morning, the first wave of 214 aircraft came roaring from the Pacific Ocean to attack the US Navy at Pearl Harbour. This was followed an hour later by a second wave of 170 more. The total surprise of this raid caught the Americans with their proverbial pants down and chaos ensued. Two hours later, 2,403 USA personnel had died, 1,178 were wounded, and the 65 aeroplanes on the ground destroyed. The loss of two battleships and the disabling of another six was a blow but fortunately three aircraft carriers were not in port and the Navy still had 20 cruisers and 65 destroyers in good fighting order.

America was now ready to join our war! Within a short time the GI Joes were over-paid, over-sexed, and over here. They had elegant serge uniforms. They had chewing gum. They had nylon stockings, and they had money. They also had American accents and every girl thought that if she married an American soldier, she would live in Hollywood after the war. Some were lucky and did marry nice guys and build a new life on the other side of the Atlantic but there were more who were left holding the baby when the hostilities were over.

Not only did the fighting men of the United States of America come to the aid of the party, they also brought their entertainers and radio shows to entertain their comrades and lighten our dreary lives.

In addition to hearing the American comedy shows, the Big Bands of Benny Goodman, Artie Shaw, The Dorsey Brothers, Glenn Miller and the rest, I listened to the news and had a keen, and oddly adult, interest in the progress of the war. My first moment of elation, as for many people, was hearing on the early morning news that El Alamein in North Africa had been wrested from enemy hands. From that moment Bernard Law Montgomery was one of my heroes. I liked General Alexander because he was handsome but on the 6th of June 1944 when I heard about the landings in Normandy, Dwight D. Eisenhower was entered into my book of favourites. Once Russia had been betrayed by Hitler with the Operation Barbarossa invasion of their country and joined the Allied nations in their fight against the Nazis, we all loved 'Uncle Joe Stalin', the big Russian bear, who later proved to be an even worse monster than our mutual foe.

We used to go to the cinema a good deal and there we could see newsreels of the action, albeit a week or more late. My most vivid memories were pictures of the devastated Russian countryside and the white clad Russian soldiers camouflaged to blend in with the environment of dense snow. I also clearly remember the eruption of Vesuvius and the rivers of molten lava creeping inexorably down the mountainside after the Allied troops had landed in Italy. Most of all, I recall the horrific sight of Belsen, the emaciated survivors and the bodies being bulldozed into mass graves. I have heard that there are those today who would argue that these camps did not exist and that the film evidence is a fake. Try telling that to any of the few survivors who are still alive today.

There were lighter sides to this child's war: one incident has always stuck in my mind. My parents were wont to pick up stray servicemen, on leave but with nowhere to go, and bring them home for a couple of days. One Christmas morning I awoke early, as is de rigeur for small children on that day of days. I had suffered greatly from toothache as a child and failing any other solution; a swab of neat whisky was applied to the offending tooth. I developed a taste for Scotch at an early age and thanks to Grandad's black market connections, we always had some in the sideboard.

This particular Christmas, I decided to creep downstairs and lighten the dawn hours with a wee dram, so I set off very, very quietly. I opened the dining room door, then the sideboard door and kneeled on the floor to get out the bottle. Pulling the cork, I drank from the bottle-neck, and was replacing the bottle when my eyes became accustomed to the light. I then saw a soldier: well, a man wearing a khaki battledress top, lying on the hearth-rug covered by my eiderdown, propped up on his elbow, looking at me.

"Good Morning" I said - I was a very well brought up little girl.
"Good Morning" he replied.
"Happy Christmas" I said, full of seasonal spirit and a generous mouthful of Scotch.

"Same to you" he said, with which I went back to bed. I doubt whether he ever told my parents, they never mentioned it to me. I expect he went back to sleep and on waking later, concluded that it was an unlikely story. He had not really seen an eight year-old girl slugging Scotch out of the bottle at six in the morning and it was all a dream. Mind you, his name was Jock: maybe he was used to dreaming odd dreams when under the influence of a wee dram.

Another Christmas, we had a sailor called Danny but the house always seemed to be full of young men, ostensibly friends of my half-cousin, Joy. Personally, I think they were far more interested in my mother. At least one, an eighteen-year-old named Geoff, with whom I was also madly in love when I was eight years old, was besotted with her. I know that Joy never forgave the devilish older woman for stealing her boyfriend. Many years later, when I was eighteen, I met Geoff again. He was portly and balding and I think it amused him to entertain me now I was almost a grown up. He did not admit to any hanky-panky involving my mother, but he did not deny it either. I failed to tell him that I had heard his voice in my parent's bedroom one sleepless night during the time when Johnnie was in Walsall. Discretion is the better part of valour whatever that means and my mother always denied any impropriety.

Probably my saddest day listening to the news on the Forces program, was Sunday the 15th of December 1944. The previous day in freezing weather Major Glenn Miller had set off on a flight to France, where he and his orchestra were scheduled to play for the Allied troops who were there on active service. The aeroplane disappeared and no trace of it or its occupants has ever been found. I was devastated and wept buckets. His music lives on through recordings and a tribute band which tours constantly.

The following day, at 5:30 a.m. there was a sudden explosion of gunfire in the Ardennes and a fierce battle started. 2,000 guns and 600,000 German troops made a totally unexpected attack on the Allied soldiers in a last ditch attempt to regain the upper hand and prevent the assault on the Rhine and the advance to Berlin. The battle raged for weeks leaving 8,000 American dead and another 70,000 missing or wounded, not to mention the German losses. During that winter, 9,000 of the enemy had been shot as deserters by their own comrades.

When victory over Hitler and Nazi Germany was announced, all the regulations prohibiting bonfires went to the wind and there was a wonderful blaze at the bottom of our street, on what had been a building site before war broke out. Of course we had a few months to go before the war in the Pacific was done although the island hopping policy had recaptured many Pacific islands. In spite of heavy bombing raids on Japan's major cities causing massive destruction and loss of life, their national spirit prevailed. This dedication to the Emperor decreed that only he could accept surrender and since he enjoyed a godlike status, how could non-believers persuade him to admit defeat?

In great secrecy, a nuclear weapon using uranium and code named Little Boy was ready for use. Another, Fat Boy, which had been developed in a separate line of research and employing plutonium, could also be ready for use by late July. Their use was justified at the time when the only alternative strategy open to the Allies was to make a land invasion in two stages on the individual islands of Japan. In view of the Japanese fanatical devotion to their leader and the attendant willingness to lay down their lives for him, it was estimated that there would be a likely loss of around 69,000 American lives in the first attack alone. Losses during a future attack on Honshu when the enemy had reached a more desperate level of suicidal zeal, was incalculable.

A decision was reached and, on August 6th 1945, the 'Enola Gay' a B-29, piloted by Paul Tibbets of the American Air Force, carried 'Little Boy', the first weapon of mass destruction to Japan. Between 60,000 and 80,000 people died, either at the time of the bombing or in the weeks that followed but still there was no surrender. A few days later on August 9th a group of three B-29 bombers carried 'Fat Boy', the plutonium bomb, to Nagasaki where the damage was somewhat less, possibly due to the more hilly nature of the area. While 35,000 were killed or injured in this attack, it must be remembered that the real numbers of casualties resulting from those two fateful days was far greater than the figures suggested since cases of radiation sickness, birth abnormalities, cancer, and many other conditions continued to emerge for years afterwards.

On August 8th, Russia declared war on Japan and with massive force mounted an attack on the Japanese Army in Manchuria via the Gobi Desert. The Emperor had now been convinced that the time to surrender had arrived. Emperor Hirohito himself made a recorded broadcast to his people, his first radio message in ten years of his reign, at noon of August 15th to announce capitulation and the forthcoming occupation of their country by Allied forces. The official documents were signed on board the USS battleship Missouri on September 2nd. Just a day and three hours short of six years since Great Britain had declared war against Hitler.

It was all over and cities, lives, and families could be rebuilt, or were gone forever. Today, vast cemeteries all over the world bear witness to the tragic loss of life and the sacrifice made by hundreds of thousands, nay, millions of young men from many countries to which they would never return. Wives had lost their husbands and husbands had sometimes lost their entire families in the bombing of our cities and towns. How many mothers would mourn their sons and daughters, and countless children would reach adulthood having no memory of their fathers.

CHAPTER 4
THE DANCING YEARS

A year before the war came to an end, my mother decided to make a final effort to interest me in the ways of Terpsichore. She took me along to a ballroom dancing studio in the centre of Leeds, at which she had made friends with the Principal, Miss Josephine Dyson. It was suggested to me that I could take private lessons and therefore demonstrate my ineptitude in the seclusion of an empty room. Empty, that is but for the teacher and myself. The idea had a certain appeal and so I agreed.

The Budding Ballerina

Miss Dyson was a loose limbed lady with a nose of admirable proportions and muscular legs, which I discovered to have been the result of her early ballet training. I duly learned the basic steps of the Waltz, Quickstep, and Foxtrot and turned out to be a surprisingly apt pupil though somewhat stiff and unbending. In an attempt to unstiffen and bend me, Miss Dyson suggested a few ballet exercises designed to stretch the tight tendons in my legs. Or was it actually a clever ploy to get me interested in Ballet? Whatever the real reason, it worked, the somewhat punishing stretching and leg lifting which is far from comfortable, painful even, had some weird appeal for me. Maybe I saw this as the flagellation I deserved for being less than perfect or perhaps it was merely that for the first time I appeared to be successful in some field of physical exercise.

My expertise in the playground or on the sports field had been less than rewarding and suggestions that, with my long legs, I should be a good runner only served to highlight my obvious failure. The thought of vaulting over a large leather obstruction known as a horse, filled me with dread and the deep conviction that I was about to go splat, like a cartoon cat chasing a mouse. Of course, the dancing was non-competitive and there was no other more talented child with whom I could unfavourably compare myself so I listened with joy when Jo Dyson told me that I showed great promise and could aspire to being a ballet dancer if I worked at it.

My mother was delighted; all her thwarted ambitions could now be realised. Were they insane? I already took size six shoes and was tall and sturdily built. Not fat, you understand, but not ballerina-slim. The idea of any male dancer of average size ever being able to lift me gracefully in the air, even in 1944 when it all started, was ludicrous. I probably weighed more than the run-of-the-mill ballerina before I was eleven years old and certainly had bigger feet, but I was too young to see the problems and the two adults were driven by ambitions of their own. My mother had seized the opportunity to formalise her expertise in this noble art of dancing and Jo needed help in the dancing school and no doubt some support in her rather arid personal life. My mother's own private life had taken a turn for the worse when my father was transferred back to Leeds and was able to live at home. There would be no more going out dancing two or three times a week as she had done during the early years of the war. Johnnie made an effort to join and took ballroom dancing lessons himself from Jo, but by this time the rot had well and truly set in to my parents marriage and no amount of proficiency on the dance floor was going to save it.

The question of my further ballet training soon came up. Jo lacked the competence to see me on my way to the Royal Ballet, and there was also the small question of my academic career for which I was eminently more suited than for the corps de ballet or the chorus line. My grandparents, both pairs, and my father, felt that I should pursue a normal school career and take dancing lessons in the evenings and at weekends. But, I had been introduced to a far more exciting idea through a specific journal, 'The Dancing Times', given to me by the architects of my future. In this publication were advertisements for various training schools as well as for ballet shoes, and dresses etc. Somewhat surprisingly, my mother, who had remarked on my unsuitability for frilly frocks and part clothes, was now quite able to envisage me in a tutu.

There were, at the time, three residential establishments which combined a formal education with a comprehensive training in the performing arts. All of these were in the South of England, a very significant fact because had the moment to make a choice arrived a few months earlier, the result would have been very different. It was now the early summer of 1945, D-Day had come and gone, and victory in Europe was already celebrated. So, the threat of bombing no longer existed, and there was little to prohibit my going south to complete my education. I was drawn into an elaborate plan to present my father and my grandparents with a fait accompli. My mother wrote off for curricula, and entry requirements, while in the meantime I sat the entrance examination for the previous school of my choice, Leeds Girls High School, which awarded only six such places each year. Once more, I did not get a place. I was good but not that good.

However, I was up to par for Allerton High School but my desire to attend that particular establishment was equal to my desire to have my backside rubbed with a brick. The uniform was bottle green, and I did not see myself in green. In addition, it occurred to me that the school would be full of beastly girls waiting to push me around and expecting me to join in games. What horror! The idea of a small select group of dancing daughters was far more inviting, especially as there were younger children than little me at these select establishments. I was sold on the idea and so devoted to my mother who had convinced me of her place at the right hand of God, that the pleas and very real tears shed by Johnnie and all the grandparents fell on my deaf ears. Dorothy, my mother, had to be right and I was totally obsessed with seeing the whole scheme through. In addition, as soon as I was safely tucked away in deepest Sussex any plans for an escape from an unrewarding marriage could begin to take shape, though I was unaware of that at the time.

We Three Musketeers travelled down to London, then on to East Grinstead, having made a choice of training school, which stood in an idyllic setting, at the top of a long drive bordered by rhododendrons and surrounded by unspoilt Sussex countryside. The house itself, Charters Towers, had an imposing hall with a magnificent fireplace, heavily carved and holding silver cups, evidence of the achievements of past and present pupils. The student residents numbered thirty-seven when I started in the September of 1945. Some of them were quite old, having been forced to abandon their dancing studies in 1939 with the outbreak of war. They had now returned in order to complete their training, having spent the intervening years in the armed forces or in factories making munitions. It was a strange mixture of ages and socio- economic backgrounds. I was enthralled by the whole atmosphere and was thrilled when the Principal, Noreen Bush and her husband Victor Leopold, who was in charge of the day-to-day management of the school, agreed to accept me as a pupil. I presumed that they had seen some talent in my oversized form but I fear that it was the lure of another set of fees that was the real attraction.

In fairness, not every student was filled with a desire to tread the boards. Someone has to teach, and there were several older pupils who were destined to do just that. I think that the September intake numbered around six so the school was not exactly a major money-spinner at that time, the fees were around £36 per term of twelve weeks. We had to take sheets, towels, pillowcases, blankets and our ration books plus a box in which to keep our personal junk. The bulk of this went in a trunk and was sent in advance by rail, the rest accompanied Mummy and me on the train.

The preceding three months had been traumatic for me. Guilt was laid on me by both sets of grandparents. How could I be so wicked as to leave them after all the love they had bestowed on me? My father was less verbal but I think he was afraid to argue with his formidable wife in case he incurred her wrath and brought down Armageddon on himself and his tribe. He might as well have had his say: his days as a married man were numbered anyway, but he hung on to what he had. It wasn't as though there was another man or that he was a drunk or a wife beater. On the surface all was sweetness and light and I suppose that at that time I never suspected that life might change so dramatically.

September 1945 altered my life permanently. It was goodbye to any childhood, although I was only eleven years old. We pupils at 'Bush-Davies Schools' were not ordinary girls. There was no tennis at the weekends for us: we had made a life choice, and we were as committed as nuns in a convent. Our gods were those of the dance, our temples were the classrooms and our instruments were our bodies. These tender forms had to be trained and maintained to the limit of our physical ability, and that limit was constantly pushed further. We attended dancing classes every day, after school and after tea as well, and on Saturday mornings. If you had an exam looming up, it could be Sunday too.

We learned ballet, tap, musical comedy, which was a sort of ballet to modern music but without the technique and discipline, national dances, and character dancing which again was ballet-based. All of this was supported by daily 'Limbering' classes, which entailed doing exercises either standing or lying on the floor. These were designed to develop strength in the muscles and suppleness in the joints and tendons and probably resulted in many a later back condition and arthritis. This regime of exercise was incredibly hard work and physically punishing but it was part of the life which I had chosen and I would not have given in and admitted defeat. It was hell!

I hated being away from home. I was sleeping in a dormitory with nine other girls ranging from eight years old to twelve, with lights out at 7:30 p.m., and everybody up and rushing for the bathroom as the bell rang at 7:30 a.m. There were the usual assortment of tyrants, bullies, wimps, and pacifists. Many of the bullies were in the clique of the boss's daughter, Jane, a younger girl than her followers and Chief Tyrant. I soon aligned myself with Clodagh Early, a girl slightly my senior and built like a rugby forward, the second in a large family, who took no shit from anyone. She had a keen sense of right and if she bore down on you, hasty removal of one's person would possibly avert the need for emergency surgery. She was terrifying. Also in our small clan was Mary, a thin, pale, bespectacled child also from Worthing, Clodagh's hometown, so she also came into the class of Clodagh's protected species. We also had the advantage of superior intellect and stuck together academically until Mary packed it all in and returned to normal life, leaving the two of us to go on to School Certificate and glory.

Our academic studies, such as they were, took place in a wooden building reached by walking along a covered way from the back of the house. It was impossible for all the school age pupils to go to school together, there was only one full-time teacher, the headmaster, Mr B, who was ultimately dismissed due to his penchant for massaging his crotch with the foot of whichever little girl was being treated to some private tuition at the time. Maybe his transgressions were even more spectacular but I can only speak from my own experience and the facts were never made public, naturally.

We had one or two part-time teachers. There was one young man who had done a quick teacher training course. He was totally fazed by being surrounded by theatrical little girls who came to school in ballet practise clothes, ready to rush off into the ballet studio as soon as the 3:30 p.m. bell rang. For the first few months, we attended school in relays: some in the morning, some in the afternoon. The other half of the day was spent in the dancing studios. To most of the children this sketchy education probably mattered little. After all, it seemed irrelevant to have a degree, if you were in the corps de ballet or the chorus and none of us and few parents could see further than the immediate future. Need I say that my mother viewed it very differently? I was streets ahead of most of the kids of my own age, most of whom were not very well endowed academically speaking, with the notable exception of Clodagh and Mary. My progress was down to the pace of the average clunk-head, but salvation came in the shape of an extraordinarily talented woman of indeterminate age with red hair and a face of such amazing mobility that her unloveliness became a plus.

Clodagh and Mary knew Miss Raby from their hometown of Worthing. I seem to recall that she taught ballroom dancing there, and the other two girls were reasonably competent on the ballroom floor, another thing we had in common. Ann Raby started her career as teacher to potential ballerinas on a very part-time basis, coming from Worthing to East Grinstead in her rather racy car. Remember, this was only shortly after the end of the war and cars were at a premium. Maybe she had owned it before 1939 and kept it mothballed during the hostilities. We never asked her what she had done in those years, but I imagine that it was something amazing.

Initially, she taught us French during the day and ballroom dancing at night. She was very highly qualified in that art, being not a mere Associate of the professional society, not even a Member, but a Fellow of the Imperial Society of Teachers of Dancing, the toughest examinations board in the country at the time. Her French accent was excellent and I was one of her star pupils but then I was a star at everything except Geography and Maths. This latter subject was a mystery to me in spite of being first-class at the mechanics of figures. Addition, division, and multiplication were a piece of cake due to the teaching methods of the period: times-tables were learned like nursery rhymes and once learned lay ready to leap to one's assistance whenever needed.

Miss Raby soon shouldered the responsibility for teaching Maths and discovered that my talents were beyond those of my contemporaries so I was promoted to the Upper form whose youngest member was a year or more older than Clodagh, who was promoted with me. This was where the trouble started. The rest of the class was comparatively clued up regarding Algebra and Geometry and I was a total novice. I was struggling from day one and could never come to terms with the concept of using letters to represent numbers, and putting brackets round others. In addition to this, a feeling of panic pervaded my being at the thought of angles and hypotenuses. Case in point, I can spell it but I don't know what it is. By the time I was fourteen years old, Miss Raby admitted defeat, and I bade farewell to Maths forever. However I can still tell what so many times so and so is, well before my grandchildren can punch the numbers into their calculators.

Miss Raby also took over teaching English and her interpretation of Shylock and others made Shakespeare tolerable. Her reading of Toad of Toad Hall and her characterisation made her the face of Toad forever in my mind. During all the years that she taught at Charters Towers, she was never seen before six p.m. without her graduate gown billowing around her and she flapped down the covered way to the schoolhouse like a giant bat. In fact she only took it off for the ballroom lessons and when she joined in some of our ballet classes at which time she donned tights and tunics like the rest of us and just mucked in. She was certainly in her later forties, and I regret that we did not appreciate her very special talents at the time. I owe her a very great deal.

She assumed the mantle of headship, following the removal of the other oddball teacher Doctor B, an ex-pat Czech, who also had considerable extra-curricular interest in some of his pupils and their studies in anatomy. One of his subjects naturally enough, had been biology, at which I was quite a star, so I was relieved to find that Miss Raby could teach that, too. I later discovered that she would read up a chapter at night then deliver the lesson to me the following day. By doing just this she managed to teach me through to getting a Credit in the School Certificate examinations. These were the immediate forerunner to 'O' levels, only harder, because we had to pass in six subjects at one sitting over a period of about four or five days. For almost two years before these exams, the last ever before the new system came in, in 1950, Clodagh and I worked in isolation under Miss Raby's tutelage because we were so far in advance of the rest of our peers that regular lessons, with few exceptions were not practicable. We had the work set for the day then we would go in search of a quiet spot anywhere in the school. Sometimes this would be the staff dining room, their private lounge, or the student common room. It was a weird school life but a great preparation for my long-term future. When eighteen years later, I decided to study alone for 'A' levels I knew all about the self-discipline needed to succeed.

During these more academic years the dancing took more of a back seat, though it was still very much a part of the curriculum I was not pulled out of school for ballet lesson. The school needed our scholastic achievements in order to gain approval by the local Education Authority. This fact gave us a very strong bargaining position when needed, for instance when we wanted to leave the afternoon before half term started, or when we both decided to discard our school uniform in favour of rather smart grey suits and no school tie or hat. This was all accepted without comment; I even got away with being seen smoking out of the dormitory window by the cook. I know that she reported it to Miss Bush that evening, because I slept in the dorm over the kitchen and overheard the loud-voiced cook telling the tale.

The following morning, Miss Bush was leaving to go on an examining tour and she came up to the dorm, ostensibly to say goodbye. She was a tiny bird-like creature with a violent temper, a hooked nose, and black Italian eyes. She patted my cheek and said "You're a wicked girl, Taylor" and that was that. She rattled off, the huge gold charm bracelet on her wrist jangling and her high heels tapping on the polished floor. I think that she was only four feet ten inches tall but had been a real live ballerina in her time and Mr Leopold, her husband, was a world-class tap dancer. Their married name was Kimm, but we only knew that because their daughter was Jane Kimm. Their son, Paul Kimm, a pupil at Oundle School was in the choir at the wedding of Princess Elizabeth and the entire school managed to fit into the staff lounge to watch the royal wedding on their television.

On the subject of 'dorms', I had seen one which was called the Tower room when we visited the school and I thought it was most romantic. Throughout my days at 'Bush' it was the one dorm I longed to occupy and the only one which was never graced with my presence. I did serve a spell in Noah's Ark, right opposite, which was in the eaves and boarded from top to bottom in pitch pine. In the summer it was as hot as Hades and in the winter we slept in our socks and gloves to try to keep warm.

Shortly after my arrival at school, always known to us as 'Bush' as an abbreviation of 'The Bush-Davies Schools', I was introduced to what the old hands referred to as the 'Inter Comps'. I used to see these words listed as a class on the blackboard where the days' dancing classes were chalked each morning. I could not imagine what sort of dancing inter-comps could be. It emerged that this was another abbreviation, this time for Inter-Schools Competitions, a regular event staged in London involving two full days of competitions in the various disciplines between the East Grinstead and Romford branches of the school.

Miss Davies ran the Romford school and they excelled in the tap and musical comedy events, as we did in the more classical events. The two heads used to visit the other establishment fairly regularly and Marjorie Davies was a great favourite due to the fact that she didn't shout much and never whacked our disobedient limbs with a cane or her hard bony, taloned, little hands as Miss Bush was wont to do. Her mother, known as Auntie Taffy, lived at our school and used to play the piano for assembly on Sundays. She would sometimes entertain us with her fine singing and always referred to us as "you chaps".

My first 'inter-comps' took place in the first November I was at school. Quite a baptism of fire in fact, because I was plunged into the whole work ethic that has dominated my life. You work until the job is done or until you have rehearsed to the point of exhaustion. You do not complain when your feet are bloody and sore, and you do not say "but I haven't had my supper" or "it's time I was in bed" or "I don't feel like it". You just get on with what you have to do because the show must go on. It was an invaluable lesson and a very exciting time. The whole atmosphere of tension and anticipation. The costume try-ons. The creeping out of the dorm to watch the rehearsals in the hall and being spotted by Noreen Bush who would then roar "Get those children back to bed".

Some of the performances were of a very high standard. This was no provincial dancing class: we expected to graduate to win the best jobs available in our chosen branch of show business, either as performers or as teachers. In order to achieve those ends we knew that hard work, stamina and total dedication were necessary adjuncts to any talent we might have had. I learned at a very early stage that success does not come to he who waits, it comes to those who work for it, and the harder you work the more likely it is that you will win.

Eventually, the day of the competitions arrived and the entire school boarded a bus at an early hour in order to reach London by 9:30 a.m.: competitors and non-combatants alike. I was one of the latter, still being at the stage of sorting out my left foot from my right and keeping in time with music. However, we were all excited at the smell of the greasepaint and the murmur of the crowd which was already gathering in The Toynbee Hall. Parents had come from all over the country, mine from Leeds and many more from slightly less distant parts. We friends from the North were in a minority and of course, the Romford branch had no problems with distance so the opposition were well supported.

There was some rare talent amongst them, only one of whom I ever heard of after I left school. This was a girl named Doreen Hinton later known as Pip Hinton, who had a fairly steady career. I was in a show with her at one stage or maybe I should say, on one stage, which we shared with a very amusing young comedian who went on to great heights as Norman Vaughan. The other exceptional performers were Mareda Osborne, who was a lovely-looking dark-haired child, Brian Lindsey, the only boy in the competition and Kay Henderson. Where did they go to?

At the end of the day, we climbed on the bus once more, and journeyed back to East Grinstead to repeat the whole thing the following morning. This was show business! Strangely, I still had absolutely no desire to ever perform on a stage myself.

I don't remember if we ever had another 'inter-comps', because the next year the school participated in a national event of a similar nature known as 'The Sunshine Comps'. The theatrical profession has long supported an organisation known as The Sunshine Homes for Blind Babies and the competitions were one of the many events which brought in much needed funds. There were heats all over England and as many of us were entered for an event as possible, It was performing experience and as long as we didn't disgrace the school or make complete fools of ourselves, we could learn something. Even one of our teachers, Miss Gwen, entered. We hated her: her sister Miss Kath was prettier and not such a bully.

In addition to all the dancing classes provided at the school, there was also the option to take Drama and Elocution lessons from a visiting teacher, Miss Pauline Bird. She was nicknamed Dickie, of course. I was in like Flynn and began my association with the spoken word, a very wise move, as it turned out. I could have had piano lessons but didn't and have never regretted it but I did take up horse riding, the only thing I did that wasn't career related.

We had about five Shirleys, strangely, the only name that proliferated at the school, so most of us became known by our surnames, as a nickname. Fortunately none of us had a ghastly moniker. The oldest inhabitant was Shirley Searle, and it would have been pointless calling her Searley, so she kept her original name. I was Taylor, and there was Jordan, and Kay, and Cookie. For some reason, my father and his brother always called each other Taylor and years later I was also endowed with this honour and was always called Taylor by my first husband. We had some odd nicknames among the pupils. There was Dildy Smith (Hilda),and Pike Moore (Mary), and Moody Ellis (Muriel). Over the years, I have encountered many similar nommes de guerre, but my all-time favourite pseudonym was that of one of my son's schoolmates, who rejoiced in the title 'Wonky' Wildsmith.

In addition to the 'comps' we had other performances, mostly at the school itself. These were rarely dance-oriented but mainly Drama, or music or mime. All the pupils of Dickie Bird would do excerpts from plays and one of them included a line that has stayed with me for the rest of my days. The scene involved the Bronte sisters. Emily is being pressurised to have her work published, as her sister Anne implores her to agree, "It is wicked to hide your light under a bushel" she cries. Damned right. If you have a gift, you should spread it about and stop being so wrapped up in it yourself. Maybe it was Anne who was responsible for the publication of Emily's only novel, 'Wuthering Heights'?

Occasionally we invited an audience of very special people and the dramas were followed by ballroom dancing. Our guests were some gentlemen who later became known to the public as 'McIndoe's Guinea Pigs' and they were residents at a special unit in the Victoria Hospital in East Grinstead. Most of these men were pilots or other aircrew who had suffered terrible burns in their aircraft and were undergoing reconstructive surgery in the hands of the great Archibald McIndoe, whose surgery was still very much in the experimental stage. Hence the guinea-pig reference. When we encountered these tragically damaged men on our Saturday trips into the town, it was difficult to neither stare at their terrible disfigurement nor to obviously avoid looking. Keep in mind that these were comparatively recent burns and these boys were not pretty, their faces were red and purple, sometimes with twisted or missing ears, noses or lips. Their hands might be mangled and claw like but the scars on their souls were not on display. Just walking down the street of a country town must have required great courage, so we tried to do our bit.

After the Easter holidays, I returned to school not realising that it would be the last time my 'home' would be 18 Moor Allerton Drive, Leeds. By the time half-term arrived in early June, my mother and Jo Dyson had bought a dancing school in Maidstone, Kent and escaped from Leeds. With them went my oak toy box, a chest of drawers, her sewing machine and a couple of hundred pounds, raised on the mortgage, and left for Johnnie to pay off. She might have got more if she had waited for the due processes of the divorce court, but the law and the rights of married women were very different in those days and I think she reckoned that a bird in the hand was the best option. I am sure that Dorothy felt that she had earned the money having rescued her in-laws from bankruptcy and looked after her absentee brother and sister in-law's house for the duration of the war. Naturally Johnnie was stricken but I had been carefully indoctrinated and felt little guilt or regret at his plight. I tried to compensate many years later. Too much later.

Among the items which moved South with us were some pieces of jewellery, among them a ring given to me by Grannie Ada and a beautiful gold charm bracelet, a gift to my mother from her father-in-law, my Grandad Taylor. These were never seen again, the story being that they had been sent in a drawer of a wardrobe and been stolen. I'm sorry but I don't buy that one at all. Only an idiot would despatch such things in a removal van and my mother was far from being that stupid. The sale of unwanted gold would have raised much-needed funds.

My return journeys to school were now shorter and lonelier. There was no-one going my way. First a bus into the town, then another to Tunbridge Wells, a quick dash across the road and yet another bus to Maidstone. Sometimes the trip was done by train up to London, then back down to Maidstone passing a small airfield en-route. This boasted a tiny building, which housed the local flyers no doubt, and just a few years later it started accommodating charter flights to far off places, like Jersey and Guernsey. Like Topsy, it growed and it growed, and now we call it Gatwick Airport.

It was great fun being in a position of privilege as the daughter of one of the partners in the dancing school but it was a life very different to that of the average child, so no change there. One difference was that most people who want to learn ballroom dancing have a day-job, so lessons have to be in the evening with a few exceptions. One of these exceptions was a portly gentleman called George who was obviously besotted with my mother. He used to take us out during the day and she kept him on a string. There was another George at the same time, a miller, very handsome in a country lad way, he was in his thirties and single. He told Dorothy that he was an expert in tossing sacks of flour about, in an effort to impress her but she pointed out that she was not a sack of flour and was unimpressed with his romantic advances. However there was another pupil with whom she was more impressed. This one was about twenty-six, tall, dark and handsome, his good looks only marred by a nose which had obviously encountered an immovable object some years earlier. Within a few months, his fate was signed, sealed, and almost delivered.

I do not know the truth about the split up with Jo Dyson. Dorothy's version of the story was that Jo had turned strange and became mentally unstable, claiming that my mother was trying to poison her. Strange: I would have thought that she would have got used to Dorothy's cooking by that time. I suspect that Jo had nurtured a slightly proprietary attitude verging on the possessive: are we talking latent lesbianism? Are we talking latent? I don't know, and there is no answer to be had after all these years. However, Dorothy moved out of the house they had shared and when I came home for the next holiday I found that I was now living in a bed-sitting room in a very unsalubrious part of town.

Number 13, Church Street, was a terraced house which sat back from the pavement by a couple of yards, and was only minutes from the town centre. The kitchen was in the cellar, and there was no bathroom. There was a toilet in a shed at the bottom of the garden and the chamber-pot was under the bed. The room that was to be my home was about twelve feet square and held a bed, two fireside chairs, the sewing machine, my chest of drawers from my bedroom in Leeds, and the toy box. There was a gas-ring and a gas-fire, and a built-in cupboard that acted as a wardrobe. In spite of this comedown in our circumstances, we managed quite well. Dorothy secured a post as secretary to the local big-noise dentist, which turned out to be a lucky break since he serviced the dentition of Maidstone's finest and many useful contacts were made. It was while we were living in these straightened circumstances that I learned, painfully, that grown-ups are not perfect, though I always presumed that my own mother was above criticism, because that was what she had always told me.

The handsome young man with the re-arranged nose had succeeded where others had failed and was 'walking out' with my mother, in a manner of speaking. One Saturday night, during the school holidays, she went out with Reg, ostensibly to a party and promised that she would be back by 10.30 p.m. I was still awake and waiting at 2:30 a.m. when she came in. Perhaps that was where the rot set in to our relationship. I had always thought that a promise was not to be given lightly and was shattered to realise that my mother could let me down. Reg became a permanent feature in our lives and, when I wrote this, he was still in mine. In the later years, I was essential part of his life but in those early days I suppose I was an encumbrance. Eventually he moved in to another room in the house but I knew that during the term, when I was at school, he slept in my place in the double bed. They did not always remember to remove his pyjamas from between the sheets before I arrived home for the holiday.

In 1949, Johnnie agreed to divorce my mother on grounds of desertion. So, she and Reg married and remained so until her death in 2000. From the moment that Reg came into our lives I felt as though I had lost my other half and I longed to have a love of my own. There were times when Dorothy and Reg would take me dancing to the local ballroom where I could show off my skill and get to dance with real live men, and this was where I first encountered Stanley, Reg's younger brother. I worshipped from afar for nearly a year, and finally, my patience paid off though what a 23 year-old could see in a flat-chested and unworldly 15-year old I cannot imagine. It certainly was not sex. I was very innocent, as fifteen year-olds should be. Maybe my big attraction was my amazing dancing ability; he was a keen dancer, so I was a useful partner

By the time Dorothy and Reg married in April 1949, Stanley and I were a steady pair. I am positive that his older brother, and no doubt my mother, had threatened him with instant emasculation if he ever over-stepped the mark. The first and maybe only time his hands landed on my unclothed boobs I thought that I had lost my virginity. It was just as well Stanley was restrained in his amorous advances since Dorothy and Reg were quite happy to let me go up to the room he occupied at the weekends, early on Sunday morning, and climb in with him for an hour or more. Poor man, he must have been a saint. A year or so later she was lecturing me about morals and quite forgetting the fact that all eyes had been blind when the occasion suited her.

Stanley was not the first man I had been out with although some previous expeditions had been engineered. One night I was co-opted to accompany the dentist's son to a very smart do, all ball gowns and black tie. Frightfully lovely darling. I suppose that the one thing in my favour was that I spoke with a voice untainted by any local accent and in grammatically correct English. I felt totally out of my depth, but I must have behaved acceptably because shortly afterwards I received another invitation, this time from the Mayor. Would I partner his son to a function? Mrs Mayor had me in for inspection mind you, tea and crumpets in the drawing room. I found these dates profoundly discomfiting especially as I was collected by Prince Charming in a taxi from my ghastly bed sitting room.

A few nights later, a visit to the theatre was arranged and again the embarrassment of being escorted to and from my lodging house and the lack of knowledge about what drink to order and when. Nobody had ever explained that port should only be consumed following a meal. Bob Day, the young man, was charming, very academically bright and ahead of his age group. He took a commission in the army and lost a leg while on manoeuvres before he was nineteen. I last saw him on a train to London en route to collect his spare artificial limb.

So, on rolled the dancing years, with frequent examinations in the various branches of the art and in Drama and Poetry, at which I was quite a whiz. During those boarding school days in the term at least, entertainment was carefully monitored. We were taken en masse to see 'Henry V', a splendid and spectacular film in which Laurence Olivier gave a rousing performance intended to inspire patriotism and confidence in a nation bruised and scarred by five years of war. Another time we went to a symphony concert at The Davis Theatre in Croydon, and to the same venue on several occasions to see the ballet. The performance of Bizet's 'Carmen' by the Roland Petit Company was particularly significant because it starred Petit's wife Renée Jeanmaire, who was extraordinarily unlike any ballet dancer seen before. She wore her hair very short, in what she popularised as the 'Gamin' cut. Then she became internationally known, and appeared in the film 'Hans Christian Andersen'. Many years later, in year 2000, Zizi Jeanmaire, as she became known, was still a headliner, but as a singer in American nightclubs.

The ballet itself was overtly sexual and very avant-garde for its time. Even though I was uninformed about the mechanics of that sphere of activity, the choreography left little doubt as to what was being portrayed and I was deeply impressed or should I say shocked? My only sex education came in the form of three small booklets which gave me the unvarnished fact. I was horrified on two counts. First and foremost, the revelation regarding physical performance and more importantly, the fact that my mother had no word to say on the subject. I naturally concluded that the whole exercise was shameful and unspeakable. During the holidays, I still spent a lot of time in the cinema and in the library, both of which are the refuges of the lonely. In the latter establishment, I filled in the gaps in my sex education, not the practical side of course, but at least the more academic side of things became clearer. At the time, few libraries held any copies of the more illuminating leg-over manuals.

Eventually, the time to prove that my academic ability was up to par arrived, and Clodagh and I were entered in the December sittings of the School Certificate exams. We travelled to Worthing and stayed the week at her home. It was the final sitting before the introduction of 'O' levels and, before my sixteenth birthday arrived, I had the good news that I had passed all six subjects, five with high grades. Well done, Miss Raby! This meant that on my return to school, all the stops were out to push me through the last dancing exams that would qualify me for a teaching career if I chose to take that option. By the end of March 1950 I had gained professional teaching qualifications in Ballet and Stage Dancing. In the former, it was the Intermediate Examination of The Royal

Mother & Daughter, 1945

Academy of Dancing, and achieved only after much hard work and effort and done in the three months after my great academic success. I knew that the Advanced Certificate was way beyond my ability.

I really had outgrown my own strength by that time, I was five feet nine inches tall and the Ballet was not going to be for me. Even getting tights big enough was a problem. Talking tights, let me make you aware of one of the tricks of the trade at that time. To ensure that ones hose were wrinkle free, we used a method of tightening up the already tight tights, girding up our loins in a literal sense. This involved putting pennies inside, at the groin, poking the penny through the fabric to the front and capturing this by wrapping elastic or tape around the coin, which was about one inch across. Once secure, the tape was led across ones lower body to the next groin and the process repeated. Round to the nether regions and so on, using from four to six pennies in all. Strung up like a chicken ready for the roasting dish, one would then attempt to move in a suitably swan-like and graceful manner. On the occasion of my last ballet exam, I waddled into the studio at Romford, having travelled up from school on the train on a foggy, cold, February morning. I stood at the barre waiting to perform, fully aware of my incompetence.

"We will start with pliés" said our examiner. For the edification of the uninformed a plié (plee-ay) is a deep bend with the back ramrod straight and the feet and knees pointing east/west while the rest of the body faces north/south. As I went down, gracefully lowering my arms, there was a dreadful ripping sound accompanied by a rush of cool air to my nether regions. I had ripped the borrowed tights from knee to knee and they hung in tatters, flapping around my thighs. The examiner said: "Just carry on dear and don't worry about it". Easy for her to say: she was not nithered with the cold, terrified, and standing with her underwear in rags. However, the show must go on. I passed, probably with a sympathy vote. I scraped through with 68 marks: a pass was 65, and it was the lowest mark I had ever had. I didn't care; I was sick of the whole thing and just wanted a chance to stop being at school. I had developed a yearning to try my hand or should I say my feet, treading the boards and being a real live performer.

For some months, I had trudged round rehearsal rooms and empty stages, strutting my inadequate stuff and hoping that nobody would notice that I stood head and shoulders above every other hopeful candidate. Fortunately, the school was by this time associated with another influential member of the profession who now specialised in fixing up jobs for the less talented. I left school at Easter having been selected to join the chorus of a prestigious production in Blackpool, the following June. I was 16 years and 3 months old. Look out world, here comes Taylor.

CHAPTER 5
THERE'S NO BUSINESS LIKE SHOW BUSINESS

I spent a sort of gap period at home, psyching myself up for my great moment, my grand entrance into the world of entertainment. At the end of May, I packed my clothes and travelled to Leeds for a short sojourn with my relatives and my adoring and much maligned father. It was his job to deliver me to Blackpool where I was to make my debut, the first of his many trips to that resort. We set off in the breakfast hours of Sunday morning and arrived in the resort around lunchtime. This was before motorways and bypasses so the journey took almost three hours. We located some 'digs', the term by which stage lodgings was known, and I was installed in a very pleasant out-of-town bungalow whose owner was a motherly lady of ample proportions, Mrs Haslam.

There were two other girls from the show there, who were old hands with both Blackpool and Mrs Haslam. The next day we were joined by one more, a girl from my alma mater, Jo Orrin. We had been fortunate to have been auditioned by a colleague of the Misses Bush and Davies, whose job it was to fix up as many aspiring performers as possible with suitable employment. I had been up to London for other auditions and had already developed a sag in my knees in an effort to minimise my height so that I did not tower over all the other aspiring high kickers.

It had been a little intimidating for a sixteen-year-old to be trudging round the London streets at that time because audition land was in Soho, where the local ladies of ill repute hung around in doorways waiting for the punters. The additional problem that one had when walking from one audition to another in this district was the black fishnet tights. These were the most flattering leg-wear for me for the audition but de rigueur for the local floosies. Since time was of the essence and there was a distinct shortage of it between one theatre and the next, it was necessary to put on whatever street clothes were essential for the journey but keep on the tights. It was not at all unusual for me to get propositioned en route. In retrospect, I would have made considerably more money in the oldest profession but I was a nice girl at the time.

Some auditions were in rehearsal rooms, some were on stage at the most famous theatres in the land so I can truthfully say that I have appeared on stage at the Palladium, the Coliseum, the Royal Opera House and others. Regrettably, my only recognition came in the words "Thank you, dear. Next."

The worst part of going to auditions was actually walking in and feeling that every eye in the room was turned on me. In all probability, this was because we were all hoping for the same job and everyone needed to weigh up the competition. I found this scrutiny unnerving so I decided to take charge of the situation and confront my fear by calling the shots. I reasoned that as soon as the assembled company had looked at me my worries about whether they would do so, no longer existed. It would be all over and I'd have nothing left to fear but my own lack of ability or looks.

I adopted a strategy that involved flinging open the door to the stage or rehearsal room, standing very still and tall until every eye was on me, all the while scanning the room. When I had allowed time for most eyes to be upon me, I waved flamboyantly to an imaginary friend in the farthest corner. When my audience turned to see whom I had greeted, I slipped in and started to prepare for the forthcoming ordeal. It worked for me and years later someone said of me, that I never just walked in to a room, I always made an entrance. Old habits die hard. Inside many extroverts, there's an introvert desperately hoping that no one will see through the bullshit and recognise the quivering jelly underneath.

That first weekend of my stage career, Johnnie stayed the night in a hotel and so we were able to enjoy Sunday afternoon in Blackpool, the first time I had been there since 1943. We had coffee at the Savoy Cafe, lunch at another restaurant, the best seats in a cinema and an evening meal at yet another eating house, Nicky's Chicken Grill, which was to become a favourite after-the-show eating house for the cast. Johnnie never stinted on anything and it was lovely to revel in all the luxury after the years of economising. The following morning, I reported at the appointed rehearsal room and began learning six or seven routines for the show, which was called 'Fiesta at the Coconut Grove'.

The stars were Jimmy Jewell and Ben Warris, a well-known comedy duo. The supporting artists included Robert Wilson, a Scots singer of radio fame, who took the stage wearing hairy legs and a skirt. By the way, he also wore tartan jockey shorts. One spectacular couple were an American brother and (very fat) sister act who did amazing acrobatic routines on roller skates which one would imagine a lady of such ample proportions would find dangerous if not suicidal. Imagine standing in the wings and seeing a sixteen stone blonde standing on her hands, which were clutching roller skates, approaching you at a terrifying speed. Another American, a ventriloquist, also had a spot on the bill and a Spanish couple, Elsa and Waldo, did a comedy dance act. Waldo also had a busy time pursuing any likely female and since he owned a huge Cadillac, he had a certain pulling-power. We saw nothing of these speciality acts until the dress rehearsal.

Les Girls numbered sixteen and I was the baby of the company, which did not stop one of the stars of the show attempting to grope me in the wings, not that I was the only recipient of his unwelcome attentions. Toward the end of the second week our brand new costumes arrived in the care of the boss and staff of the costumiers, all male. We were summoned to the dressing room at the Hippodrome and given our clothes to try on. The men did not leave the room. I was shaken, but stripped down to my underwear and stepped into the first costume, a two piece affair consisting of a bra top with one frilled sleeve and panties with a floor length multi frilled skirt attached only at the back. Mine was purple, and very Copacabaña.

Unexpectedly, as I stood in my new finery, a middle-aged gentleman came over to me, kneeled down, and stuck his hand up one leg of the bottom half of my outfit. I was horrified. Removing a pin from his mouth, he said, "We need about an inch out of here" matching actions to words and moving on to the other leg. I was too stunned to demur and it went from bad to worse. "Get your bra off, love, it can be seen. Yes, now." I thought I was fairly un-bashful having gone to boarding school but other girls are one thing, strange men were something else entirely. I decided that if it was alright for the old hands, it would have to be alright for me.

During the two weeks of learning and rehearsal we gathered every day in some rooms to perfect our routines and a local aficionado brought us bagels every mid-morning at his own expense. The choreographer invented these dance routines as she went along as far as I know, though how she remembered what everyone was supposed to be doing remains a mystery. I guess that like other skills, it is all a matter of use and experience.

Our producer was a gentleman of distinction, Robert Nesbitt, who was also the producer of the ongoing show at the London Hippodrome. When we finally graduated to rehearsing in the theatre, he would sit in the stalls, always dressed immaculately in a dark suit and looking like a well-to-do businessman. He was always a perfect gentleman, he never swore, raised his voice, or spoke any vulgarisms. He looked and behaved more like a barrister than a show biz whiz. They don't make them like that any more. The Saturday before we were due to open, we were still hard at it on stage, at midnight and someone sent out for sandwiches to boost our flagging blood sugar levels, I never knew who paid for them but I always suspected that Mr Nisbett organised it.

The dress rehearsal itself was on a Sunday and we were hard at work all day, as we had been during the preceding days. Johnnie had arrived from Leeds at lunchtime and was allowed to watch the proceedings. A dress rehearsal is a full run through, with no stops for corrections or comments, if there is anything wrong it has to wait until the next morning. During previous rehearsals, it became clear that in the two parts of opening number when we had to do a fast change, there was insufficient time to rush down to the girls dressing room in the bowels of the theatre, change and get back in time for our next entrance. The first part of the opening number entailed four items of clothing, bra top with one sleeve, one glove, briefs with floor-length skirt, and a hat. The second outfit was a red and white striped leotard, like a one-piece swimsuit, white gloves, and a top hat. Again no bra could be worn and we needed the services of the dressers to make the change in the allotted time. We had 30 seconds to do it!

Our head-girl, Lorna, who was the appointed leader of our team, agreed that we would perform this striptease on the side of the stage assisted by the two dressers as long as the male stagehands were nowhere within viewing distance. The discarded costumes were to be flung on to sheets for removal when we were once more tripping the light fantastic. Right, sorted. Sixteen dancers, two dressers. This was an unlikely scenario for a successful quick change.

The dress rehearsal is a non-stop run through as on the night, so we got under way with the opening number in our lovely Latin-American costumes. As the music finished we all made our exit, some stage left, and some stage right. In spite of carefully laid plans there were stagehands everywhere and a large sheet spread out ready to receive our discarded apparel. The dressers stood expectantly, one of them and eight of us on each side of the stage. There was absolutely no time for modesty so we started ripping off clothing and within seconds we each had a stagehand pulling off our tops, hats and briefs and pushing us into the next lot. They were doggedly cramming our hats on, zipping us up, and tucking any stray parts of our persons into the leotard. The show's the thing and convention has no role when the production is at risk. Nothing more was ever said about the lack of privacy and by the time the show opened the next night, we each had our own dresser, the particular stagehand who had jumped into the breach at the dress rehearsal.

My faithful father was there to see my debut, leaving after the show at 10.30 p.m. in order to drive more than eighty miles back to Leeds. He had to be up by 5:00 a.m. to go to the market, and he did this every alternate weekend until the last performance on October 16th.

Dorothy and Reg never came, but I suppose it was a long way to Blackpool. She had a full time job, and money was in short supply and lots of other reasons. Allegedly. I only know that if my only daughter was fulfilling all my dreams and ambitions, I would have been there for her, even if I had invented an illness and borrowed the money. There was enough money to pay for a tail suit for Reg but as I said, I took a back seat when he came along. I don't remember being overtly aware of how I felt then but I was used to it at the time and I'm probably just having an elderly bitch about how badly done to I am, or was.

Although we only had one free night a week, which was Sunday, I never missed my social life. In fact since I had never had a social life to speak of, it was nice not to expect one. Of course there were the 'stage-door Johnnies' who used to wait for the end of the show in the hope that they could pick up a companion for supper and possibly breakfast too. Another girl and I risked it one night, the chaps were middle aged and we reckoned that if things turned difficult we could outwit or outrun them. Fortunately they did not press themselves and their attentions on us too strenuously and we arrived home in pristine condition. Many of the cinemas and theatres had a 'free list', which wasn't a list at all; it really just meant that any performer from the other shows could have a free seat, usually at the afternoon performances. We might see a matinée, or a film, or sometimes Sunday specials with big stars in them. Frank Sinatra came one Sunday but I can assure you there was no free list on that occasion. There was an American Air Force base near Warrington and no shortage of takers for the seats.

In all, there were eight live theatres in Blackpool, most doing two performances a day, the cream of the entertainment industry was glad to be there for the summer. Blackpool had a longer season than elsewhere because when all the rest had closed, this resort still had its star attraction to finish with. As the schools reopened for the autumn term, the lights went on in Blackpool. There were miles of illuminations and it was the only spectacle of its size and style in the country, although these days I understand that Morecambe puts on a good show. Unfortunately, the weather always causes some damage but that is the price to be paid for the windy, wet, western location.

I was fortunate to have the chance of a little unusual extra-curricular activity. We had a real live orchestra as did all the stage shows at the time, and one of the musicians, a clarinettist of mature years, had a tandem. He was experiencing difficulty in finding a back-seat pedaller, and came down to the dressing room to ask for volunteers. No one did. So I did. We used to cycle to St Anne's which boasted a large boating lake, where Zacco hired a sailboat for a couple of hours and I was first mate. It was glorious weather, and sometimes we arrived back at the theatre sunburned and wind-blown, only just in time for the six o'clock show.

A 'first' of some significance for me was my encounter with men who were sexually different. I had never heard of such things, hardly surprising when one considers the paucity of any sex education in my life, and I was truly astonished to find that there were two so-called 'queers' in the show. One of these two was Geoffrey, who was totally overt and talked about his sexual encounters without embarrassment. The other was a sweet young chap named Johnny, a much younger man who went on to have his own team of dancers and appear on that new fangled thing ...... the television. He was a lovely lad and was probably still struggling with the question of whether he was one of the boys or one of the girls.

Every year in Blackpool there was a Variety Club event in aid if their charities such as the Sunshine Homes aforementioned in the preceding chapter. This was the News of the World Garden Party, sponsored by that newspaper. The stars came from all over the country and fortunately, in 1950, the year I was able to attend, the weather was perfect. We all assembled at a point in town to be taken to the park where the event was to be held and taxis, coaches and horse drawn carriages drew up as we waited to board. As luck would have it, I drew a horse and carriage and Richard Attenborough as my companion. Of course he wasn't the monumental star he is today but he was a film star nevertheless. He politely kissed me goodbye when we arrived and went our separate ways. It was a wonderful day, the stars mixed with the chorus girls and I sat talking to two of the biggest name producers in the business, George and Alfred Black. It was quite an experience for a sixteen-year-old.

On October 16th the show had closed and we all had to find another job. I had been picked out for a trial for a new company for a production of 'Kiss Me Kate'. This was an adaptation of 'The Taming of the Shrew', which was playing in the West End at the time. It was a great opportunity so I stayed on in Blackpool for a few days learning the dances before transferring to London for rehearsals on stage. The bombshell fell when one more routine was introduced, which involved the girls starting their contribution seated on the floor and then being lifted on to shoulders of their male partner. I have to say that my other half did a valiant job and actually got me where I was supposed to be once or twice. However, the idea of anyone hauling a five-feet nine tall package weighing 150 lbs on to their shoulder was frankly ludicrous, so the chorus manager had to 'let me go'.

The endless round of auditions and agents offices started again and I was fairly fortunate in that I had another job, for the festive season, fixed up before too long. It was early December before rehearsals started so I had a 'resting' period, which was something of a drag in the County Town of Kent. I knew few people of my own age and was probably viewed with suspicion by most of the populace. Nice girls did not go on the stage even though we had moved from the bedsit to a spacious semi in a nice part of the town. Maidstonians, and Southerners in general, are more reserved than my native Yorkshiremen, and I felt something of a social pariah. I got used to not quite fitting in or to being "not quite our class, darling" and I decided at quite an early age that if you can't join them, beat them. I had learned this one at school when I found that all the other fifteen and sixteen-year-olds had been allowed to join the local Youth Club but I was excluded on the grounds that I was "too sophisticated". Excluded by my peers, not the Youth Leader. "I'll show you, you bastards! I don't need you." They made it quite clear that they considered me to be 'different', so I decided that I would be as different as I wanted to be.

The new show was a pantomime, 'Aladdin', with Joan Dowling as the principal boy. She was a real actress, a tiny, fairly plain bundle of talent who had starred in a British film 'No Room at the Inn'. She was word perfect the first time she came to rehearsals and gave all she had every time unlike many so called stars who only want to walk through a role until the dress rehearsal. Sadly, a short time after this, she committed suicide while her husband, Harry Fowler of 'Army Game' fame, was spending the night at the Turkish baths. It sounded like marital problems to me, but we never saw any hint of that when he came to the theatre to collect her. They had both been child actors and sort of grew up together.

Once again I was looking for digs and I viewed some desolate places, eventually taking a bedsit in Hammersmith, a few minutes walk from the Kings Theatre where I was to be appearing. It was awful; the cooker was communal, as were the ablutions, the former being located on the landing outside my room. I had a double bed, however, and at the first rehearsal I found two flat-mates, one of who was a total stranger and the other Valerie Bonner, lately of Charters Towers. We all slept together in the double bed and I was in charge of shopping and cooking and the others seemed quite happy for me to be boss lady. After all I was nearly seventeen and I had considerable bedsit experience.

So, now there were more dance routines to be learned and more rehearsals. This time I travelled up to London every day from Maidstone, moving into my garret during the frenzy of the final week of preparations. Our Widow Twanky was one Clarkson Rose, an old timer of considerable experience. He used to have his own seaside show called 'Twinkle' and I remember going to see it in Llandudno when I was on a rare holiday during the war. If he had been an actor, he would have been an 'actor / manager' but as he wasn't a stand-up comedian, more of a sit-com type, I don't know what title was bestowed on him. I think his ego far outweighed his talent and I doubt that his career was going anywhere but down, but he gave an acceptable performance as the Dame. This particular show was notable in my own career because it gave me two opportunities to step on the ladder of success both of which I spectacularly ignored. Nay, turned down.

One of the acts in the panto included an old acquaintance, Nona, from the Blackpool show, where she began an affair with the male American roller skater, Dick Remy. In the London show she had become the sole female in a long established variety act known as Wilson, Keppel, and Betty. I had seen this trio many times when I was a child. The two scrawny males, Wilson and Keppel, were dressed as comic Egyptians and their lady companion sported flowing harem garb. Sand was thrown on to the stage and they then performed a comic sand dancing routine, which remained unchanged from one decade to the next. About three weeks from the closing night, Nona wanted to leave and join Dick when he returned to America but she had to find another Betty for the act. She asked me, maybe because the role had been traditionally filled by a girl who was taller than the two men, to increase the comic effect, or perhaps out of some loyalty to a past colleague. I promised to think about it. She who hesitates is lost and within 24 hours another girl was approached and accepted.

In the same show, for some reason I knew all the lines and moves of the second 'boy', the friend of Aladdin. Remember in those days, leggy females played the two dashing hero figures and men played the 'Dame' and other comic characters. The young lady who had the part was taken ill and a desperate stage manager came to the morning rehearsal call to ask if anyone could step into the breach. I dithered but Una did not hesitate, so she went on that night and did a sound performance. It will no doubt astonish those who know me that I lacked the get up and go, to go and get it. I resolved to develop a little more pushiness but another chance at greatness never came my way as long as I was in the theatrical profession.

My social life during the run of the pantomime was nil, we did a daily matinée so the cinema was a no-no and I used to go home to Maidstone after the Saturday night show or on the milk train to Leeds for a day of pampering. My only social encounter was while walking back to the bedsit one night on New Year's Eve, having returned from Kent because we had a show next day. Out of the darkness a male voice spoke to me "You all alone, and sure if it isn't New Year's Eve". I turned and found a pleasant if ordinary chap catching up with me and he told me he was on the way to a local pub for a predominantly Irish shindig. Would I like to go? Well it seemed more fun than going to the bedsit alone, so I said yes. It was all singing all dancing and with the exception of yours truly, all Irish. At throwing out time, my escort duly took me home, demurely kissed me goodnight, and we each went our own ways, never to meet again. I suppose I was lucky, I dread to think of the alternative.

I did have three other memorable Sunday evenings, however, one of which was a Sunday special performance by Ram Gopal and his Indian ballet company. This was absolutely unlike anything I had previously seen, we did not have the Asian population in this country at that time so 'Bombay Dreams' would not have had the popular appeal that it enjoys in the 21st century. The second Sunday special was Ralph Reader and his 'Gang Show' a wonderfully professional entertainment performed by Boy Scouts and Scoutmasters. The third Sunday special was a joy. There was a comedian called Cheerful Charlie Chester whose career as a broadcaster spanned several decades, and one memorable night he held the stage without any supporting artists, for nearly three hours.

A decent wage for a chorus dancer at the time was about five pounds a week, which did not leave much after two pounds and ten shillings (£2.50) or more, was used in paying for digs. So, getting paid six pounds with an extra ten shillings for the matinée in Blackpool and the same in London was indeed riches. The average shop assistant was paid about three pounds a week, if that, but of course they did not have to worry about finding a new job every three months. Fortunately, I was a great saver, and very disciplined, a lifelong habit to this day and so I always had my savings to fall back on when I was out of work. At the end of the pantomime the endless round of agents and auditions began again and I have to say that several encounters in agents' offices were hazardous; many of these men had little interest in my dancing ability. There were also the nights when I felt unwilling to go home to the somewhat censorious atmosphere of my mother's house and I decided to stay in London. However my savings did not run to hotels and I've slept in some pretty odd places.

Among these was the office of one Charlie Harvard; an agent who booked mainly circus acts. He was never less than the perfect gentleman to me and would take me to shows or dinner and drop me off at the office to sleep on his casting couch with strict instructions to be gone before the cleaner turned up. One morning, I was having a wash and brush up at Piccadilly tube station, when a policewoman walked in and gave me the third degree. Another time Charlie could not oblige but phoned a man who could and I went all the way to Potters Bar to stay with a Jewish tailor called Harry. Somehow I managed to come through all this with my virginity intact. I imagine it was my naiveté that saved me, I still believed in fairies.

On one occasion, I had arranged to meet a jazz band and their coach, the bus kind, in Cambridge Circus at midnight, for a free ride up to Leeds. Charlie took me out for a meal and dropped me off at ten-to-twelve and drove away. Five minutes later he came back to make sure that I was going to be alright. He stopped the car by the kerb and I went over to assure him that I was fine, so he went on his way. Within half a minute, the cops arrived. Was the man soliciting? Was I soliciting? Who was I? Where did I live? Where was I going? And please get in the car - we're going to the cop shop. I finally persuaded a small red-haired copper that I was capable of taking care of myself and departed for Kings Cross under escort.

The big problem was that I was a shilling short of my train fare to Leeds. Somewhat desperate I approached a pleasant looking older lady, asked her for a loan and her address, and without the latter finally boarded the train for the North. I don't know why I didn't get a ticket to Wakefield and ring my long-suffering father to come and get me. I could have ended up in pocket, but I was not in the habit of crying for help.

I had managed to contact the famous Uncle Willie Henshall and paid a visit to his office but he pointed out that my training had over qualified me for a chorus line job in one of his shows, which were strictly second rate. However, I finally managed to find myself a second rate job without his help. A new production was being staged for the purpose of reviving the jaded career of a well-known but passé comic by the name of Bunny Doyle, who had been a successful pantomime Dame when I was a small girl. I was offered the job of a showgirl, that is to say, a tall, long legged lovely who stood around on stage wearing very little and requiring no talent at all but oddly, attracting a higher wage than the hard working dancers. Well, a girl has to eat, so I took the job.

The show was called 'Non-Stop Hollywood' and it all seemed very glamorous, particularly when we were taken to Heathrow Airport to pose on the latest airliner for publicity photographs. I think that the aeroplane was a Constellation. It was huge and we were photographed on the steps as though we were just leaving for America. In fact the furthest we went was Tonypandy in South Wales by way of Hereford and Ramsgate where the show opened. Holiday towns out of season are dire places to be and Ramsgate was no exception. However on the opening night I managed to liven things up a bit.

As I explained, a showgirl is required to do little except stand around or glide gracefully across the stage looking aloof and elegant while wearing the skimpiest clothes. At that time all ones personal bits had to be covered, this was long before 'Hair'. On the first night, the Watch Committee came to the show to ensure that nothing naughty was said, seen, or done and that the show was fit for the eyes of the local populace. One Mick Mulligan, of 'Magnolia Jazz Band' fame, underwrote the finances of this epic production and he was posted in the wings, very close to where I was standing trying to look like a totem pole. The star of the show supposedly arrived at an Indian reservation and as he stepped out of a puff of smoke, we totem poles were to fling our arms above our heads, adding to the effect.

My costume consisted of a bikini bottom and a brief strapless brassiere. This flimsy top half gave up the ghost as we flung up our arms, and it went flying across the stage leaving me illegally underdressed. With great control I crossed my arms over my naked bits as Mick Mulligan hissed at me "Don't move, the Watch Committee's in. For God's sake keep still." I kept still. From then on we had to wear gold sequinned stars stuck to our boobs with spirit gum in case it ever happened again, which it didn't. I never found out if the Watch Committee had noticed and the show closed three weeks later so I was back to pounding the streets, chasing from audition to audition. During the brief run, I had become enamoured of the drummer, a romance that was going nowhere even if the show had run for years, so I expect he was happy enough to see us going our separate ways. I never heard or saw anything more of him but there is a bright young thing film director who is the right age to be his son, same surname, and quite an unusual one, same looks, a dead ringer in fact. Just think I could have been his mother and then I'd have got to go to premieres and all that jazz!

The next job I got was in a small select summer show in Bognor Regis. The star was a very elegant and classy comedian named Tommy Fields, brother of the famous Gracie. He did his act in white tie and tails but had some hilarious routines with the also-ran comic, one Norman Vaughan who later became famous for his compèring of Sunday

59

Night at the London Palladium and for his catch phrases "Swinging" and "Dodgy". Norman was one of those funny-men who was always funny: it wasn't just an act he did when the curtain went up. He was painfully thin but was very well catered for in the lunchbox department to which he referred as "my brother", of which more later. His side-kick in the show was Pip Hinton, formerly known as Doreen, late of the Romford branch of my alma mater. Norman was a big pal of Dick Emery: he was the comedian in our sister show at Southsea, and was a regular visitor to Bognor.

The two shows had the same producer, Dick Hurran, who also produced The Folies Bergère in the West End. He was a very different animal to the suave and elegant Robert Nesbitt. Dickie was unashamedly transatlantic, casually dressed, and very hands-on. Not literally, we were never in danger of getting groped, but leaping on to the stage, all singing, all dancing and made no bones of the fact that the more buttock our costumes exposed the better he and the audience would like it. We were of the opinion that he was seriously misjudging the taste of the Royal Bognor Regis clientele but he had his way.

We were a small troupe, only four of us, each with a publicity photograph outside the theatre. The company boasted a tenor singing old favourites from Lehar and Strauss, and we had a soprano who did likewise. Sometimes they did it together and we ladies of the chorus might flit about on stage in filmy costumes, simulating romantic dream sequences to the strains of The Merry Widow or The Chocolate Soldier. Remember this was before Elvis Presley, Buddy Holly and long before The Beatles. The latest show business sensation a hard of hearing knock-kneed young singer called Johnny Ray and Nat King Cole was thrilling us with "Too Young".

We worked hard for our pay; we had a repertoire of three shows which rotated so that anyone on a two-week holiday got to see all three. The locals could see them all, hopefully forgetting what the first one had been about by the time that they had seen the third and coming again and again throughout the twelve week run. I had a lovely social life in Bognor, one of the stagehands was young and well-educated, and had an open topped sports car. He also had friends, one of whom was a very upper crust type who used to race his Jowett Javelin. Frightfully lovely, darling. Then one weekend he was racing, and I never saw him again. After Bill, I fell madly in love with a naval type, Fleet Air Arm actually, who had a flying accident which resulted in him losing a small toe. In the meantime I moved in with his Mother and lived in luxury while waiting for Hylton to recover. His father, deceased, had been a Harley Street consultant and the house was very gracious living. There was a breakfast room, and washbasins in the bedrooms; even Clodagh's house did not have those. Hylton was stricken with appendicitis while still in Haslar, the naval hospital at Portsmouth and I faithfully visited him Wednesdays and Sundays.

He came home eventually but I don't think I came up to the moral standards he expected of a chorus girl, or down to them, and he ditched me for another member of the cast. I wouldn't have thought she would have filled the bill either but it wasn't something we discussed in those days. I had briefly, very briefly lost my maidenhood to the drummer but I had no intention of making a habit of it and was hoping the lapse of morality might disappear into the mists of time. In spite of having enjoyed a fairly easy relationship with my mother, she had opted out of discussing the birds and the bees, so I was rather uninformed about sexual behaviour. I certainly could never have discussed anything of that nature with her. She finally "just happened to find" some contraceptive pessaries, purchased only in case I ever needed them, in one of my drawers. This discovery occasioned one of the Oscar-winning tragedy performances which I was becoming used to.

Eventually, my mother and Reg came to see me perform. Since Bognor was not a million miles from Maidstone they decided to make this their summer holiday. They were both miserable all week, and I was made to feel guilty that I was the reason for them to be spending seven days in Bognor. Another God-given opportunity to play the martyr. Why they didn't just come one Saturday night, stay over, and go home on Sunday, I don't know, but they never did that even when I was in London, from where a late train or bus was available. I used to catch the bus after the show on a Saturday night and walk alone at 1:00 a.m. from the bus terminus in Maidstone, a distance of a mile or more. Happy days!

Johnny, on the other hand, had travelled down from Leeds to see me and spent a week in one of the better hotels. We had a splendid time sunning ourselves during the day and meeting after the show in the bar of his hotel for a drink together. The staff thought I was his bit of stuff and he never disenchanted them. He could hardly announce my age because of the licensing laws. He looked far younger than his years and I looked older than mine so we just went along with the game.

The last night of the show arrived and I had decided that my foray into showbiz was over, so it was a very special night indeed. The Royal Yacht Club members were regular clients and we had been invited to their club parties during the season. Another one was planned for this final night. It was traditional for practical jokes to be played during the final performance and Tommy and Norman were the chief culprits. During Tommy's solo, where he entertained in evening dress, singing and playing the piano, Norman was under the stage pushing long objects like feathers and a Union Jack which unfurled as it emerged from a hole normally used to anchor props. Tommy was oblivious to what was happening and astonished that he was getting laughs where none was called for but he finally spotted one of the causes of amusement, crept, grabbed it and shouted "I'll get my own back, Norman". He did.

Later in the show, Norman and Pip did a duet with a story line. They were supposedly a young show business couple struggling to find work and were standing on the station with no future bookings. They decide to abandon their show business hopes and find other employment. Suddenly their future looks better as a Telegram boy comes onstage with a telegram offering them a long-term booking. Cue for song. Norman always opened the piece of paper and read it out to Pip, but this time Tommy had substituted the original with the message "I have an opening for your brother" and Norman fell about laughing. Remember that "My brother" was Norman's pet name for his male member. The show normally closed at 10:15 p.m., but this night it was 11 o'clock before the audience left. We had a backstage party, then off to the Yacht Club for a late supper, and that was the end of that.

I had decided that being a dance teacher was less stressful and better paid than my on-off stage career but I did not have a clear idea of what I was going to do. I need not have worried; my mother took over, organised my immediate future, and then later was very bitter that I had some plans of my own stemming from her intervention. If she had kept out of it I may very probably have stayed in Maidstone and eventually married the boys next door, or someone my mother approved of more than my ultimate choice.

CHAPTER 6
"THE LIGHT FANTASTIC"

I don't really remember how or why, but my entire family happened to be in the same town at the same time. My mother and Reg were in Leeds to see Grannie Ada who was presumably practising her swan song yet again and I was in that fair city staying with Johnnie. One evening whilst I was otherwise engaged, Dorothy and Reg went to a dance studio in the town owned by a Mr. Leonard Cave. By the end of the evening my fate was sealed and I had little say in the matter, having been taught from an early age that mother knew best and that I must never, never argue, on pain of being sent to Coventry and being stripped of my decorations. The plan was this: I was to come to Leeds to serve an apprenticeship with Mr Cave in order to qualify for the teaching examinations set by the major Ballroom Dancing societies and live with Johnnie during the period of my professional training. Having used his generosity and goodwill, I would return to Maidstone, open a dancing school and once again fulfil my mother's dreams. Maybe she would come to see my triumph if I was that close to home.

It did not work out like that! The training was destined to take far longer than had been expected because as long as I remained unqualified, my pay remained low. In the meantime, I became accustomed to being mistress in my father's house and master of my own fate. My parent did not censure the hours I kept with the friends I chose. Deep joy!

The Central School of Dancing was located in a basement in the centre of the city. Because it was a cellar, one would have expected a concrete floor. Unexpectedly, it had a parquet floor that was fine for dancing on for a couple of hours but which proved hard on the feet when one was teaching all day. I believe that, in the past, the room had been a part of a multiple men's outfitters, Montague Burtons, and this may account for the parquet floor. There was no natural lighting because that was not possible below street level. At night, for the public classes, the studio was illuminated by strings of coloured light bulbs. This gave the place an air of slight sleaziness in marked contrast to the studio of the main opposition which held the crown for dance competition successes, and was bright and airy and out of town. I didn't care; I would have felt threatened by that school and by its formidable Principal, Miss Olga Sheard, a former professional competition winner. In fact I felt intimidated by her pupils, never mind the teachers.

Many of these dancers used a strange stance, obviously dictated by their instructors but, I suspect misinterpreted by the pupils. This entailed the female half of the couple leaning as far back from the waist as her roll-ons or corsets would allow while the male partner stood in a rigid and slightly backward leaning position. It was just as well they both knew the order of the steps to be performed because the lady's ears were so far away from the gentleman's mouth that she couldn't possibly hear him if he was to speak to her. In stark contrasts to the upper body, the lower halves were joined as if by superglue because being welded at the hip is an essential part of the steering system in this noble art.

Contrary to popular belief, the dancer who is 'leading' (that is, the man or female who is dancing the man's steps) does not guide his partner by using a strong-arm approach but by pushing her along or around with his pelvis. In the meantime, the lady, as she is called, snuggles into extremely close contact from her bosom to her knee leaving her to work out for herself whether her partner has half a toilet roll in his pocket or is fantasising about what he'd rather be doing. I must point out that at this stage of my development it never occurred to me that the poor chap I was telling to snuggle in had any other thought in his mind other than learning to dance correctly and it was years before I understood what men meant when they said I was sexy to dance with. Sorry guys, I didn't know there was any other way: dancing was dancing to me and not a part of sexual foreplay. Not that I knew anything about that either.

So, at the age of seventeen years and nine months I found myself mistress of my childhood home and a budding teacher of ballroom dancing. Len Cave kept me budding for quite some time, about two years, because I was doing a professional job at an amateur's wages. I started out by helping at the evening 'Beginners' classes three times a week. Within a very short time I took over the duties of teaching these hopefuls the basic steps of the Waltz and the Quickstep. During the dark nights of the winter months I regularly had as many as a hundred boys aged seventeen to thirty odd standing behind me following every step and chipping in with wisecracks for half an hour at a time, three times a week. My expertise with repartee improved quickly though it had been some years since I first experienced the sweetness of success in that field of endeavour. Oddly, that was also in the ballroom.

My mother had taken me to a tea dance and one of her acquaintances came over to speak to us. I was, at the time, well aware of my shortcomings in the glamour stakes. Freckles, pigtails and big feet do not make a thing of beauty. The gentleman commented that I would have to watch out for the wolves when I got older. I was furious because it seemed a real put-down to me but I replied, "Better let the wolves look out for themselves" and had the pleasure of seeing his jaw drop. I think Mummy-dearest was mildly surprised too, but from then on I decided on the tough-guy approach to the opposition. However, it was to be several years before I learned the real power of my verbal ability.

Johnnie was delighted to have me back in the fold but I had been well indoctrinated to perceive him as a heartless profligate who had rejected all ideas of domestic bliss long before my arrival in his life. There had been no forgiveness from his ex-wife and I was programmed to carry on the feud so I took advantage of the situation. The house in Moor Allerton Drive had not changed since 1945 and so I set about rectifying the situation immediately by going to a fairly expensive department store where I had frequently lunched with my paternal grandparents during my early years. I selected a new living room carpet and told the assistant to bill it to Mrs Taylor's account and deliver it forthwith.

I think this faintly amused my Grandmother, but the carpet duly arrived and was followed shortly by a single bed and a dressing table to replace the furniture that had ostensibly been sent to me at school. I knew nothing of housekeeping or cooking; I had never been permitted to practise these skills in case the results were inferior to those achieved by my mother. On occasions when I had sought to help by dusting, she would take one look then get out the duster and do it again. A great confidence booster. I could fry chops and boil potatoes, do bacon and egg, and soon learned to cook a roast, but my great achievement was to turn the scraps of this last one into a curry, courtesy of Connie, the mother of my last love, Hylton.

Johnnie was amazingly tolerant and he was fairly handy in the galley himself so between us we managed quite well. On Monday and Wednesday, he only worked in the morning so we would meet for lunch and then go to a matinée at a cinema afterwards, in the best seats of course. We were regular customers at Matthias Robinson's, an upmarket department store, and we became known to the manageress, a tall blonde lady of imposing proportions. On my eighteenth birthday, a Monday, we lunched there and Johnnie presented me with a diamond ring, a family heirloom of some considerable carat-age which had been given to him on his own eighteenth birthday. I was thrilled to receive it and immediately put it on my third finger right hand, where it sits at this moment. The manageress came to the table, not having worked out which hand was which and said, "Congratulations, I hope you'll be very happy". I was too astonished to reply, but Johnnie didn't pause for a moment. "Thank you, I'm sure we will" he replied.

I can't imagine what she made of us, he was five feet three, I was five feet nine and although I looked as though I was in my twenties, he certainly looked in his mid thirties though he was in fact forty-four. We must have been a slightly odd couple but since he was always dressed in immaculate hand made suits she possibly thought I was marrying him for his money. Unfortunately I lost him to another woman soon afterwards, but I got to keep the ring of course and now wear it every day. It is a very eye-catching rock.

Jimmy, an attractive rogue

My duties at the dance studio increased but as this involved working evenings I had little social life. Again. At first my father picked me up at ten thirty and then gave me driving lessons, in the dark. The first time I drove in daylight I was horrified at the amount of potential victims who thronged the streets. Sometimes he would wake me up at six o'clock on Sunday mornings to practice reversing into people's gateways while they slept the sleep of the hung-over: his own needs for sleep were slight. He worked on the principle that if you woke up, you obviously did not need any more sleep. If he went to bed at 10:30 p.m., he would be awake by 3:00 a.m., and be sitting up in bed doing the accounts for the shop in the market. He had joined the family business in 1947 having returned to printing after the end of the war and found it less than satisfying. After all, it hardly compared to roaring round Harewood in a Cromwell tank.

Food used to magically appear. My father did all the buying for the shop and a huge paper sack full of fruit and vegetables came to our house every week. This continued until the sale of the shop in 1967 at which time he was suddenly unemployed. I never had to buy greengroceries, or a Christmas tree, or a turkey for the festivities until then and it came as a severe blow, I can assure you.

I found out that the dance hall to which my father had trailed my mother before I was born was now called the Astoria Ballroom and had a public dance on Tuesday nights from seven-thirty until eleven: price two shillings (10p in today's money). That's for me I thought. I'll go and strut my stuff and show them what a real dancer can do. It is very lonely standing in a dance hall hoping that someone will come and ask you to dance, but if you aren't there they can't ask, so you have to gird up your loins and take your courage in both hands and various other clichéd terms if you want to succeed. If you don't take a chance, you don't stand a chance, how's that for another one?

On that very first Tuesday, I stood on the balcony surveying the possibilities, wearing my spectacles, since I was optically challenged. Having sussed out the possible talent, I would then take off the specs, and make my way downstairs to the arena, where I waited to be mobbed by anxious young men desperate to whisk me on to the floor. I'm glad I'm not young any more. Years later I solved that particular problem by not bothering to wait for some spotty youth to fulfil my dreams. I simply decided who was going to be the lucky man and approached him myself. It always worked and if they thought that my invitation implied more than a bop that was their bad luck ... or their good luck, depending on how I felt about it.

That first night, chance would have it that there was a skinny little weed present, known to his peers as Little Jimmy. He was a motor mechanic who suffered from asthma and dermatitis and had all the grace and charm of a camel. I felt sorry for him. He had very little going for him except a classic ballroom dancing posture and lovely movement, but he was a mite vertically-challenged as far as I was concerned. He would only dance the Samba with me because in that dance no body contact is necessary so the height difference was not a problem. Because the Olga Sheard studio was in the vicinity, many of the pupils frequented the Astoria Ballroom, so the standard of expertise was pretty high. The real dancers were there at the kick-off and dominated the floor until the masses arrived at around eight o'clock. I had to leave at a quarter-to-eleven in order to catch the last tram home and very few young men had cars in those far-off days. If one was escorted home, on the tram, it meant that there was a long walk ahead for one's gallant swain, so it didn't happen too often. After dancing with a girl a gentleman might indicate his interest by asking if his partner would like to go up on the balcony for a coffee: alcohol was only allowed at private functions in those long gone days. If you agreed to this refreshment, you were stuck with him until home time, at which point, beating a hasty retreat was the order of the day unless an unlikely passion had stirred one's being.

I used to go for coffee with Little Jimmy on a regular basis because it seemed that no one else would, he was very gauche and seemed immature and unsure of himself. He always wore a suit when he was out in the evening but with a hand knitted pullover for heavens sake, hardly the epitome of sartorial elegance. His father had a garage nearby but Jimmy worked for someone else and seemed to live in a state of constant war with his parent. He had the reputation of being a very promising young golfer, which surprised me. Socially he seemed an unlikely golf-club type and certainly not my class, darling!

Meanwhile, my proficiency as a dance teacher went from strength to strength but there was no sign of the tuition promised. However, I had bought the textbook and was able to put my "learning from manuals" skill into action. There is a lot more to ballroom dancing than floating round in time to the music. There is the question of precisely how much turn is made between one step and the next, which part of the foot the step uses, whether the body is rising or falling and which way the body is moving in relation to the feet. A teacher has to know all this for both the man's steps and the lady's, which are not always the exact opposite. In addition, one has to develop a truly essential skill. This entails knowing when your pupil or partner is going to make a total cock-up and finding a speedy way of getting your own feet out of harm's way. Open-toed dance shoes were very fashionable at the time and I was constantly having my stockings laddered from the toes up. Steel reinforced boots would have been more appropriate.

On my eighteenth birthday I had a party, my first since 1945. I only knew people who came to the studio so it was a small gathering, I didn't even have a man in my life to invite. However, one of the girls knew a spare man and she gave me his number to ring. He had the most sexy, sophisticated, voice I had ever heard and I pictured him speaking to me on the phone perched on the edge of his desk wearing a smart blue suit, probably sporting a Clark Gable moustache. He was a press photographer, an older man of about twenty-six, maybe more and I couldn't wait to meet him. This was more my style than a scaly-skinned, undersized, motor mechanic. He certainly was not invited.

The night arrived and so did the guests, with the exception of George, the man of mystery. Finally, there was a knock on the door and I rushed excitedly to welcome this attractive hunk. I hope I did not show my astonishment. George stood there, immaculate in a brown suit and cream shirt, brown tie and shoes and possessed of a face that one could only describe as homely. Clark Gable he wasn't but he came in full of charm and took possession of the only remaining chair. This came to be known as George's chair and is now, more than fifty years later, known simply as 'George'. Where his namesake is I know not: it is sad to lose track of old friends. I last saw him when he came fifty miles to take the photographs of my daughter's wedding.

The evening went with a swing and later in the week George rang and arranged a date. Unfortunately dates with George often turned into press assignments. On this first occasion we went roaring off to Bawtry, near Doncaster to photograph a body recovered from the river but I cared little since I was already madly in love with this fascinating older man. Unfortunately for me the dates, working or pleasure were few and far between and while finding me amusing and cute, George was not looking for a steady relation-ship. I finally gave up hoping and took up with a stunning naval type by the name of Bernard. Many years later, George took my wedding photographs and had the nerve to say, "It's a good man that can take my girl away from me". He did finally marry but it was a short-lived union: I suspect that he was too set in his ways to make a success of a partnership.

Bernard was not officer material. He couldn't dance, and was undoubtedly no Einstein but certainly a thing of considerable beauty, and he had a physical appeal that was remarkable. We enjoyed several passionate weeks interspersed with his periodic returns to duty. However, when he started talking engagement rings I had to back off. I was more interested in ensnaring George into that happy state and I was still pursuing that objective during Bernard's absences. I suppose that strictly speaking, I was two-timing the poor man but I had made it clear that matrimony was not on the agenda.

My connection with the navy was short lived: he was great for a snogging session but otherwise had little potential. For some months, my father had been involved with the wife of one of his friends from the early 1930's, Benny, who was now stricken with some paralysing disease and confined to a wheelchair. Johnnie had met the lady and a friend of hers on a night out in some local hostelry. He took Eileen home and spent time with his old friend who asked Johnnie to do them a kindness and take his wife out for a drink now and again.

I remembered her from my early childhood as a very pretty platinum blond, petite and elegant and was shocked at the change. She had grown very stout, her hair was coarse and her face exhibited the ravages of too many cigarettes and far too much alcohol, in fact I do not recall seeing her sober. She was enormously grateful to Johnnie for his attention to both Ben and herself and became besotted and very dependant on him. I disapproved strongly but at last my father had someone in his life to care for and to love and I could hardly expect him to remain available for me for the rest of his days. We still had some nights out. We went greyhound-racing, to see wrestling and boxing matches, and once to a rugby match. Johnnie also played golf; he and Uncle Clifford were then the only non-Jewish members of Moor Allerton Golf Club.

I did have someone new in my life, but not a man. One day coming home on the tram, I had struck up a conversation with a girl about my own age and before we parted company we arranged to meet again. She had been turned out of home because of a relationship with a man disapproved of by her strict Roman Catholic parents, and was living in digs. The relationship was over but she preferred not to ask if she could return to the fold. Instead she moved in with me and we enjoyed a friendship for many years. Annie remains another lost love I last saw when she had her first baby. Why do we let our precious friends get away?

Annie had not enjoyed the privileged life that I had experienced, being the eldest of a large family with no well off grandparents to subsidise her. For the first time in my life I had a sister, we shared a bed and a life, although of course Anne worked during the day and I at night. I suppose that nowadays two grown women sharing a bed might imply something unusual in the relationship, but rest assured that we were both strictly heterosexual and within a short time we both had permanent boyfriends. Naturally we went to the Astoria together and it was great not to be alone either on walking in or leaving to run for the last tram home. Anne took ballroom dancing lessons from my boss. It was a period of contentment that lasted for a couple of years, even after we both had men in our lives. Mine was the first to appear on the scene: in fact, he was part of the scenery. Perhaps I should have left it that way.

Little Jimmy was at the Astoria most Tuesday nights. On one occasion, I must have gone alone, and I was dancing with an older chap, a regular of no importance to me. As we danced past the bandstand which was the cliques hangout, Jimmy mouthed to me "I'm taking you home". Surprised, I said nothing but at the end of the evening I climbed on the back of his motorbike and was escorted to my door. We stood talking for a while and then he disappeared into the night with a Triumphant roar of exhaust fumes. Funny boy I thought, no smooching, no fumbling, no anything. Not my type anyway

However, he must have had some sort of interest because he took me home again the next week, and the next, but still no action. I decided to go on the attack and pinned him against the wall demanding some sort of response. That's what I got ..... some sort of response. But, it was as adventurous as kissing my elderly relatives. No wonder he hasn't got a girlfriend, I thought. I felt sorry for him: he was unattractive and socially inept. I decided to take him under my wing. At that point, although he was already twenty, his hormones kicked in. He suddenly sprouted body hair, grew about three inches, and lost the eczema. He also lost his virginity. I of course was one jump ahead, and no pun is intended.

So romance, or a semblance of it, had finally come to me, my road-to-hell paved with good intentions. We certainly shared a considerable lust and very little else, but at that time my idea of happy ever after was coloured by Hollywood movies and the attitude " I'll never stop loving you, even if you steal my money, let me down, beat me up. I don't mind if you have several other women on the go and are a general all-round rat. I'd rather be miserable with you than happy without you." How pathetic can one get? There are still women with that philosophy, they are known as battered wives, if not physically then mentally.

We had only Tuesday and Sunday together at first, and Jimmy's father wanted him home by 11:00 p.m. or very shortly after. This meant that on some nights I would be collected from the studio around 10:30 p.m. and whisked home on the motorbike in time for a frantic fumble before Cinderfella had to rush off into the night again. Sometimes he was well past pumpkin-time and Father Webster would become enraged and abusive, stopping just short of inflicting grievous bodily harm on his eldest son. His method of establishing who was the boss involved punching and laying about the offender with a belt. He was a charming man to meet in public and a well-known bastard in business and to his family. I later turned out to be the only person who could handle him, probably because he didn't frighten me and I could out-manoeuvre him verbally.

Eventually, years later, Anne ended up back in a lonely bed sitting room again. She did marry, having abandoned her Catholic faith and taken up Methodism, to fit in with her husband. Although she is godmother to my eldest son, she has never seen my other two children. What a bonny girl she was, dark hair and full mouth, a little on the heavy side from the waist up with slim hips and legs. Quite the opposite of me, I still had difficulty finding enough busty substance to fill a bra but had a back end to ensure comfort rather than speed.

It was not far into our relationship that Jimmy, no longer quite so little, had an almighty bust up with Harry, his father and moved out of the family home and into lodgings only a few streets from my home. Unfortunately, Harry did not intend to employ him and thus give him an easy ride in life. This was a wise decision in fact because family and work rarely mix well together, but of course Jimmy did not see it that way at the time. His younger brother, Brian, was an articled clerk to an accountant and totally different to his older brother. He never seemed to incur the Old Man's wrath, and was bright, well educated, and spoke so quickly that he was almost incomprehensible. Demons and sprockets!

The first time my mother met him she commented "You married the wrong one, dear" Unfortunately for him, the time came when Harry wanted Brian in the business and pulled him out of his articles before he was qualified. This was a ghastly mistake for which a price was to be paid years later when the business collapsed, leaving Brian unqualified and having to take a menial job and study for his accountancy exams while trying to support a wife and family.

Harry was quite mad and had a very poor opinion of his wife and family, who he treated like skivvies. I was the only one who gave him as good as I got and consequently used to be dispatched to intervene on behalf of the others, having been fully-briefed beforehand on the business matters concerned. He was a bully and a tyrant, but deep down had a great desire to be loved. He should have married someone more like himself with opinions and the intelligence to put their ideas forward. Edna was a nice woman, a former midwife, so not stupid. Maybe by the time I knew her she was just worn down and was taking the easy way out, keeping her mouth shut and rifling his wallet every night. She had no refrigerator or washing machine, items not to be found in every household at that time but this was a home in which one would expect to find modern luxuries. Harry later told me that he had not purchased these things because Edna would have broken or misused them. She contented herself with buying extremely expensive clothes from the haul of pound notes removed from Harry's wallet, or from the brown paper parcels of bank notes that he kept hidden around the house. Did he know?

She was generous with the money and used to pay for lovely garments for me too, which would have otherwise been quite out of my financial reach. She might spend two and a half times the average man's weekly wages on a suit, and three weeks wages on a coat. She had no freedom at all. Every day Harry came home for lunch and expected a good meal on the table and each evening he demanded a high tea, always cooked, so if she wanted to go to the town she had to fit that in somewhere between meals. Later on, when Brian worked at the garage, lunch started at 12:30 p.m. with the arrival of Keith, the foreman, followed by Brian at 1:00 p.m., then Harry at 1:30 p.m. There was no question of her ever getting a day off unless we were going to Darlington to visit her family, maybe once a year.

The Darlington crowd was great, all fairly successful in their chosen fields of endeavour. Uncle Bill was an estate agent, and he also had a furniture showroom. He was a gentleman in every way. He and his wife never had any children and both died at a fairly early age. Jimmy looked like his Uncle Bill, but Bill's charm was real and reflected the nice person he was. Uncle Joe was smaller and physically less imposing but a hardworking and successful motor trader who owned a big car auction business and was married to Nora, the sister of Bill's wife Betty. They had two children, Diana and Denis, nice people who had grown up with a little culture and class. Auntie Kath had not done quite so well. Her husband, Dick, had nothing much to commend him but they owned the corner shop and lived with Granny Haithwaite, whom I suspect had purchased said shop to give Dick a job. Grannie H had a favourite grandson: the eldest, Jimmy, who had spent some of the war years along with his mother and Brian, living with her when Harry was in the army, defusing bombs. She was often called upon to finance some of her grandson's schemes. I maintained contact with the Darlington branch of the family for years but haven't been in touch for a long time now.

Eventually I passed my professional teaching exams with quite remarkable distinction and my relationship with Little Jimmy continued its rocky ride. There were constant rows and estrangements followed by reconciliation. I had created a Frankenstein's Monster and was rapidly losing control. He had come out of the motor trade and was drifting, still hoping that one day he would be welcomed back into the fold and win his rightful place in Daddy's business. He had a spell as a salesman, selling golf gloves and grips for the shafts of golf clubs but was barely scraping by. I'm sure his mother raided the coffers for his benefit and I paid for any nights out together. In the light of information received long after, I suspect that there were other fillies in his stable, all paying their share, one of these I discovered at the time and scotched the game by befriending her.

We made a trip to Maidstone to visit and introduce my beloved to my mother who was deeply unimpressed with my choice of boyfriend, especially as he left a cigarette burning on the bedroom windowsill and scorched the immaculate white paintwork. She was pleasant enough but it was obvious to me that she considered this young man a most unsuitable swain for her daughter, and of course like every other girl through the ages, I knew best. This time she really was right.

I have no recollection of how Jimmy managed to support himself at that time but, as always, he was never without money to buy beer. However salvation of a sort was to come in the shape of a fellow golfer and former schoolmate, called Derek, the only surviving child of middle class parents who doted on him. He was a very able salesman, a brilliant raconteur and gave the impression of being well educated and socially adept. He landed a job as a representative for a well-known local tailoring company, and used to do the rounds of retail outlets exhibiting his samples and taking orders. He soon found that there was extra fun money to be made by selling the odd waterproof coat, perhaps, for a few pounds, no questions asked. Of course his sideline increased his income and simultaneously the desire for more, and more. One problem was that his sample case grew increasingly heavy as his customer's demands for cheap coats exceeded his carrying ability but help was at hand.

Little Jimmy had a car, courtesy of Grannie Haithwaite and he was unemployed, what could be better than to combine the salesman and the chauffeur and double the takings? The coats were leaving their rightful home at a rate of maybe fifty a week and sometimes more. Life took on a different aspect. No more scraping up the price of a drink or hanging around with equally impoverished friends, we now mixed with a more elite crowd, all working for Daddy in long established businesses and running nice cars and suitably glamorous girlfriends. However we did have a second 'in-crowd'. They were all sales representatives with company cars, with one notable exception, Harry, who aspired to be a writer and who was intense and earnest. Much more of him later.

On Saturday night, it was the rule that we telephoned John, the leader of the pack, to establish where and when we would all meet and the venue was always fairly upmarket and often some miles away from Leeds. I was still under orders to drink only tonic water or dry ginger because they were the cheapest drinks to be had and God forbid that Jimmy's beer money should be wasted on me. Once again I was mixing with folk who had grown up in a world very different to mine and I felt intimidated. They had never lived in a bedsit in a rough area and the girls certainly did not make their own clothes as I did. By hand. Some weekends we all repaired to Scarborough after the bars closed and stayed the night at a hotel. By this time I had Saturday night free. In spite of morals not being quite as free as they are today, largely due to contraception being less easily available, the girls used to sleep with their male friends. I have no memory of how the registers were signed: in those days people who shared a room were expected to be married.

One August Bank Holiday, at the time, the first weekend in that month, we were staying at the Prince of Wales Hotel. Derek, who had acquired a nickname that sticks to this day, The Jerk, was there without a female companion and several other members of the clan were either at the same hotel or others around the town. There were also two unattached young ladies, both fat lumps of amazing awfulness, who shared a room, so precluding any unwelcome advances from Derek. They thought!

The whole crowd was dining at another hotel, either The Grand or The Royal, memory fails me, and it was a black-tie job and ball gowns for the ladies. Jimmy had only brought brown brogues and paid the Boots at our hotel to polish them with black wax at night then restore them to brown before breakfast. Derek was the proud owner of a white tuxedo and was sporting it in the bar during the cocktail hour. Or two. By the time we persuaded him to get in the car for the very short ride to the dinner venue, he was extremely well-oiled and feeling no pain. This was just as well since on our arrival, in the pouring rain, he opened the door of the car and fell in a heap in the gutter. Totally undaunted, he shook himself, straightened his hair and walked in as though he owned the place and proceeded to entertain everyone with his wit through the evening. By the time we got him back to base camp, he was paralytic and we put him to bed and went down to the dispense bar to enjoy a nightcap.

Half an hour later, there was a frantic phone call from the room shared by the two fat friends. Could someone please go and remove Derek from one of their beds. Jimmy and I went and found that, inebriated as he was, he had still found the bed of the less-offensive of the pair and not that of the ugly sister. In fairness he was dressed for the occasion and was wearing pink and grey striped pyjamas with a breast pocket stuffed with five-pound notes, those big white ones. Quite why he was carrying so much collateral I don't know: either he felt that only a fool would be parted from his money or perhaps he hoped to buy his lady's favours if his charm failed.

Jimmy told him to get out of bed and vacate the premises and this request was met with stage snores, so I stepped in to the breach. Dressed all in black, I leaned over him and with barely suppressed fury assured him that unless he cleared off immediately, I personally would knock his teeth down his throat. Derek opened his eye, looked at me for a few seconds, and meekly complied. I will never know why. I was just grateful that physical persuasion had not been called for and my bluff called. I gathered up the fivers from the bed, thrust them back in his pocket, and escorted the miscreant back to his room.

We returned to the dispense bar, the only one open at that time of night, but within minutes Jerk appeared, carrying his golf clubs. He was still dressed in his pyjamas, the legs of which were rolled up to his crotch. He was not a tall man and the bag of clubs was not very different in height, maybe this explained in part at least, his deep desire to be noticed. This particular night he gave a virtuoso performance, telling jokes and doing impressions of communications between Air Traffic Control at South Cerny and a pilot. He had served in the RAF during his National Service (the compulsory military training served by all but the medically-exempt young men over the age of eighteen) and loved to give the impression that he had been an officer. In truth, he never elevated himself above the rank of Private, although he was capable of ingratiating himself into all classes of society. The evening finally drew to a close at about 2:30 a.m. with Derek hitting three-penny pieces with a golf iron through the open window. To the younger reader, it should be explained that the three-penny bit was a twelve-sided nickel-brass coin, 23 mm. across and 2.5 mm. thick. It was easily balanced on a flat surface such as, in this case, a beer mat. But, it was a very small target, especially for a golfer in Derek's state of inebriation. He hit every one, until his amused audience had emptied their pockets. The next morning, he was down to breakfast bright and early, ready for a round of real golf before lunch. Unfortunately trouble was waiting around the corner for him and his cohorts.

In his absence on holiday, some inquiring employee at the clothing firm had noted the disappearance of a considerable amount of stock and the police were called in to investigate. The result was a dismissal, a trial, a charge of stealing twenty-four, yes, only twenty-four raincoats, all the police could prove. Jimmy was charged with receiving stolen goods but Derek insisted that his friend had been a totally innocent party and got him off the hook. I was at the trial: many of Derek's pals were there, and many plain clothes policemen. There were more stolen raincoats in the court than Derek was charged with stealing, and every copper was wearing one and keeping schtum. I was just relieved that Jimmy got away with it. We were all waiting outside to see the culprit off to jail and, as he climbed in the Black Maria, he turned round, grinned broadly and drew his forefinger across his throat in the classic gesture and we all applauded.

Earlier that year, I had become weary of being expected to work eleven hours a day in a cavern and I had flounced out of my job with no clear idea of how I was going to support myself. I sold encyclopaedias door-to-door, waited on tables in a cafe, persuaded hard-up housewives to run catalogues, and worked as an assistant in a chemist's shop. Eventually I landed a job as a demonstrator with a major company, bringing their new invention to the notice of shoppers in better class stores. This innovative device took the form of a sponge mop with a handle to squeeze it out. Very plush and upmarket, but correspondingly expensive. I am ashamed to say that, totally lacking in integrity, I walked out on that job without giving notice. I felt bad about my behaviour and have tried to compensate by being totally reliable ever since.

Jimmy and I became engaged. I bought the ring, naturally, and he too eventually got a decent job as a representative for a major tobacco company. He went off every Sunday night until Friday, traditionally 'the boys night out', so I did not see him until Saturday night, when I was graced by his company. On Sundays, he played golf all day until it was time to return to whatever town the team were working in. A fine romance, indeed. I found out, much later, that he spent so long in the North-east that he had time to become engaged to a girl in West Hartlepool, though where she thought he went at the weekends, I cannot imagine. There was a rail strike at the time, so maybe he stayed up there sometimes, as the reps were not allowed to bring the cars home and had to travel by train.

Another period, he was in Norwich for a long spell and I used to go down there on the afternoon train from Leeds to London, getting off at Peterborough. After that I had to change trains and then make the cross-country trek to East Anglia. It was a six-hour journey. At the time that part of the country was swarming with American Air Force personnel, who invaded the town at the weekend armed with vodka, cigarettes, chocolate and nylon stockings with the intention of persuading some local lovely to share this bounty and then favour the giver with sexual thanks.

One of these was a master sergeant from Texas named Bill, who was forty-ish, stocky, and balding, and Jimmy had befriended him or visa versa. He was always much the worse for wear by the time I arrived and, even if he had found the girl he longed for, I doubt whether he would have been capable of fulfilling his dreams, but he lived in hope. We used to meet in the best hotel in town, at that time the Great Eastern and one time as I walked in I heard Bill's unmistakable tones coming from a phone booth in the hotel reception . He was obviously trying to call a taxi and was having difficulty due to the effect of something he had drunk "Hell, I don't know where I am, just come and get me" he roared. Unsurprisingly the taxi never arrived.

The great love affair was still off and on. If I had had any pride at all I would have ended the whole sordid episode but my sense of morality told me that if someone was getting the goodies, they should have to pay for them, and nice girls expected marriage if they had given their all. I kept telling myself that I could make Jimmy into a better man but ignored the fact that he had no desire to become better and was totally unready for a real commitment.

During one of our 'off' periods, I met someone else, Don W, who was handsome, witty, knowledgeable, and came from the sort of background of which my mother would approve. The only odd thing about him was his job. He was the only child of older parents. His father was dead and Don had inherited his business and ran it with the help of an elderly assistant. This establishment was situated in a narrow alley just off Briggate, the main shopping street in Leeds, and sold very specific items, condoms, and other types of contraceptives. It was known as the 'prevention and cure shop', since it was just possible that a cure for the condition not prevented might be obtained there. At least a part of Don's working week was taken up with decanting bulk boxes of cheap condoms into small envelopes. Stack 'em high and sell 'em cheap. Within a week I was swept off my feet and on to the pillion seat of a Harley Davidson 1000cc motorbike, wearing a fresh engagement ring, shorts, and ex- RAF flying boots and was on my way to the South of France.

CHAPTER 7
FROM HERE TO MATERNITY

All our clothes, and a certain amount of food, were packed into panniers and a suitcase or two and we set off on the great adventure at about 10:00 a.m. one Sunday morning, reaching Maidstone at teatime. I thought that I was unlikely to ever sit again. Several unaccustomed hours on a motorbike can have that effect, but joy of joys, my mother was instantly delighted with Don. Mind you she would have welcomed Quasimodo if he replaced the previous claimant to my affections. Don and I planned to get married within a couple of months of our return from the holiday, which was scheduled to last three weeks and had been arranged in a hurry as far as I was concerned. Maybe deep down I welcomed the opportunity to escape from a relationship which was deeply unsatisfactory, so I dare not hang about in case I had a change of heart. I think that this was the reason that I had abandoned the job demonstrating Minit Mops and just run for the hills, in this case, the Alps.

We stayed overnight in Maidstone because our flight left the next morning from a tiny airport at Lydd in Kent, now known as Ashford International. "Flight?" I sense you thinking. Yes, in those days it was possible to drive the vehicle on to a 'plane and fly with it to one of many European destinations. Our port of call was Calais Marck where we enjoyed a steaming bowl of hot chocolate before setting off on our momentous journey. It was around this time that Don started to lose some of his appeal. The sophistication was, like beauty, only skin deep and out of his own environment he seemed quite gauche and inexperienced. He spoke not a word of French and so I took over all communication duties but at least he was expert at erecting the tent, at which I was a complete novice. The first night we pitched up in a field near a river and washed in the running water. The other essential ablutions were effected under cover of the shrubbery. The second day we covered another three hundred miles on the old main road to the South. There were no motorways in those days but mile upon mile of tree lined absolutely straight highways.

On the third day as we approached Avignon, we were overtaken by a German registered Opel carrying a driver and four passengers. Some time later, it was our turn to pass them and then theirs again by which stage we had begun to wave as we went past each other. Eventually we pulled alongside, with me doing the international gesture for "How about a drink?" A few miles down the road we all pulled into a café-cum-bar, and introduced ourselves. Three of the occupants of the Opel were German and the others were Belgian, en-route to Marseilles from where two Belgians and one German were travelling by boat to North Africa to participate in an archaeological dig. I found it rather strange drinking with people who had been our sworn enemies a few years earlier, but they were all very pleasant and spoke good English.

After a pleasant hour or so we waved goodbye and all went on our way but within a few miles the Harley started to give some trouble and we were brought to a halt miles from anywhere. It was already dusk and it seemed as though our only course of action was to pull the bike off the road and pitch the tent for the night and then deal with the problem in daylight.

We were feeling pretty desperate and wondering what to do when a car came down the road towards us from the direction in which we would have liked to be going and the Opel pulled in. They had thought it strange that after keeping up with them for hours we had, metaphorically speaking, suddenly disappeared off their screen. After fifteen minutes they had come back to look for us. A towrope was attached to the bike, and Don sat on it to keep it under control. I sat in the front of the car, a very large one, thank goodness and in darkness with the radio playing we set off towards Aix en Provence. This was a truly eerie experience; I was seated in totally luxurious modern comfort with men from the master-race who would have been taking me to possible interrogation and imprisonment eight years earlier. I never found out what their occupation was but the car was better than anything available in England at the time and certainly would have been completely out of the reach of any of my acquaintances. I had never even been in a car with a radio before!

Eventually we reached Aix. Our saviours all spoke French and English, so one of the men went with Don and the bike to a garage, arranging for a repair early the next morning and another one of the party found us a hotel. Once again we all sat down for a drink by which time it was late at night and for the second time we bade farewell. The following morning all was well, the bike had been repaired and we resumed our journey over the winding roads of the Alps, dropping down to the magic of the Côte d'Azur, the most spectacular place I had ever seen. I had found the ride round the multitudinous curves and corners of the mountain roads, quite terrifying but had steeled myself to lean into the bends and was fortunately distracted by the sight of the bays and the sea below us, which was immensely exciting. It was our fifth day on the road since leaving England and the unexpected stop at Aix en Provence had dictated the time of our arrival on the Riviera, which was early afternoon, giving us plenty of time to find a campsite and to drive around gawking at the millionaires yachts and incredible hotels.

There was still a shortage of new cars and most of these went to large companies to transport their burgeoning sales forces. In consequence, second-hand car dealers enjoyed a huge boom and if, as Harry Webster had done, a pre-war garage owner had 'mothballed' his stock when called up to serve in His Majesty's Forces, he was in clover, with a few old vehicles at nearly new prices. Some fortunate young people did have their own cars, often open-topped, and usually a present from Daddy and we saw several upwardly mobile MG-owners with their glamorous companions on our travels. It was of little importance that we were on a motorbike. We were there, and the experience was breathtaking to me. Nowadays it would carry more clout being on a Harley Davidson than in an MG, since the Harley has become a cult machine.

I must confess that the idea of the trip was probably more appealing to me than my companion was but I could not have one without the other. The young can be very mercenary.

We found a campsite in Cannes with combined showers and toilets. There were footrests and a hole and you either stood or squatted, depending on the precise definition of your call to nature or you simply stood naked and pulled the shower cord which was located next to the flushing cord. Before too long I had used the facilities for an elimination exercise and fully dressed in my transparent nylon panties, all I wore the whole time we stayed there, I pulled the cord. The wrong cord. At least I showered all at the same time, and did my laundry. After a few days to recover from the journey, we set off again to complete the trip which had been intended to finish in Capri. This turned out to be an over confident estimate of our staying power, but fools rush in where angels fear to tread. We made a leisurely trip through Monaco, I couldn't believe the policemen were real, they all looked like film stars, dark hair, sun-tanned, flashing their pearly teeth at every female and all resplendent in their navy and white uniforms.

From Cannes, we travelled to Italy and the heavens opened, making the sun baked roads slippery and treacherous and the overloaded Harley difficult to control. We were going through a tunnel near Savona when the wheels hit a patch of oil and skidded. The bike went down, Don and I ended up on the road, and I could have reached out and touched a huge lorry as it passed close to my head but we quickly recovered and climbed back on. Fortunately, nothing had come loose and we were able to beat a careful retreat from the scene and get back to open road.

About two miles further on when we had left the city limits behind, the same thing happened. This time there was no traffic, and we decided that discretion being the better part of valour, we would abandon the journey for the night and find somewhere to lay our heads. Chance would have it that we were close to a pub, Italian style, so we pulled in and I managed to ask if there was a campsite nearby. The landlord nodded excitedly and led us out to his back yard, not a camping place, but at least a place of haven for the night. We thanked him, pitched the tent and, fortified with large quantities of vino rosso, we slept. Intermittently. All through the night we were woken by the sound of Italian two-stroke motor cycle maniacs trying to take a bend or attempting to beat the barriers at a level crossing which we had failed to notice as we arrived.

The following day we discovered that our holiday home was just across the road from steep cliffs leading down to a totally secluded beach, with the railway running along the top. Climbing down was not a problem for two fit young people and clothes became unnecessary. Imagine the rail passengers looking out of their windows on to visitor unfriendly beaches and then finding themselves waving to two naked and wildly gesticulating savages on the sand below. We spent two nights there and then decided to return to paradise, to the tender mercies of M'sieu at the site in Cannes. There had been few other campers there when we made our first stop but when we returned the place was deserted but for le Patron himself, who we never saw wearing anything other than a low slung bikini and a great deal of body hair. His arms seemed to be substantially longer than average and his hirsuteness made him look like a gorilla. Nevertheless, he was very pleasant and constantly gave us huge amounts of wine which he brewed in a gigantic vat on the site, presumably from the previous years home grown grapes We stayed another week there then set off for England, home and beauty.

On the way, while still in southern France, we had stopped for a break at the roadside when a Frenchman of the agricultural variety approached us. Thanks to my schoolgirl French I was able to converse with him. He produced from his pocket,a shell casing in which there was the burial certificate of an unidentified American soldier, which he had found while working the land. He wanted to know what to do with it so I suggested that he took it to the nearest Mairie. He gave us a very graphic description of the American bombing raids on the area with many 'Boom Booms', and confirmed that there was no love lost on our transatlantic cousins.

The rest of the trip was achieved without incident until our arrival at the diminutive airfield for the flight home. They had closed it in our absence so we had to drive to Boulogne and reached there just in the nick of time for the flight to Lympne, also in Kent and slightly closer to Maidstone which, again, was to be a staging post. Unfortunately for me I had developed honeymoon-itis, known as cystitis to the more informed, and it was deemed wise to take a rest cure and travel back to Leeds on the train. However, since I was under twenty one, my mother gave Don a letter of permission for me to marry so that he could start the formal matrimonial arrangements in my absence and the following week she and I bought some splendid cream and gold brocade for my wedding dress. I drew a picture of the gown I wanted and a professional dressmaker set about the task.

We had an engagement party when I got home, the banns had been called at least once at St. Johns, Moortown, the five-diamond antique ring was on my finger and then the telephone rang. It was Jimmy, and, a few surreptitious meetings later, one romance was off, and one was back on. It was sheer animal appeal, I don't think we ever really liked each other but we could not keep away. My mother must have been devastated but I have to say that there were no recriminations. Don eventually married and went into the priesthood but died in his early sixties from cancer. I never saw him again after ditching him in such a cavalier fashion, which was amazing when we still went around with the same crowd.

In this particular set of acquaintances was a couple of amazing attractiveness, David Nelmes, and his lady, Shirley Carter. He was like an illustration from a magazine romance, very tall with blonde hair and elegantly chiselled features, always immaculately dressed and the epitome of the clean-cut hero. Shirley was also stunning, as dark as David was fair, with big brown eyes, dark curly hair, and a perfect figure. She also had a biting wit and was nobody's fool: she terrified me. After spending time trying to make the best of my meagre assets before a night out, I would achieve a modicum of satisfaction with my appearance and sally forth with reasonable confidence.

Then Shirley and David would turn up and I wished I had stayed at home with a good book. Many years later she told me that her own feelings had been the same as mine. I didn't like her much at the time but she was Cinderella and I was an Ugly Sister, so what's to like? A few years later, we both had babies of similar ages so we developed some common ground and are still in contact, only a slight change in her hair colour marks the passing of fifty years, when last seen she was as slim and stunning as ever.

My relationship with Jimmy resumed its unsatisfactory progress but by the time the New Year and my birthday arrived I found that I was pregnant. Not a happy state of affairs in those days. Unmarried mothers were definitely not our class darling, but I assumed that in view of our long relationship, a wedding was in sight. I had the dress, unused from the last planned ceremony so it could all be arranged quite easily. The flowers were ordered and the taxi to transport me to the register office and I organised the licence. Johnnie brought in three bottles of sherry for us to have small a reception at the house in Moor Allerton Drive. I bought a couple of new detachable collars for Jimmy's shirt so that at least he would look tidy and delivered them to him in the Fforde Greene pub on the Thursday night. He had gone along with the plan and we were set to live at Johnnie's until we could finance an alternative.

I arrived home that night, having seen my intended half an hour before to be greeted by my father and Eileen, his lady friend. They handed me a large gin and suggested I sit down as they had something to tell me. The something was a telegram which was simple and to the point. "Wedding off - see you Sunday". A few moments later the phone rang and it was one of the boys who had been in the pub, who had rung to apologise, as he had known about the message waiting for me when I got home. I was devastated but the unpardonable bastard had the nerve to take me out on the Saturday night with Carl and Pam, some other friends, and I was stupid and beaten enough to go. Many years later, the same Pam and Jimmy were married and when she used to jestingly complain about him, I always replied that she had known him long enough to know better. However, she stuck by him until his untimely end. She was the best wife he had: at least she had some sort of control, and she was always a good friend to me and the best hairdresser I ever had.

So, meanwhile back at the camp, the heroine is with child and the bridegroom does not want to be Daddy. The alternatives? Disgrace, not just on me but the entire family or an illegal abortion. Luckily I had a friend who had endured the same traumatic experience and she assured me she could do the job of terminating my condition. One Saturday afternoon, armed with an enema syringe and a small packet of Lux flakes dissolved in a pint of very hot water, but, I must add, cooled before use, I subjected myself to a do it yourself abortion. Not exactly myself, Maureen was on the business end of the syringe. The following day was hell, Jimmy's mother came to join both Pam and her sister Pat, who were giving their support but getting a little worried and by about two-o clock in the afternoon it was all over. The reluctant bridegroom never mentioned it again. Bastard, and I still married him.

I think that the next time it happened, he did not have the bottle to refuse to make an honest woman of me. What about me? Was I so desperate for love and to belong to someone that anyone would do? The answer to that is quite obviously yes, but there was an element of tragi-romance which could have appealed to me. I had spent so long immersed in films and books that I suspect those stories were my reality . I expected to be treated badly, to be pushed around physically as well as emotionally. I had been told, in my childhood, that my father had apparently not wished to own me, and that it was on the cards that I was a foundling who had appeared on the doorstep unsolicited and did not really belong to anyone. I was obviously a bitter disappointment to my mother in every way, so it was unsurprising that I felt worthless and undeserving of real love. Thus, I settled for anything I could get.

I suppose I have been fortunate that, after a period of mourning my misfortune, I have always had the ability to pick myself up, shake myself off, and start all over again, is there a viable option? Life goes on and the sooner you can get on with it the less time you have to weep about what has been. Maybe my way of coping is to put a funny hat on and make everybody laugh, so that I don't have time to grieve or to face up to the reality of loss. Do not misunderstand, I have grieved for what has gone but often for lost loves and I soon learned that another one comes along if you wait a while. I mourned the loss of my unborn child but I always knew that other chances would follow and fulfil a lifetime ambition, to be a Mummy and have someone to love forever.

So I picked myself up and landed a good job as a demonstrator with an international food company, I think that my rounded vowels and lack of regional accent were the key factor. However, the Area Manager, who was hiring, had an eye for a decent pair of legs and possibly considered me a likely candidate for his harem of 'nieces'. His first name was Rex, so he naturally had the nickname 'Sexy Rexy' though he was more often known as Dickie, to alliterate with his surname. Apart from the odd risqué remark, he never gave me any hassle. Mind you I was six inches taller than he and treated him as a rather tiresome little boy who had to be humoured. Fortunately, I proved to be a dynamic sales lady, especially in the Northeast where the locals and I took to each other at first meeting, much to the joy of the sales reps. However before I journeyed north, I went on a training course along with others, to the company headquarters in Hayes, Middlesex. I learned how to make a good cup of instant coffee, always mix with a little cold water before pouring hot water into the cup. I was shown how to make a mousse from jelly and whisked up evaporated milk and how to make packet soup, a totally new invention at that time.

My first assignment was to join another young lady, known as 'Dickie's Demon Demonstrator' in Scarborough. She was charged with showing me the ropes for a week and then I was on my own. We were always booked in to good hotels but it is a rather lonely life, living out of a suitcase and not knowing anyone in town. My second week was in Doncaster and I did not feel too uncomfortable sitting alone at the bar with a dry ginger before retiring to my room with my radio, a tin of fruit, one of evaporated milk and a book. Sometimes the local sales representative for the company would take me to the cinema or I went alone, but in Middlesborough I had quite a busy social life. The various salesmen used to meet for lunch in the basement restaurant of the store where I was working and I came to know them, so they would invite me along for a drink now and then or to join them at the cinema, no strings attached.

I had been provided with a large wicker skip on small wheels, reminiscent of the ones that the laundry used to arrive in at boarding school, in which my essential equipment was transported. This gear consisted of several large glass dishes in which to display my mousses or mice, all decorated with tinned fruit,(if there was any to spare after my voracious appetite had been satisfied,) a whisk, various mixing bowls, paper plates and plastic spoons, a standby supply of fruit and Ideal Milk and glacé cherries. Not forgetting my bright yellow overall. Fortunately because the skip had wheels, if a porter was not available, it could be hauled, with difficulty, from platform to platform. I used to leave it in the left luggage office at the station on a Saturday night until Monday morning. I also had my suitcase to carry and usually a portable radio of gargantuan proportions, I could not risk missing the Goon Show. I used to travel by train then taxi to the store, to arrive by lunchtime on Mondays and then set off home at five o clock on a Saturday and get home just in time for a night out with Jimmy, who had landed back in Leeds on Friday night.

We did not see much of each other but I still managed to get pregnant again before too long, though in fairness, I am sure that Easter weekend was to blame. It must have been all the chocolate that made me careless. This time there was no going back, I don't think he would have dared. So with a month to go, a wedding was arranged, not as planned at the register office, but in splendid style in church, with a reception at The Mansion in Roundhay Park. This was all courtesy of the dreaded Harry, who had telephoned me to arrange a clandestine meeting, just we two, at which he asked me to postpone the nuptials in order to give time to arrange a reception that would satisfy him. I explained that a postponement was out of the question but suggested that I personally would organise a fitting celebration in less than three weeks. Considering that I had only Monday mornings to do it, I think it was a small triumph.

The leading men were in morning suits and I asked a girl I knew to be bridesmaid because she had a dress that was suitable. It all went without a hitch though I was enormously relieved to find that Jimmy had actually arrived at the church before I did, albeit somewhat glassy-eyed because of his pre-nuptial carousing. The whole day was reasonably successful, although my father whispered in my ear "When you want a divorce, Colin Cummings is the man to see", a sign of things to come, perhaps. My mother did not come to the wedding, unsurprisingly, so I did not bother asking her the second time I entered the marriage stakes - have I just given away the plot?

After a very pleasant lunch at which Derek, who was out of prison by this time, did what he was good at and made a speech, and my old friend George took the photographs.

82

"Happy is the Bride

Eventually, we took off for a weekend at the St. Nicholas in Scarborough. It was the first time I ever signed the register in my single name in mistake but since confetti was still in my hair, I think the receptionist was convinced that I was Mrs. Webster. Jimmy had taken his golf clubs with him: God forbid that he should miss his Sunday golf. Before dinner, the bridesmaid and her boyfriend arrived so we could not possibly suffer from boredom with each other's company. Two days later I was back at work and now respectably married, planning my first visit to an antenatal clinic.

We lived with Johnnie which worked out fairly well because neither one of us were there except at weekend. My time was taken up with washing and ironing my husband's clothes in time for him to take them with him when he left immediately after Sunday dinner at about seven o'clock. I continued a Monday to Friday life of living in good hotels and fiddling my expense account by over- buying from the shop the fruit, cream and evaporated milk that I needed for my demonstration. On Saturday, before leaving, I traded in the excess for staples such as butter, sugar and bacon to take home for the weekend. I had an allowance for lunch and dinner at night which was a set amount so I economised and made a profit. I haven't changed, but my money management enabled me to save enough for the deposit on a house by the time I left the firm to have my baby.

In the months before that happened I continued to haul my skip and my suitcase around the north of England. I spent much of my time in the Middlesborough area which was very handy for visiting my relatives-in-law in Darlington, and for going out with a particular representative who enjoyed letting his friends think that he was having an affair with a pregnant woman. In reality we were never more than drinking pals.

I had an easy pregnancy, no morning sickness and the only fads I had were that I could only drink tea from a metal pot and smoke only Turkish cigarettes. Since I only used about ten a week, it was of little importance. I kept very slim until I was about six months into my term and then, when the baby turned into the head down mode, I blossomed overnight into a huge creature who could not see the ground in front of me. I managed to make the trip to Maidstone to visit my mother and developed another fad. I started drinking beer, something I had always found extremely distasteful in spite of many attempts to come to terms with the taste. This disappeared the day after I gave birth and only returned when I was expecting my third child.

B-Day was to be December 16th but I knew that it would be later in spite of predictions to the contrary on account of my enormity. I had no intention of being in St. James' hospital for Christmas! Jimmy found a puppy wandering on the golf course and brought it home, a wee black bundle that we named Bobby. I felt that we must report the find to the police and a few days later someone came for him. I was heartbroken but soon I was to have a real live doll to play with who was going to fill my life.

On Christmas Eve we went out for a drink and were invited to a party but my husband did not think I was in any condition to go, overdue to deliver as I was. He took me home, dropped me off at the gate and went on his own, to arrive himself at 3:00 a.m. I was furious and made it very clear, so he hit me and I fell back on to the bed, performing a neat back flip-over and landed on the floor at the other side. He played golf the following morning while I worried at the sudden cessation of foetal movement and we lunched at his parent's home. Boxing Day went past without incident but on the night of the 27th as we prepared for bed, I noted a small show of blood.

In a state of near panic, the expectant father packed me into the car and took me to the hospital where I spent a miserable 36 hours waiting for something to happen. Eventually after much gas and air, Pethedine and pushing something did happen and I held my son, 9 lbs 7 ounces of brown eyed, tanned, and lovely baby. It would be a long time before I needed anyone else in my life. In fairness, I have to report that Jimmy arrived un-summoned and talked his way in to see me: you must remember that visiting hours were totally rigid in those days and the idea of the father actually being in the room at the point of delivery was unheard of. The feeling was that he had done his bit being there at the point of conception.

He was always there when the children were born, and the only time I ever saw a tear in his eye was when the midwife made our daughter's arrival known to him.

CHAPTER 8
"HAPPY EVER AFTER"

At the time that I gave birth to my first baby, it was standard practice to keep the new mother in bed for three days and in hospital for at least eight. In view of the fact that there was an acute shortage of bed space, this was remarkable. Only first timers or women who had already experienced difficulties in their previous pregnancy or those who lived in very poor or overcrowded housing were allowed the privilege of delivering under clinical conditions. Visiting was limited to one hour a day, from 7:00 p.m. until 8:00 p.m., and the regime allowed no freedom regarding feeding times, nappy changes or mothering, the idea being that baby must learn to wait for food and the book said that every four hours was the norm. Why nobody ever told the babies this I cannot imagine, some of us might have snatched a little sleep from time to time but in retrospect, maybe it was all a cunning plot designed to discourage us from ever attempting to book into a maternity ward again. It certainly worked with me.

In spite of predictions from large bosomed ladies that my puny appendages would never do for breast-feeding, within forty-eight hours of delivery, I was producing enough milk for two mouths and had nipples like chapel hat pegs. The only problem was that nobody had warned me and I was severely deficient in the nursing brassiere department, so I awoke each day to a sodden and milk soaked hospital nightgown.

After three days languishing in bed, taking no exercise but that required in order to ease myself on or off the bedpan, I was permitted to swing my legs to the floor and stand up in preparation for walking to the toilet. In those first moments, I was convinced that in place of the infant who had just vacated my inner space, some sort of boulder had been installed, making it impossible for me to stand up straight and thus rendering the simple act of walking a feat of major proportions. Although my son was substantially bigger than the average newborn, I had not had an episiotomy but had sustained some minor tears, which were not stitched. Urinating was not a pleasure even when I was busting for one. At least the eventual freedom to go to the john meant that I could apply a wad of cotton wool soaked in cold water to my tender parts and hold it there to dilute the fiery flow. Evacuating the too, too-solid waste products was another story.

Every day, some bright-eyed bushy tailed nurse would ask, " Have you had a bowel movement today?" I had never had a bowel movement each day under normal circumstances and, in view of the execrable catering arrangements, a diurnal evacuation was unlikely. Add to this the fact that I, like every other about to be mother, had endured an enema which may not have meant that the bottom fell out of my world but certainly made me feel as if the world was falling out of my bottom. It cannot be surprising that a movement was not at the top of my list of priorities. Except that if the required evacuation was not achieved, remedial measures would be taken, in the form of cascara, followed by pessaries and eventually by another enema. I decided on a pleasanter way because like George Washington, I could not tell a lie. Besides, I wanted to be sure that my parts were in working order before I left the tender care of the medical establishment. Well, there was one part of me the function of which I had no desire to try out. At least, not in the immediate future.

I decided on remedial therapy of my own design. I have always been partial to liquorice, and Pomfret or Pontefract cakes were a particular favourite, but a large quantity could have a remarkable effect on ones large intestine and herein lies my fiendish plot. I asked Jimmy to bring me a couple of packets at visiting time and I consumed the lot before lights out. The following morning, full of hope and Pomfret cakes, I waddled to the ablutions, having donned my corduroy housecoat, which was smarter and rather more elegant than the average dressing gown on display and thus helped my self-esteem. I sat, hoping for a stirring in the bowel region but not a rumble, so, unwilling to strain the parts involved; I went into the washbasin area and took off my housecoat. I could not believe my eyes. The front of my hospital nightgown was sodden, as expected.

What was not normal was the colour; the wet patches were grey, with black around the edges. This was what you get from eating all that liquorice, I said to myself. What effect will it have on my poor baby? I panicked. I slipped my housecoat back on rushed out to find a nurse, grabbing the first one I saw. Almost in tears, I told the tale to which she listened patiently, then said, "In view of the fact that your dressing gown is black, I think that it is the dye from that which has so efficiently tinted the nightie, dear. I wouldn't worry about the baby either. Hopefully you will get diarrhoea before he does". I was relieved. However, not in terms of defecation, though after a dose of cascara and a superhuman effort, which brought tears to my eyes, I managed to answer "Yes" to the next enquiry.

The night before my dismissal from the tender care of the angels of mercy, the new father brought me a dress to wear to go home in, though how I squeezed into it the Lord only knows. I had gained a monumental four stones during my pregnancy and was still wearing two of them nine days after delivery. I felt quite sylph-like.

In the morning of my departure into the real world, there was a ritual Jewish circumcision in a side room down the ward. The father and other male relatives came along and the Rabbi took the already screaming infant to the slaughter, no anaesthetic was administered although a nurse told me that the baby had been lightly drugged. Imagine, you male readers, someone is snipping off a portion of your dick, what sort of commotion would you make? I was profoundly distressed, particularly since my husband had insisted that any sons we had, should be subjected to the chop, a practice well-advised in the sand and heat of the desert but not really vital in the twentieth century, unless medically appropriate.

By the time my great grandmother, the redoubtable Ma, had arrived with my father for press photographs to be taken, I had recovered sufficient composure to pose for the photographer. Following the announcement of the birth in the newspaper, the press photographer had come to catch me with the oldest and the youngest of five living generations of our family and preserve the moment for posterity. I took my son home and a nightmare, in which he was the only gleam of light, began.

At the time, early in 1957, although Korean War was over, there was still an ongoing problem with the

Ma, Me & Russell, January 1957

Russians. Communism was the bogeyman word for much of the world and I was con-vinced that my child could be taken from me and brought up in a gulag or commune. Maybe I had spent too much of my life under wartime conditions or perhaps it was good old postnatal depression but a real fear of losing the ones I love surfaced at that time. A more sinister and darkly psychological explanation would be that the deprivation of love had been a real threat to me since childhood when it was used to ensure my compliance and good behaviour and now for the first time it had metamorphosed into a deep rooted terror. I still live with it and the loss of my loved ones is the only thing I am truly afraid of.

Within days of my arrival home when sleep was at a premium, Jimmy developed pneumonia and was raving and hallucinating. At one point, while standing at the top of the stairs, he hurled a large coal effect electric fire at me. Fortunately, apart from the odd dent or two on the fire, I managed to escape relatively unscathed.

Somehow we all survived the experience of his illness and he was never poorly again, I will say that for him. He was not a man to make a fuss over a slight cold: he suffered only with hangovers. Eventually, as all babies do, Russell settled into a routine and grew big and sunny-natured, I disregarded established feeding routines and filled his belly with cereal from the time he was four weeks old, by which time he had reached weaning weight.

Around February 1957, we moved into our own house, 76, The Drive, Roundhay, a small semi-detached house built in 1930 and costing , when we bought it, the princely sum of £1650. By squirreling my salary away and living on the expenses allowance when I was working I had saved enough for the deposit. After paying the solicitor's fees there was about fifty pounds left for improvements. I had a new sink unit, lino for the kitchen and paid a decorator to paint the bathroom. Our mortgage repayments were in today's money, £8.22 a month, which was one quarter of a month's wages for Jimmy. Only the husband's earnings were taken into account in those days, and money was very tight. I had been lucky, my Granny Taylor gave me £100 to buy carpets so I had a carpet square for the living room, one for our bedroom and a fitted carpet in the hall stairs and landing. Not synthetic, there was no such thing in those days. No, it was decent quality Axminster, though bought at a good discount, courtesy of someone we knew.

I had bought the old three-piece suite from Johnnie for three pounds and he gave me the bedroom furniture that I had slept with for most of my life. My mother had sent me two pairs of blankets when we were married which she paid for weekly, good quality bed wear was very expensive, and money was tight in Maidstone. My mother-in-law paid for curtains to be made. The baby's room was carpeted with red car carpet, and the other two rooms were unfurnished. The only heating was the coal fire, and the electric one recently used as a missile. This was very useful for those times in the early hours when babies demanded attention, but it was rather expensive to run.

By this time, if I remember correctly, Harry had relented and taken his eldest son back into the family business but it was a very uneasy peace. Business was still good, the hours were not excessive, and the workplace was only a few minutes away by car. The garage was open from 8:30 a.m. until 5:30 p.m., and also on Saturday mornings. After work, an obligatory call was made at a hostelry not far from the garage, The Gipton. This routine operated on Saturday lunchtimes and every night at 5:30 p.m., delaying my husband's arrival home for an evening meal until 7:00 p.m. He had usually gone out again for the evenings drinking by 8:00 p.m., and the sign of the swinging golf clubs claimed him Saturday afternoon and most of Sunday. I saw very little of my spouse and Russell saw even less. At first, there was an hour or so after the evening meal when I was privileged to share his company but by the time the nights were lighter, he stopped coming home for a meal at all and would roll in after closing time around 10.45 p.m. So, it was Russell and me against the rest. Mother-in-law was sympathetic but had long been resigned to this way of life and her approach was to grit one's teeth and think of England.

During the day, I wheeled the pram to the shops, sometimes to Moortown or to Talbot Road or Street Lane Parade and I went to the baby clinic. Somewhere along the way I met up with Shirley Carter, now Nelmes, who had a baby two months older than Russell. She still looked as glamorous as ever and was as terrifying as always in her competence. However we started to meet up, sometimes we walked the prams to the park or just to each other's homes. I'm not really the 'get together with the girls' type but anything was better than the unrelenting loneliness.

She loaned me a book one day as I left the flat where they lived when their children were small. It was a thriller written by Harry Patterson, the aspiring writer, who I had last seen on a tram (a wheel-less electric vehicle which ran on steel tracks and received its power from overhead cables) a few years previously. On that occasion, I had asked him how things were; he had gone to a teacher training college so I presumed he was a teacher. He replied that he was working as a telephone operator for the Post Office so that he could spend more time on his writing and that he had had a play accepted by the BBC. I stifled my cynicism and was suitably approving. The book I borrowed was "Soft Wind from the Sea" I believe, and it was as good as many that I had read. It would certainly have made a decent 'B' movie, the sort which used to support the main feature in the cinema at that time. I returned the book and, though I met Harry once or twice on the shopping parade, I never asked him again about his writing. None of us took it very seriously.

About twenty-five years later, David and Shirley came to visit us when we were having one of our huge parties and they stayed the night. After breakfast the next day I asked, "How's Harry Patterson, do you ever see him?"
"My God" she replied, "don't you know? He's been at the top of the best-sellers list for months now, writing under the name Jack Higgins."

The book was called 'The Eagle Has Landed' and was the first of many best-sellers. It was later filmed, and this was very successful too. Which just goes to show you, never laugh at any one's ambitions: Harry is laughing all the way to the bank. He probably owns the bank!

We last saw him in Jersey quite by accident. His silver convertible went past as we were leaving a tourist shop near St. Ouens Bay in Jersey and we gave chase in our rented Ford Fiesta. This would have been an impossible task anywhere else, but on Jersey's country roads, not too difficult. He still looked shaggy-haired and intense, wearing his trademark horn-rimmed spectacles and laughed like a drain when I recounted our meeting on the tram. "I shall not forget your name," he said. "I've just finished a book about a plot to kidnap the Duke of Windsor" (I later found out it was called 'To Catch a King'). He gave us his telephone number and took off in his very expensive motor. I do not think he has ever equalled 'The Eagle Has Landed' but he is still an international best seller and his books are always a good read.

Meanwhile it is June 1957, I am almost a single parent, the marriage is a disaster and I would like to get out of it but what would we live on and where would we go. Social Services did not provide their bounty in those days and having made one's bed there was nowhere else to lie. I went to Maidstone to visit my mother but could hardly cry on her shoulder, since she had warned me years earlier of the mistake I was making. So, I came home after a short break and decided to consult a solicitor. I had been subjected to verbal and physical abuse, much of which was in the frightened presence of my child, but as a witness he was not very much use in the legal sense. I do not think, in retrospect that my own attitude had helped in these ghastly situations. I was equally volatile and was naturally frightened, but not prepared to be pushed around. I am not proud of my behaviour at the time

I used to think that I might do my tormentor actual physical harm at some stage, and certainly was not above laying into him with my fists or anything else which was available at the time. Once, in the middle of a row, while I was clearing up after a meal of cold beef and chips, I picked up the chip pan in order to put it away. It was still full of hot fat and I was amazed when my co-combatant hurriedly backed away. I realised that he really believed that I intended to throw the hot oil at him. He often recalled the moment in later, and mellower, years and was always convinced of my determination to win the point by any means available to me. He even cited my aggression as being a definite plus when compared to his second wife, Pamela One, who, so he told me, cried when there were angry words. Much later, I found a far more successful way to deal with his outbursts, a patient tolerance, as though he was a slightly naughty child, had the required effect and I did not have to lose my temper and pride.

The solicitor that I consulted, in York, agreed to act on my behalf and suggested that I gave the matter careful thought. Whilst I was doing just that, I found myself pregnant, again. I felt totally trapped in a situation wherein I was a housekeeper and nursemaid who was expected to welcome the sexual advances of a man who reeked of beer, cigarettes and fish and chips when he finally came home, having not set eyes on him since break-fast time. I had no place to run to, so I had to make the best of what I had.

Fortunately, at this time I often had the use of a car, courtesy of Harry and Woodland Garage. Though I did not have a full licence I drove legally due to an event which is now part of history. There had been a conflict out in Egypt, known as the Suez Crisis, during which time the Canal was closed and supplies of oil from the Gulf States were impeded, so petrol was rationed. The Government decided that any provisional licence holder who had held this license before the edict was issued and already had some experience, could drive unattended by a fully licensed driver.

I spent quite a bit of time emulating my father in his tank driving days but my chariot was a Ford V8 Pilot, a former police car and a wagon of epic proportions and potential speed, much of which I utilised. I actually attempted to pass my driving test in it on two occasions. During the course of the first, the examiner was unimpressed by me reversing round a corner at 20 miles an hour then ramming on the anchors. This manoeuvre resulted in him sliding off the seat, (no seat belts in those days) and landing in a heap under the dashboard. The second time, I was seven months pregnant and could barely squeeze in behind the steering wheel. The examiner was a dour gentleman who, en route to the car from the Test Centre asked if I could read the number plate of a certain vehicle in front. Of course I could. It was the V8 Pilot, so I read it and then explained that it was the car in which we were going to take a ride. "It's an ex-police car," I said. He concurred, and added, "I took delivery of that car from the Ford works at Dagenham, when it was brand new and I drove it for two years when I was in the Police Force". Thank you and goodnight, I thought.

He was obviously unimpressed with my driving though in fairness to him, he took me down a very wide road to perform my three-point turn, and failed me anyway. Two years later, having taken lessons in an attempt to modify my technique to match my learner status I made a third assault on the test in a driving school vehicle of modest size, a Morris Minor. This was IT: I had to pass! Once again pregnant and with three infants, a car was a must. The same examiner walked out as last time. "Hello, Mr Myers," I said, " I always seem to be pregnant when I see you".

"Nothing to do with me, young lady. Can you read the number of the car over there?" He must have been having a good day; I passed.

During the second pregnancy, I grew rather less than I did the first time around which was unsurprising since my darling boy was turning into some kind of monster. Maybe he felt threatened by my growing lump or perhaps it was the volatile atmosphere in the house but whatever the reason, my golden child became a little tarnished at the edges and started to present some challenging behaviour. In order to prepare him for the coming event I acquired a dolly from the little girl next door for him to identify with and told him that Mummy was going to have a baby so here was one for him. It was a black doll so he told everyone that his sibling was definitely going to be of similar colouring. It has just occurred to me that this could have been the reason for the difficult behaviour which accelerated after the arrival of our new family member. I had always put this down to jealousy, but perhaps it was not that emotion at all but bitter disappointment at discovering that his new brother was as white as the driven snow.

Due to an acute shortage of hospital beds there was no way that I was going to be allowed to produce my second infant in hospital nor did I want to, so arrangements were made with the midwife to do a home delivery. Boxes of wadding, sanitary wear and brown paper arrived in cardboard cartons to await the eventful day. No, the brown paper was not to parcel up the new arrival should it prove less than satisfactory when delivered, to be forwarded to another recipient. The packaging was to play the role of a reasonably waterproof sheet at the moment of truth. Imagine being born on a sheet of brown paper, it's the sort of thing you might never live down.

I was determined that I would not call for medical attention at too early a stage. When I arose in the morning of B-Day, suspecting that the game was afoot, I despatched Russell with his father, having explained to our son who the strange man was, to the care of my mother in law for the day. That was fine because as is the way with grandmothers, she thought that the sun radiated from his anus and did so to the end of her life, in fact she liked both the boys. It was only Dani, for whom she had little time.

With the traditional energy spurt at these moments, when the effort should be saved for the forthcoming battle, I decided to wash down the bathroom walls and was still there, balancing on the edge of the bath when the pupil midwife arrived. She was not impressed by my gallant display of good housekeeping but I got it finished before we went downstairs for a cup of coffee. I was convinced that the longer I kept upright, the more easily the baby would make its way down the birth canal. Gravity must help after all, so

I walked up and down the hall singing loudly in order to control my breathing.

At 4:00 p.m., the nurse suggested a hot bath and went upstairs to run one for me but unfortunately she let it run too far and it was unpleasantly tepid when I lowered myself in. At least it washed away the remains of my pubic fuzz which she had found time to eliminate along with the contents of my bowels, but not in quite the same way of course. The brown paper was waiting for me as I lay my weary body to rest at last but I soon got rid of that as with a whoosh like Niagara going over the Falls, my waters broke. Within thirty minutes it was all over. Under the influence of a drug called Pethedine and an inhaled pain reliever known as gas and air, I had hallucinated that I was squeezing a tablet of soap out of my hand, in the bath. However the bit that was squeezing was not a hand and the object getting the push was no bar of soap. Through a drug-induced haze, I thought very clearly that my effort might well have resulted in the poor child being precipitated right off the end of the bed. In reality all was well.

He appeared to be in good shape and at least arrived the right way up. This was fortunate as during the earlier months I had fallen down the stairs feet first and flipped him over so the clinic doctor had done a little manipulation to try to right him, not being entirely successful in her efforts. In effect, he had been lying in the womb, face front instead of facing the back in the proscribed fashion. This resulted in the infant nose beings pushed up in a most unbecoming way, giving my second son a very angry look. In addition to his glowering aspect he sported a mop of reddish blonde hair. With the early evening sun pouring through the window and casting its rosy light on the already fiery tresses, I felt as if I had produced an alien. When in repose, his skin took on the pale apricot shade of ancient alabaster and on opening the black orbs when he awoke, he looked just like a bush baby.

So, now we were three and from the start Russell was determined to shower his little brother with tokens of his esteem. Huge toy trucks and tankers would descend on Brad's unsuspecting form and very rapidly I learned to shout "Gently" each time my eldest son approached bearing gifts. Within a very short time Number One Son had concluded that "Gently" was the name of his new companion. Just as quickly, he cottoned on to the fact that once ensconced in the armchair with a bared breast and a suckling infant, all hell would have to break loose before I would move, so this was when he elected to do all the forbidden things hitherto banned. I fought back by arming myself with a supply of missiles such as wooden bricks and soft-ish toys which I aimed and launched at him to try to re-establish supremacy. Later on, I gave him some good hidings. I'd be in jail nowadays.

In the meantime, Bradley, who had started life at a mere nine and three-quarter pounds had gained vast amounts of weight on my involuntary demand-feeding regime and looked like a prize-fighter. I say my involuntary regime, because I would not, by choice, have fed him every two hours. But, it was the only way of keeping him quiet. Having looked angry on arrival, he was angry until he was able to sit up and either feed or entertain himself. He was probably bored rigid and, since he has never tolerated fools willingly, probably had no desire to do so then. He too was subjected to me filling his unsuspecting stomach with baby cereal, though a week or so earlier than Russell, but he was weaning weight at three weeks old.

I also alleviated some of the night-feed problem by staying in the spare bedroom for a week or two and simply hauling him into bed with me and sticking a nipple in his mouth. The big problem was that with only a sixteen-month gap between my sons, I still had broken nights when Russell was teething as well as having to feed the new ever-open mouth. Jimmy said that he would get up to tend the older child and his needs as I had to do the honours for the baby so that was nice, wasn't it? The first night it happened, the master of the house arose, stubbed his toe on the dressing table, swore, farted and disappeared downstairs with his eldest son, leaving me awake and worrying whether my child would survive the ordeal. I decided that it would be easier if I simply took sole responsibility so father never did the night shift again, though one Sunday morning he gave me a lie in and got the boys up and gave them their breakfast while I languished in bed.

At the time Brad would produce positively Chaucerian nappies but on this occasion he saved it until his father sat him on the potty. Two hours later Jimmy came to wake me up and said that the poor child had been sitting on the Jeremiah since they arrived downstairs and could I please get up to lift him off and dispose of the fallout. Brad sported a red ring around his backside, which took some hours to subside.

I usually tried to catch up on my sleep during the day by leaving the boys playing on the living room floor while I climbed into the playpen out of their way and caught forty winks. Brad never slept for more than about half an hour during the day and was so demanding that I could not even turn my back on him without him voicing his disapproval. I even had to take him to the toilet with me, a far cry from my lovely sunny eldest son, who was beginning to show the dark side of his moon.

By now we had a telephone, again courtesy of Harry who presumably wanted to keep tabs on his eldest son and one day I was talking to the latter while the children were playing elsewhere. Russell appeared carrying what I took to be a new potato and said something unintelligible. I smiled approvingly and he returned to the living room. When I reached the scene, Brad was sitting propped up by cushions with raw egg streaming down his face. What I had mistaken for a spud was a fresh egg liberally coated with farmyard muck, which Russell had obviously cracked on top of Brad's totally unfazed head.

On another occasion, when I was on the phone, Russell came to me and said something and smiled. I smiled back and said, "Yes". The weather was glorious and he was running around the garden stark naked but when I put the phone down he was nowhere to be found. I ran to the bottom of the driveway and looked up and down the road. There was a choice of four directions he could have taken. Leaving the sleeping baby, I ran towards the busiest thoroughfare and spied a policeman (those were the days!). I explained my plight and was just describing my son's appearance when a little girl emerged from a drive holding a naked boy by the hand. My naked boy. I guess the copper was glad that I had arrived before he had the job of escorting an eighteen month-old wearing nothing but his birthday suit, round the streets trying to find the rightful owner.

Unlike his older brother, Bradley did not enjoy being thrown in the air or bounced on a mattress; he was frightened by sudden movements and yet seemed oblivious to doors slamming and other loud noises. Was my son hard of hearing, I wondered? My Grandmother Ada was reassuring, "Ee, he's just like your mother's cousin David, same colour hair and all. He was mentally deficient, you know."

Thank you, just what a mother needs telling. Later on, he would strip his baby sister down to her nappy so that he could run around the house in her pink, frilly, knickers and dress. I feared that what I had here was a deaf, retarded, transvestite. Thankfully I was wrong on all points. I think. He is extremely well-informed, knowledgeable, and academically successful and I tested his hearing years ago. I do not know whether he now sleeps in his wife's nightie or his own but his sexual orientation is not in any doubt.

Brad never trusted anyone else with his safety; he would not hold your hand and never sat down in the bath until he was about five years old. I soon learned that if he fell, I should not attempt to pick him up - anyone who did so was beaten off by his flailing fists. There were one or two occasions when my apparent lack of sympathy would bring an onlooker rushing to his aid but they soon learned their lesson.

Russell had talked early, walked before he was a year old and was an all round

Full House

outgoing chap who had the happy knack of saying the right thing in order to make a good impression. He has not changed. Brad seemed to lack any desire to walk or maybe his short stout little legs would not support the height and weight of his upper body. However, one day when he was almost sixteen months old, he stood up and hiked across the lawn, came to a stop, took a moment to consider the options then executed a sharp about turn and walked back. I think he had watched and worked out

94

how to do it all. Then, when he was quite sure, he made his move. This was the pattern for all his skills whereas Russell wanted immediate gratification. How you bodge it doesn't matter, just get it done. Like his mother, I'm afraid.

Brad viewed the art of conversation in much the same way most people see a visit to the dentist: speech was avoided if at all possible. He learned to say "More" when he realised that this sound issuing from his lips ensured that another spoonful of food would be delivered to his already full mouth. Apart from this he hardly ever spoke to anyone other than his brother and me. One fateful day, a lady spoke to him and he gave her his "Are you stupid?" withering look.

"Oh, are you shy?" she said, and my heart sank.

"Yes," said Brad, with a satisfied expression on his face, "I'm shy". He had no idea what it meant but he decided that if being shy gave him an excuse to refrain from talking to undesirables, then shy he would be. This lasted until he was about fourteen. Sometimes, to show that he was not a totally unmannered ignoramus, he would push a note under the door to inform the visitor of his affliction.

In the meantime, things were rocky at Woodland Garage and came to a head during the winter of 1958. Harry suggested that Jimmy should depart forthwith and agreed to help him set up on his own if premises could be found. Eventually we found a run-own garage at Bramley on the Bradford side of Leeds and obtained a loan from a petrol company. Somehow cars appeared on the forecourt and Broad Lane Garage opened for business. Now, instead of leaving the house at eight thirty and coming home at eleven at night, the hours stretched from seven thirty until the early hours of the next day. The after-hours clubs had opened and the excuse was always 'business'.

I was scared when I was alone in the house at night and sometimes would go to sleep on the hearthrug rather than open the living room door and go upstairs. Jimmy did not bother waking me; he might have had to explain where he had been so I used to wake up at three o clock in the morning stiff and cold. We must have jogged along reasonably well; I took the line of least resistance. It was easy really, I had given up trying to have a normal marriage, and he had the freedom to do what he wanted to do over at the other side of the city. He did tell me years later that he had another child in Bramley. Regardless of any financial problems we had, there was always enough money for golf trips.

My next-door neighbour, Amy Hill, had been awful to me when we first moved in to our house. She often stood in the garden telling her dog how dreadful I was, loudly enough so that I could not fail to hear. One of the problems was the noise that occurs in any household with a small child. At one stage Russell, upon awakening in the early morning, would shake the cot by holding the top and rocking the entire structure, thus lifting it off the floor and then letting go. This resulted in a resounding crash when it resumed its normal orientation to which she took exception, although his bedroom was on the outside of the house and not adjoining her rooms. She expressed her displeasure by turning on her vacuum cleaner and standing it on the bare floor of her front bedroom and leaving it to run. I wonder why a polite enquiry as to whether there might be some means of curtailing his exuberance, could not have preceded her retaliation. I did find a way of inhibiting this noisy exercise, however. I nailed the cot to the floor and ignored her verbal attacks.

Another of Russell's noisy tricks involved jumping from the second or third step of the staircase, down to the hall. This created a satisfying thud but was prohibited for fear of incurring the wrath of the ungodly, next door. My eldest son therefore talked his young brother into doing the actual jumping so that when I arrived on the scene he could innocently say, "It wasn't me, Mummy". He was a poor liar, in those days. His expertise in this particular field of endeavour improved a good deal over the years.

I should have immediately used my old technique of winning the enemy over to my side which eventually, I did, inadvertently. The day after I passed my driving test, I went to the garage at Broad Lane to collect a car for my own use. As if by magic, Amy decided that I might prove very useful for trips to the town and days out, so it was pumpkin-time in reverse. She became my fairy godmother, which also brought her certain other advantages. These included drinking the whisky when she was babysitting, which would not have been so bad if she had not tried to cover the spirit level by watering it down. However, I could cope with her smarminess better than her outright bitchiness so it was a case of making the best of things.

Before Amy took over the nanny-ing duties, we had a local teenager who used to do the honours. She was very attractive and used to invite her boyfriend or friends round to pass the time. Jimmy took her home, by car, although it was only a few streets away, and she made it very clear to him that a quickie was not out of the question if he was so inclined. He told me about this but treated it as a joke, after all she was barely sixteen, and anyway he was certainly not missing long enough to have taken her up on the offer. Whether they ever met at any other time I don't know but she certainly pursued him even to the local pub at Bramley where she met other members of the clan, one of whom she later married. This husband, on his second time around, was only a year or two older than her father. The last time I ever saw her it was eleven years later when she came to visit me after I met David, and she tried to exert her charm on him and seduce him on the stairs. In broad daylight if you please.

Amy sidled into her role during another pregnancy and the one pleasant memory I have of her is Christmas Eve 1959. We went out leaving her in charge and when we arrived home she was in the kitchen in a black dress and white apron, doing her old retainer act with everything prepared for the lunch next day and the turkey in the oven part-cooked and smelling delicious. Her own household was somewhat unusual. Her husband slept in one bedroom, she in another and Arthur, the lodger, in the third,

Allegedly. I think the lodger was the more popular of the two men in her life but I only set eyes on Mr Hill on very rare occasions, Arthur did the gardening and any household repairs. It was a strange set-up.

I loved my boys but still wanted a little girl and one day I went to Leeds shopping and looked longingly at the baby dresses in Marks and Spencer. I made a decision and did not consult the donor; it was my fertile weekend so I used it. Jimmy must have thought it was his birthday (in fact it may well have been, calculating back) and by Monday morning I was in business. If the new baby was a boy I would have agreed that this was an acceptable resolution. But at least there was a chance that the little girl that I had so longed for when I was a child, might finally become a reality .

In August 1959 I took the boys to Jersey to join my mother and Reg for a holiday. Russell was two years and nine months old, Brad fifteen months. It was not easy but at least it was a holiday and the redoubtable Dorothy took control although she was recovering from the removal of a benign tumour in the rectum. We all stayed in a boarding house where breakfast was included, lunch was sandwiches made from provisions bought in the local shops, and the landlady cooked the evening meal, if we provided the raw materials. On the return aeroplane journey to Leeds/Bradford Airport, Brad screamed from take off to landing. I was pregnant and had a deep desire to throw up but somehow we survived. He was fifteen before I went on a 'plane with the children again.

The lump grew as lumps do and Jimmy spent even less time at home, sometimes ringing to say he would be away for a few days golf, only after he was en route. Maybe he kept a secret supply of clean shirts, underwear, and toiletries at the garage. There was method in his management, if he told me to my face I could object, plead, weep, or rant but it is less easy when the informant merely has to put the phone down and walk away. By the time I was seven or eight months pregnant I was seriously depressed and quite neurotic and I certainly gave vent to my feelings from time to time. One day my doctor turned up to see me. I was surprised but he told me that my husband had telephoned to request a house call because I was acting peculiarly. Doctor Black asked two things that stuck in my mind:

Q.   "How's your sex life?"
A.   "Productive."
Q.   "I don't mean that, how is it?"

I did not know what he was talking about. The word orgasm had not entered my vocabulary at that stage so what could I say. With two small children and a husband who only came home when there was nowhere else to go, my beautiful emotional experiences were few and far between. Next question please:

Q.   "How about some tranquillisers? There is a very good new one on the market."
A.   "No thank you. I'll cope."

The new wonder drug was called Thalidomide and we know all about that now. There but for the grace of God goes my little girl.

I was convinced that my new bundle of joy was female in spite of my size but in March I took the boys and Jimmy's Mum to a child's birthday party where I picked up a nasty cold and cough. Eventually I called the doctor in the hope of being prescribed some antibiotics. No chance, because I was pregnant. No pills, only cough drops, but since he was there he examined the lump. Oh yes another fine big boy. I told him that this was a fine big girl.

"No, I don't think so. Much too big to be a girl"

"We'll see," said I. I was pretty confident. I coughed and coughed, and felt that my stomach muscles were taking a beating; I could have done with a bit more sleep not less.

A week or so later, a few days before the expected date of delivery according to me, I was sitting watching television with my next-door neighbour, when a loud bang issued from my abdomen. We looked at each other in amazement but there were no other similar sounds. However the following day there was evidence that the birth was imminent and before I went to bed that night I took the precaution of giving myself a short back and sides in the business area.

It turned out to be a long labour, contrary to my expectations. I was convinced, after Brad's speedy arrival that I might be in serious danger of giving birth while I was cooking the breakfast but no such luck. I summoned assistance at 3:30 a.m., and the two nurses, Jimmy and I, sat drinking coffee and smoking until 6:30 a.m. We waited until I had seen the boys into the kitchen for their breakfast before they went to Grandma Webster's house, then the delivery team repaired to the bedroom. No Pethedine this time unfortunately, it was a long five hours. By 10.30 a.m. the midwives had decided that some help was needed and they sent for the doctor but by the time he roared up the stairs, I was sitting up and having lunch.

"How are you, are you in the second stage yet?"
I pointed to the Moses basket, "It's all over, "
I said.
" How much did he weigh?"
"SHE weighed ten pounds two ounces" I replied smugly.

She was lovely, very much like her father to look at, with dark curly hair and deep violet eyes. She was my bringer of joy. She still is.

Full house.

We did have some laughs

CHAPTER 9
"THE COUNTRY LIFE"

In spite of his apparent joy at fathering a girl, the proud parent was in the house no more than before, and now I had three children to cope with. At the time of Dani's birth, Russell was three years and three months old, Brad was twenty months and still waking up in the night teething, and Madam was just as demanding in the early evening as the elder two had been. Neither of the boys was at all jealous of their sister but, later on, she was a menace if they wanted to do something without her or play a game she was too young to join in with. Having suffered physically at the hands of my husband, I would never tolerate the boys hitting her in retaliation for her assaults on them. They were instructed to pick her up, one at her feet and one at her shoulders and firmly remove her from the scene. It seemed to work pretty well. She was uninjured, though humiliated, and learned how far she could go very quickly. However, that was much later.

When she was a very young baby, Russell used to help in his own way. On one occasion, she was screaming in the living room as I was trying to cook in the kitchen. Suddenly she stopped. Peace at last, maybe she has gone to sleep, I thought. A little voice spoke, "She's stopped crying now, hasn't she Mummy?"

Without looking round, I replied as I carried on with my task, "Yes she has Russell, she must have gone to sleep". There were a few seconds of silence as I got on with what I was doing.

Then, the little voice said, "She hasn't gone to sleep, I've brought her to see you". I whipped round and sure enough, this tot was clutching my twelve-pound infant to his middle with her feet trailing on the ground. At least he had rescued her before Brad had managed to strip her down to her vest so that he could wear her clothes.

I think that his liking for her dresses was probably related to his fondness for silky fabric. He often stood rubbing the lining of Jimmy's suit jackets between his fingers, and did go through a period of lugging his silky eiderdown around the house with him. Maybe he does wear satin nighties, after all. I must ask him; at least it would solve the birthday present problem. Which totally facetious remarks have made me think: why on earth shouldn't a man wear silk underwear or sleep in a nightgown or enjoy the texture of soft fabrics and why shouldn't a woman enjoy the feel of her man in those materials. I would rather sleep with a man who is wearing a pair of satin pyjamas than a pair made of Harris Tweed, a far more masculine accoutrement, what! I have worn men's jockey pants for years, they are far more spacious in the crotch area and don't ride up the crack like ladies knickers but I suppose I am an acknowledged eccentric so it is only to be expected. It really is time we all got rid of some of our old fashioned ideas.

Broad Lane Garage was doing well, largely due to the appearance on the scene of a clever 'salesman' called George, who needed a site where he could display and sell the rather flashy but desirable American cars which he miraculously obtained. Jimmy turned over a section of the forecourt to George and received a generous commission. It was time to become upwardly-mobile and move to a bigger and better house.

On July 17th 1960, we moved to The Laburnums, East Keswick, near to Wetherby. It was a large semi-detached house with four bedrooms, situated at the top of a private lane. Of course, the quiet country location had certain advantages for the Lord and Master. He was able to lead a life of his own and I was often housebound, dependent on public transport and no longer within walking distance of shops and friends. The next-door neighbour had three boys under eight years old, but she was not my cup of tea nor I hers. She was a twin-set and tweeds type and I was bikinis and trousers. She never wore lipstick; I never left the house without it. She spent all day cooking and cleaning even on the sunniest day; I sat in the garden or took the children on long walks to the river and did the housework at night. There was little else to do since I had no one to prepare a meal for. The evenings were very long and tedious, and I was twenty-six years old and apparently unloved in terms of having anyone who wanted to spend time with me. When he did come home my husband was reasonably pleasant, but he was often too well-oiled to do anything other than fall into bed.

During our first week at the new house, two girls had been playing peep over the gate and running off so I waylaid them and suggested that they come in and meet the family. Penny was fourteen and Janet a little younger and they became my friends for years to come. Penny had a brother John, who had been a late and unplanned addition to the family and he too is still on the fringes of our lives. He was a skinny rather tall boy, very pale complexioned and with ears that avoided any contact with the rest of his head. This gentle soul led quite a lonely existence since his parents spent rather a lot of time at the local hostelry, I felt that he did not have a great deal of joy in his life. One day he had some sort of altercation with an immovable object while in our garden and bore his injuries with remarkable stoicism so I told him how brave he was. His reply saddened me. "People laugh at me because my ears stick out, so I'm not having them laugh at me because I cry".

Down at the bottom of our lane lived Sally, the only child of older parents, so I was the only youthful resident in the lane, apart from the children, that is. We were not very welcome and even if I had lived a cloistered existence I would never have been accepted. As it was, my unconventionality immediately gave rise to gossip and criticism. I offered the spare living room for the use of some of the young teenagers to play their music and hang out, instead of standing around the village. In doing so, I immediately became the object of suspicion. My life was desperately lonely and any company was better than being alone, I was grateful if anyone wanted to spend time with me but unfortunately this lead to me making less than satisfactory liaisons.

Money became a little tight for a while and since we had a spare living room and a bedroom, I advertised the accommodation on offer in the local paper and a young couple moved in and supplemented the housekeeping money. Unfortunately they were not very bright and did not offer me any intellectual stimulation or even a modicum of social interaction. The arrangement did not last too long, because their sex-life was somewhat noisy and I never worked out whether Jean' screams expressed agony or ecstasy.

Meanwhile, the sales of large American cars continued to climb and at least, if my marriage was floundering, I was comfortable, had a car most of the time and I was taken out in a little style once a week. We had occasional late night parties. After closing time a number of acquaintances would bring beer and crowd the lane with their cars, much to the irritation of the other residents. At least one of these always rang the police to complain that the cars were obstructing their access or escape, not that either was on the cards at midnight, since they were all in bed before that time. In retrospect, I sympathise. If a sudden accident or heart attack had struck, there was no way that an ambulance could have got through, but when you are young that sort of thing does not worry one. It bothers me now, and I hate anyone obstructing my access at any time of day.

When I had the transport, I visited my own grandparents who still lived in the same houses that they had lived in when I was a small child and I used to go to my in-laws for lunch once a week. My father-in-law Harry and Jimmy's brother, Brian, always came in for lunch as well, and Harry wore an air of forced joviality when the children were around. I could not say that I ever liked him, if I had done so, I would have been in a minority of one.

He already financed hire purchase agreements for the car sales from Woodland Garage and I had introduced him to the concept of also financing household goods such as fireplaces, washing machines, new bathroom suites and cookers etc. I also came up with the name for that company, "North County Finance" which was very successful. At one point in 1960, his assets were in the region of £250,000. This was a huge amount of money in those days. At the time a very nice house could be bought for £3,000 and a new car for £500. He was a wealthy man, though his home boasted no fridge or washing machine and was, frankly, shabby.

Lunchtime at the Webster home had, for years, been an endurance test for the lady of the house. The first to arrive was Keith, the foreman, followed after thirty minutes by Brian, my brother in law, then Jimmy and last of all, at one thirty by the lord and master. That poor woman had a terrible time of it; she had to start cooking again by five thirty. Because she was dependent on public transport, going to town to buy a new dress was like planning a military operation. Oddly, she was allowed out in the evenings but her only friend was her cleaning lady. I suppose Harry found that very infra-dig, but she had no choice of companions and had never had the liberty to make friends outside the home. Do we make our own prisons because we cannot handle the freedom offered by the alternative?

Maybe she chose her husband in order to avoid having to make decisions herself and she was chosen because she presented no threat, intellectual or otherwise. I certainly would not have tolerated the regime under which she lived and once told Harry that I would give him half-a-crown (12.5 pence) and tell him to go for some fish and chips if I wanted to go shopping. He was surprised at my gall but took it calmly. He was extremely fussy about his food.

On one occasion when I was at the house for lunch, he complained about her cooking, which was excellent, and became loudly angry. I was sitting opposite and eventually I slammed my hand on the table and told him to shut up, in no uncertain terms. There was an ominous silence. Edna, Jim, and Brian waited for him to explode and I thought to myself "You've gone too far this time, Sir Percy" but after looking at me for several seconds, he apologised. I think that it was the first time any member of the family had stood up to him. He decided that I had some bottle. I don't know why he didn't get me to join the business but in those days, women were meant to stay home and be nursemaids, cooks, and whores for their husbands and to treat them with respect. To treat one's wife as a worthwhile human being was, in some strata of society, a sign of weakness.

Harry certainly had no friends, I never met anyone who had a pleasant word to say about him, and he had little time for the workers of the world. If a man did not have his own business, Harry was polite but condescending. It was impossible to penetrate the veneer of outward charm and find a real person underneath. Perhaps the only one who could have told us about the real Harry Webster, was his brother in law, Uncle Bill Dobson, a rare character himself. His wife, Bertha, who was Harry's sister, was a potent force and had always taken an active part in their motorcycle business. Maybe Harry should have married someone like her and was always disappointed in his choice.

One day, Harry phoned me at home and arranged to meet me, a clandestine rendezvous wherein I arrived at a predetermined spot and joined him in his car. I wondered if there was a new business venture on his mind. This time it was purely personal. He had no one to talk to, he felt distanced from his sons and considered his wife inferior in every way so would never have countenanced discussing business matters with her. I always believed that she was of average intelligence but beaten into submission and stupidity by his bullying behaviour. She just turned off and said nothing because if she gave him any argument he would not have stopped short of physical abuse.

At this meeting, the last one I ever had with him as it turned out, he told me that he felt isolated and alone, unable to discuss business affairs with anyone and that he desperately wanted to be loved. I was ill equipped to advise him, a twenty seven year old ex chorus girl is untrained in counselling and all I could do was to make comforting noises and be supportive. A week later he checked himself in to The Retreat, a private psychiatric hospital in York. Jimmy was asked to come back to Woodland Garage on a part time basis to keep things running. Brian was an accountant and had little practical experience of buying and selling cars. We went to visit the patient and, after a week or two, he came home but his older son continued to commute between Bramley and Harehills.

I joined the family for lunch on one Friday, a few weeks after this meeting with Harry and his spell in the psychiatric hospital. I do not remember how we got there this particular day but since Dani was still being transported around in a Moses Basket, a bus journey was out of the question. Maybe Jimmy came home and picked me up. I only remember that I did not have a car of my own that day. There was the usual procession of hungry bodies of which my husband was, to all intents, the penultimate one, but the time got to 1:45 p.m. and there was no sign of Harry.

It was a hot sunny day and I suggested that he might have gone for a swim at the open-air swimming pool. Just before 2:00 p.m., Jimmy rang the garage again and Brian said that his father had gone out around eleven-thirty and had taken a hacksaw and a length of hosepipe with him. We rang the police, and for some reason Jimmy decided to take me back to East Keswick there and then, probably thinking that the children and I were better at home under the circumstances. About half way there, we suddenly spotted the Oldsmobile, Harry's car, in a field and a figure apparently asleep inside. It was Harry and he was not exactly sleeping. Not so much waving, as drowning, if I may quote Sylvia Plath.

We pulled off the road and went to the car, the engine was running, and the hose was connected to the exhaust. We dragged him out on to the grass and Jimmy started to give artificial respiration while I drove back a mile down the road to a garage we had passed, in order to phone for an ambulance. Why did he do it at that particular spot, on my route home, if he intended to really end his life? If we had not waited for him to show up, I would have passed him half an hour earlier. If I wanted to commit suicide, I would go where there was no chance of being found until it was too late. In the event, it was not too late to save his life but the carbon monoxide had caused permanent brain damage. Apart from a short spell at home with a live-in minder, he spent the rest of his days in a mental hospital, happily eating sweets and awful institution food that he would have thrown at the cook in his former days.

Edna bought herself a fridge and a washing machine and started to live her own life, although she went every week to visit Harry in hospital and we used to take him out now and again. She might as well not have bothered because he never recognised anyone again. Strangely, he was good tempered and amenable, never shouted or misbehaved in the hospital. Perhaps he was finally happy.

This sudden turn-of-events meant that Jimmy eventually got what he considered to be his birthright, Woodland Garage, but, for the time being at least, the bank was blissfully unaware that the proprietor himself, was non comptis mentis. In fact, things continued as normal. Brian was the company accountant and so he kept on signing the cheques. When the bank finally found out, they foreclosed and the stops were pulled out to pay them off. Luxuries had to go. We had a very eye catching white Jaguar E-Type sports coupé at the time and Brian had a Jaguar Mark 10 saloon, also white. Jimmy bit the bullet and sold the E-Type and took over Brian's saloon instead; I expect the latter managed with what-ever was available. Poor Brian, he was always having to play second-fiddle and run around after Jimmy, a way of life in which he was trained during their childhood when asthma made life heavy going for his older brother. And everyone else.

The garage at Bramley was surviving, largely due to the chap selling American cars. This was a remarkable character who had enjoyed a chequered career, not always on the right side of the law. He and another long-standing friend ran a scam wherein they sold cars for cash, arranged a hire purchase deal, falsifying the buyers signature, then pocketed the money sent by the finance company to pay for the car. The big problem arose when the supposed buyer failed to make the repayments, being totally unaware of any finance deal in their name. Before too long, the long arm of the law reached out for the pair of them, and the only option was to disappear, which they did.

They attempted to drive across the Sahara Desert, but the vehicle was no more up to the task than they were and eventually a mechanical breakdown forced them protesting, into the hands of the local constabulary. They were deported back to the waiting arms of the law but had to work their passage as stokers. George must have enjoyed the experience because he eventually joined the Merchant Navy and attained the rank of Petty Officer. Mind you, he may well have printed his own papers. After serving time, he had a spell as a nightclub proprietor in Harrogate, where his chef was his erstwhile partner in crime, and both the club and the food were of excellent quality.

Our other ex-jailbird friend, Derek, had narrowly escaped a second spell at Her Majesty' pleasure, also by beating a hasty retreat from these shores. His sin this time was selling car light- bulbs to his customers rather than to his employer's customers. He first went to Spain, then Tangiers, and finally ended up in America where his assumed pukka English public school accent guaranteed him an immediate welcome. He was an accomplished golfer and easily found himself a job as a golf professional in a prestigious American country club. Finally when the period of just over a year which was then the time limit for bringing charges against a miscreant, was up, he came home.

Incredibly, he secured another job in the motor trade, selling an amazing new product called 'Turtle Wax', which was a car polish par excellence. Within a short time Derek, a superb salesman, was selling more bottles than any other representative in the country. Then he got his hands on the secret formula and once more enlisting his childhood friend, asked Jimmy if he would be interested in manufacturing an identical but more competitively priced product. A chemist was found who had the facilities to manufacture the polish, and a partnership set up. This included Brian, since the finance was coming from the family funds and a name was selected, 'Diamond Wax'.

This was a stroke of inspiration from one of the members of the local Drama Group with which I was associated at the time. All went well and soon there was even a TV advertisement featuring Jerk, as he had become known, polishing a car. In a short time windscreen de-icer followed the wax. Unfortunately this latter was launched during a very mild winter, and a spring that saw huge stocks of unsold de-icer. Derek came up with the idea of re-labelling it 'FLYKILLER' so I innocently asked if it would kill flies. He replied, "I don't know about killing them but it would give them a nasty headache." Sales of Diamond Wax and associated products were doing satisfactorily but once again greed won the day. One afternoon, I was in the kitchen having finished washing up, when Derek came walking unsteadily up the garden path.

He came in, very drunk, and proceeded to tell me that Jimmy was his best friend, and he loved him like a brother. By the time he had repeated these protestations of devotion, he had me up against the sink, bending backwards in a vain effort to avoid the alcoholic fumes. I was still in this apparently compromising position when the door opened again and my husband walked in. Since I only had to talk too long to the same man, when we were out, to be accused of having an affair with them, I expected the balloon to go up.

"Hello Derek" was all that was said, and then the two of them went into another room. After a while our visitor left, still staggering slightly and I got the full story.

Derek, always looking for a quick buck, had been watering down the car wax with some compatible chemical to double the amount of bottles he could sell. The complaints had come rolling in because, the contraband was more or less alright, but Derek was pocketing the cash on these sales. The rest of the stock, somewhat weakened, was going to bona-fide retailers who were marketing to the public. I understand that the innocent partners had found Derek at the Waldorf Club in Harrogate, owned by our other con-man friend George, with his trousers rolled up round his knees, wading in the indoor fountain and very, very drunk. Needless to say, the chances of Diamond Wax going on to be a market leader were well and truly scuppered.

Another interesting venture that the brothers Webster took on around the same time was dance band management or something similar. They teamed up with a very pleasant chap who had a band and arranged dances at fairly big venues, Morley Town Hall being the one that springs to mind for a particular reason. We had decided to attend this hop, so accompanied by Brian and his lady friend, we arrived outside the front entrance at about 10:15 p.m. Immaculately dressed, the men in suits and ties, the ladies in their Saturday night best, we approached the door, where we were stopped in our tracks by a uniformed commissionaire.

"You can't come in at this time of night," he said, giving the white Mark 10 Jaguar a quick once over.

"Don't worry, son, it'll be alright" said Jimmy, speaking to a man probably old enough to be his father, who seemed unconvinced that we were respectable enough to enter this hallowed place. In those days there was an unspoken rule that you could not make an entrance after pub closing time. This was a ploy to keep out the unruly element, which were much the worse for drink and so protect the innocent bopper whose only desire in life was to dance or find a popsy to take home afterwards. Only after explaining to the guardian of respectability that we were in fact the "W" in "W and A Promotions" and the transference of a ten-shilling note from one hand to another, were the assembled company permitted to join the fun and dance to a big band. Bear in mind that the age of small groups and discos was still in its infancy, The Beatles had only just hit the scene and Leeds had nothing to offer in that line so a visiting big band event was a crowd-puller.

North County Finance seemed to be doing well. There were a couple of major contracts that were pushing business in the right direction. One of these was a company called Beamur Television who rented sets to anyone who did not want to buy. The finance company started by Harry, provided the cash to enable Beamur to buy the sets in the first place. Another somewhat unlikely client was the chemist across the road from the garage, and he was selling upmarket cameras on hire purchase - allegedly. Brian handled all the finance side of the business but one day, at home with a touch of flu, Jimmy phoned him at work and asked how much Beamur Television owed the firm. "Twelve thousand" was the reply, a very large amount of money in 1962.

Two weeks later, the TV company went into liquidation so I stopped paying the rental on our set. About a year later a chap came to the door to tell me that I owed a few pounds rent and he was acting for a debt collecting agency. "Are you telling me that I owe Beamur TV three pounds ten shillings?" I asked. "Yes, that's right," he affirmed. "Can I point out to you that Beamur TV owe my husband's company £12,000 and if you think I am going to pay you £3 you are very much mistaken, " I replied. I never heard any more from them.

About two weeks after the TV company went broke, the chemist disappeared, taking approximately £22,000 worth of N.C.F. money with him. I never knew the end of that story but it broke the finance company and Brian. Not too long afterwards, he and Jimmy parted company as far as business was concerned and Brian, having failed to succeed with a venture into haulage, sold his house, and returned to accountancy. He had to complete his training and start from the bottom, with a wife and two little girls to support. All credit to them, they managed and he finally had his own firm in Otley, doing what he should have always have done, accountancy.

Meanwhile, my marriage was on the road to dusty death. We were both taking our pleasure wherever it could be found. At least I had the luxury of nice cars to ride around in, the most spectacular being a red Austin Atlantic soft-top with whitewall tyres. It was huge and did about 15 miles to the gallon, but it was very eye-catching, although it was about ten years old. It certainly confirmed my neighbours view that I was a fast bitch in a flashy car and I did not care. I was fed up with being unwanted and shut away with no one to love me. At least I was getting noticed and it was stardom in the guise of notoriety. All I ever wanted was to be a wife and mother, with a decent home and a husband to love me and I could have been happy washing his socks in an old fashioned sink. What went wrong?

It came to my ears that one neighbour, known as Fag Ash Lil, now long departed this earth, had spread the word that I was a wicked and dangerous woman. It was undoubtedly true but I was a sight more colourful than my twin set and tweedy fellow residents. Another more accepting neighbour put it to me succinctly, "A hymn of hate is being sung against you in this village" she told me.

Strangely, I never for a moment suspected that my husband was playing away from home. A surprise visit from our old friend Arthur, during the daytime when I was alone and free to talk, set me wondering but only because he put the idea into my head. To be honest, I was unconcerned. I already felt like some kind of prostitute when my husband called upon my services. I was just used to pay for my keep so I did as my mother in law had suggested some years before, I complied and it was all over in a couple of minutes. It must have been a deeply satisfying emotional experience for him, too, don't you think. How does the great passion come to this? I don't know who destroyed who, in bed at least, although I can't imagine that my resigned compliance can have done his ego any good but I did not think about things like that then, only about my own feelings of rejection and lack of love.

Our next-door neighbours put their house on the market; promotion decreed a move south for them so it seemed like a good idea for us to buy it as an investment. The property was purchased in Brian's name. I am sure that his wily brother had a good reason for this; maybe he could envisage a divorce settlement in the future. The house, a roomy semi-detached, was converted into two flats. The downstairs was immediately rented by a couple who had two Great Danes and counting. The upstairs flat was taken by three University students, two studying Law and one English, the latter being very attractive and personable, the others rather boring and stodgy. I had a young friend, Julie, the younger daughter of well off parents who owned racehorses, and she immediately fell for the English Student. He already had a steady girl at university, not that this stopped Jules. What Julie wanted, Julie got, at whatever the cost.

I spent quite a bit of time with the boys, finding their intellect and conversational level stimulating and challenging. They sometimes came around in the evening to play Lexicon; even James would stay in for a while to play and readily lost his money to them. One morning after a particularly unpleasant row at breakfast time, I went next door and ended up in floods of tears in the arms of a boring law student, who was very kind. Classic situation, 20-year-old young man comforting thirty-year-old attractive landlady, I leave the rest to your imagination. Unfortunately, I was truly besotted with him, or at least with his gentleness, intelligence and consideration for me and I, well we, really began to think that there could be a future together.

What an insane idea. What did we think we could live on until he was fully-fledged, but reality was not in the forefront of our minds at the time and the idea that I could lose my children had not occurred to me. I've since realised that there are times in life when the real world ceases to exist and one can become totally blinkered to the facts. Maybe this is when reality has become intolerable. Inevitably, our affair became obvious and my husband cottoned on to the situation. There was a dénouement and the following day I left with my little girl. I was not allowed to take the boys. I went to stay with my long-suffering father and my mother-in-law moved into my slot to run the house and look after my sons. I stuck it out for two days. My swain and I realised that it was an impossible situation and he was in fear of his tutors finding out and sending him down. It seemed that I had no choice.

It was agreed that I would return to the marital home and try to repair my marriage. I telephoned Jimmy and he came to collect me, having confiscated my car on my departure, a move no doubt calculated to help bring me to heel. That night, in bed, he made a move to re-establish marital relations, but I couldn't even submit. I asked for time but I think it was a major blow. He must have imagined that my return to the fold was due to an undying love for him rather than the surrender I had to effect in order to regain my children. In fairness, he made an effort to make it work. He helped to plant snapdragons in the garden and came home for meals. We went to look at another house and I tried to get him to involve me in the business, feeling that this might give me some sort of outlet but all to no avail.

My lost love had been forced to move out and had swapped accommodation with another student who had not been involved in my past misdemeanour and he became my friend and impartial mentor. The games of Scrabble and Lexicon resumed and afterwards Jimmy might take the students to the pub for a drink. This left me free to make a coded and prearranged phone call to a telephone box as a signal that the coast was clear for a return call, to avoid incriminating evidence on our phone bill. My partner in crime and I managed to meet once or twice during the summer vacation. We avoided discovery in spite of having a private detective put on my case who, interestingly, lied that he had followed me going to my paramours lodgings. I never went there and never would have but I did spot a car which appeared to be following me one day. It was conspicuously green with a white roof, just the job for a covert operation, but I managed to give the spy the slip by turning on to a housing estate and losing myself in the maze of street. I forget where I was headed at the time but it was a real joy knowing that my every move was being watched.

In the meantime, I was becoming increasingly dependent on my friendship with Don and needing a romantic attachment less. Jimmy equally leaned on Don and, in retrospect, I wonder if he thought that by keeping my intellectual needs satisfied he might have solved the problem. It would not be the first time that he had kept a man in-situ, even giving him a job in order to keep me off his own back. I was a commodity really, I suppose. The only time he actually asked me to stay in the marriage was in the form of a bribe. I could keep the mink stole he had borrowed for me to wear at Brian's wedding if I would stay. All I wanted was someone to tell me that I was loved and needed; I think I could have loved anyone who offered me that.

He did up the ante, however, when divorce proceedings were imminent. He came home in a glorious Jaguar XK150, all re-sprayed and chromed and said with obvious pleasure "This was going to be for you". My reply was short and succinct "Stick it up your arse" I said.

However, before that moment arrived another life change was to come about. One evening an ex-boyfriend of my young friend Julie called in, and during the course of the visit I talked about Don and what a good friend he was, generally sang his praises, I suppose. John, my visitor, told me that I was quite obviously madly in love with the object of my admiration, an accusation that I strongly refuted. The next time my friend and mentor walked in, I realised that John had not been too wide of the mark. After all, not only was he wise, erudite, and whimsical but he was undeniably gorgeous, tall, and slender with the blond high cheek-boned good looks of a Viking hero. Oh, shit!

Do the words frying pan and fire come to mind?

The major difference this time was that there were never any avowals of undying devotion, it was always made very clear to me that this young man did not include a woman nearly nine years his senior and her three children in his plans for his future. Realistically, since he expected to graduate and move on, I suppose he was in a strong position: have University scarf, will travel. Before that time, however, he was prepared to become part of the rather odd organisation which was The Odd Family Webster. I have never understood his motivation for playing his particular role as the companion of each of two people in conflict. He has always defended his involvement by insisting that the marriage was in its death throes before he came along. There was a part of me that wanted my marriage to work and with no one else to turn to, it had a very slim chance but with a new hero in my storybook, the odds were against that success.

Jimmy started suggesting that we took Don along on odd days out and he used to take him out for a drink to one or other of the pubs we frequented. He made him part of the family. In fairness to myself and to Don of course, our relationship did not descend below waist level until my other half went off to Tenerife to play golf. To my regret, Don was more interested in me on a spiritual level and frankly his superior intellect terrified me into docility in the sack. Lust was a word that was not applicable to our relationship. However, friendship lasts longer and we are still friends more than forty years later.

One day, Jimmy had to go north on business and decided to take Don with him. At the time, the family car was a Chevrolet Impala, a huge blue American car, with an automatic gearbox and power steering. It was very vulgar and extremely comfortable. On the way back down the A1, there was the unmistakable sound of a problem with the exhaust, so pulling over to the side, Jimmy the former mechanic, got out to investigate. Please bear in mind that I was not present, and can only retell this tale as I have heard it, on more than one occasion, from Don, who is always reduced to tears during his explanation. Unusually, the exhaust was not a solid piece of metal but made in a spiral similar to flue liner and the back end of it was trailing on the ground. Had I found myself in this situation, I would have picked up the trailing bit and attempted to wrench it off thus removing the cause of sparks under the car due to the friction between the metal and the road. This is what the expert attempted to do. Unfortunately, instead of breaking off, the spiral exhaust commenced to de-spiral and Jimmy backed up the road holding an apparently unending length of metal.

He was not a man given to patience and tolerance, explosions of anger were more his métier so he dropped the metal, walked to the front of the car and kicked in the headlights. Then he stood and exhibited a piece of behaviour noted by everyone who knew him and named, by Brad, I think, "The Oakwood Shuffle". This involves the rapid and repeated change of weight from one foot to the other while simultaneously scratching the head - this manoeuvre has become part of the lingua franca of the family. I have never found out how the impasse was overcome because, given Don's powers of description, anyone listening is helpless with laughter by this time and is past caring about the outcome.

A lighter moment in what was possibly the darkest period of my life.

CHAPTER 10
"BREAKOUT"

Jimmy was already running around with someone else, who was not a thing of beauty. In fact, she was known to us both as 'Horseface', which was a fairly apt description. I knew about this liaison because the chap who lived in the downstairs flat was doing some work at the garage and reported to me. Why? I would never grass on anyone in that situation, but Tony was an odd character anyway. By this time, my marriage was rolling inexorably on to its conclusion. All the children were in school, and we had had a string of au pairs who deserve a chapter to themselves.

Brainwashed by a drinking crony who had class but no money, Jimmy, who had money and no class, had decided that the boys should go to preparatory school, in the hope that they would attain maturity with both attributes. Russell had been despatched before he was eight years old, to Ghyll Royd, a prep. school in Ilkley, where he was desperately unhappy, I now know. Dani went to a private nursery school at Oakwood and then to the Convent in Wetherby. Brad also attended the same school until he was old enough to join his brother at Ghyll Royd. I thought that he was reasonably contented with this arrangement only to discover many years later, that he too had been deeply unhappy.

In retrospect, I am certain that children need to be at home with their parents at least until they are eleven and that sending any insecure child to a boarding establishment amounts to cruelty. Maybe if their father had spent more time giving us all a more fulfilled home life from day one it would have given all the children advantages that neither money nor education could buy. I regret that I cannot say with certainty that I would have been the doting wife and mother that I fondly imagined would be my role in life. It is easier to blame the other fellow than to accept your own share of the blame and in the interest of preserving the goodwill of my readers, my family, I have to shoulder my responsibility in the breakdown of my marriage.

The couple who rented the lower flat, next door, was an interesting pair. Anne had a good job as a telephone sales person for a well-known potato crisp manufacture and Tony ran a gardening business with the aid of his brother in law.

Tony was an incredible individual who had gained some engineering qualification in the RAF, but had all manner of other talents. His mother played the piano in the trio at a good quality after hours establishment but was suddenly faced with unemployment when the other band members left. At this point, Tony announced that he could play the double bass, to the surprise of his wife and his mother. The brother in law had been a member of a one hit group called The 'Cherokees', and played the guitar. He was soon co-opted. They took over the gig at the club so that after working until 2:00 a.m. Tony would drive twelve miles home and then be up to start his van with a cupful of petrol in the carburettor at 8:00 a.m. (it ran on paraffin the rest of the time) ready for a day gardening.

He possessed a photographic memory. Once he took me through my lines for a play I was learning and when I asked if we could do it again he put the book down and went through the whole scene without it. Some years later, he applied for a job as a coffee plantation manager, having had no experience of coffee other than drinking it. He asked me if I could find a book on the subject at the National Lending Library where I worked. He read the book and was offered the job. He never paid any National Insurance contributions and when the authorities caught up with him, he swore he had been out of the country and produced documentary evidence to prove it. The stamps on his passport, made with a 'John Bull' children's printing kit and a cut potato, were accepted without question. Eventually, he grew up and got a proper job with an International company. They later moved to live in Harrogate, then to Tokyo for two, years leaving their Great Dane, Corky with me. I last saw them around 1975, at which time they had a son, and a manor house in North Yorkshire.

During this time there were some interesting moments, the chronology of which have flown like migrating birds to a warmer clime. I think that on the whole they had taken place before the split up in my marriage and since it is the story that is important and not the date, I will add them here before they too follow the birds.

Brad was always good in an emergency. One day I was brushing down the stairs and Brad was standing close by on a step. Unknown to me Dani was on her way up. She was barely walking at the time but crawling up stairs is not that difficult. When she came level with me she must have decided to stand up and she then caught my eye. As I turned to see her she wobbled and toppled backwards, sliding toward the hall, but Superman leapt into action flinging himself forward on his stomach and catching his sister by the ankle, holding tightly until I came to the rescue. At which point he burst into tears. He continues to be a good man in an emergency to this day (October 2004). He was also a star turn at braving the unknown.

When he was only a baby, probably under a year old, he had managed to slide a washer from a clothes brush, on to his finger. The offending item was metal, about a half inch deep with an in-turned edge. I couldn't move it and the finger was swelling. I ran cold water on it to reduce the swelling and Jimmy greased the finger and pulled. Brad sort of moaned and I was certain that a layer of skin was going to come off. The strength needed to move the ring and the determination to do it were both more than I could have supplied but come off it did and no blood was shed.

Russell was always falling, and frequently wore the battle scars, usually the result of a sudden contact with the corner of a door or skirting board but one incident left no marks at least on the outside. Cast your mind back to the jape involving jumping off the bottom steps, barred during the Amy days but now, with halls forming the adjoining parts of the building and a noisy trio of boys next door, no longer verboten. Russell thought that it would be more exciting to jump from higher up the staircase and not taking the architectural features of staircases and the attendant bulkhead into consideration he launched himself into space. His forehead made contact with the bulkhead wall about twelve inches from the bottom and Russell dropped like a stone. He did not play that game again.

It is strange how certain events can escape ones conscious mind when it is being quite purposefully plundered in order to produce a memoir such as this. Only when watching a film last night did I remember an encounter significant if only in the cause of monumental name-dropping. The temptation to make an eleventh hour adjustment to my work of art is too great to resist.

One sunny day in the summer of 1962, I took advantage of the good weather and went to spend the afternoon at the open-air swimming pool at Roundhay Park with my little girl in tow. At one stage she wandered off a short way and joined a group of men sitting sunbathing on the grass. They were making quite a fuss of her but I felt that I should reclaim her before she made a nuisance of herself. I approached and found myself in a group of actors from the play which was currently showing at The Grand theatre in Leeds. I was welcomed into the party by a very attractive man, Simon Oates, who went on to star in a television series 'Doomwatch'. One chap was recumbent but looked up to say "hello", speaking in a Scots accent. He sported one of the hairiest chests I had ever seen, the black fuzz seeming to form a cross, from shoulder to shoulder and from neck to navel. Barry Foster, who also went on to some fame, was also there. They were all charming and polite and asked if I would like to see the play during the week.

The following day, I met Simon and we spent the afternoon together, during which time he constantly sang the praises of his fellow actor, the one lying down at the pool, who was playing the leading role in the play, a Biblical story. It was not so much his acting ability as his charisma and personality that enthralled his fellow actor. That night, I went to the theatre, having arranged to meet Simon and the cast at a cafe round the corner after the performance.

When the leading man strode out on to the stage, I was impressed. Largely by the cross of chest hair although the rest of him was stunningly attractive. Interestingly, he made no attempt to lose the Scots accent although he was playing the part of a Roman general. Simon and I arrived at the rendezvous in good time and were there when the Scotsman came down the spiral staircase into the basement coffee shop. His appearance lit up the room and he joined the group. Now I could see what Simon had been talking about. It has been said of him that the only other major star not to have been spoilt by fame was Lassie. A few months later, I went to The Odeon cinema to see him in a history making film.

His name? It was Connery, Sean Connery. I could not have let that story go untold, could I?

Meanwhile, back at the ranch life staggered on. I neither knew nor cared where my husband spent his time, but how he drove home without accident, some nights, I do know. One evening he poled in early, not having been home for a meal, threw me the car keys and five pounds and told me to take Don out. It was already about ten o clock so I went down to the pub and collected him. From there we drove seven miles to Moortown Corner and went to a club where a well-known duo was entertaining. It was around two thirty when I arrived home and as I walked into the bedroom Jimmy shot up in bed. Oh shit, I thought I'm for the high jump this time.

"Where have you been?" I was asked.
"Moortown Corner House," I replied.
"Is the car alright" was the next question.

When the answer was affirmative, the outraged husband went back to sleep. I think that put the whole situation in perspective. Some weeks later there was a dreadful row, which culminated in me being on the receiving end of a fist. A bloody nose and a black eye followed and I beat a hasty departure to the safety of Anne and Tony's flat. I went back in the morning to cook breakfast but never shared the same bed again until we were long divorced. I still kept house but did not sleep in it: in those days to do so would condone the behaviour and negate any grounds for a divorce.

In the end, it would not have mattered, because, from the legal point of view, my case was based on flimsy grounds. At that time, a divorce action required a carefully-prepared complaint with plenty of evidence. Since I had never formally objected to my husband's bad behaviour in the past, I was walking on thin ice as far as making the case stick. I have no doubt that the two solicitors put their heads together and as the price for a trouble-free divorce, I withdrew my suit and gave grounds, and agreed to Jimmy having formal custody as long as I had 'care and attention' of the children. I did not like this but was advised to do so in exchange for my freedom and the option to buy Jimmy's share of the house. This meant that I could not claim maintenance for myself but I got £4 per week for my children, plus £1 for the food for Richard, the Great Dane. If there was any such thing as Social Security, I knew nothing of it.

We continued in this atmosphere for several weeks, my mobility severely hindered because my car had again been confiscated in punishment. I can see the justice in that: the car was not mine. There was no attempt to mend the breach. Jimmy originally intended to buy me out of my half of the house, which had been transferred into joint names two years earlier, since his financial position was by then more stable. Too bad, if it had still been in my name only I would have been in a stronger position. However, he had already brought his friendly estate agent to put a low valuation on the property, pointing out all the bad points, with the intention of giving me as little as possible.

He also planned to get a housekeeper to look after him and the children and went as far as interviewing one matriarchal applicant after which he asked me if I would move back in on a permanent basis if he left. That had been the plan all along, as far as I was concerned, so I said yes. Hoist by his own petard, he then had to agree to sell to me at the price he and his bent estate agent had come up with. It was to be six hundred pounds for the settlement and I was to take over the mortgage. I had no idea where the money was coming from.

One Saturday evening, he came in for a meal, during which my young friend Julie phoned to see if I would call up to the house to visit for a couple of hours. Jimmy shook his head and said, "I'm going".

"You are going straight out?" I questioned.

"No, I'm going for good" he replied.

He went upstairs, packed his clothes into two suitcases, and walked out of the house for the last time. Much as it was what I had wanted, it was still one of the saddest sights I have ever seen.

As soon as my husband had left the house, I felt a desperate need to talk to someone. Don had gone to the pub, Julie was out and her sister Jean, who had many problems of her own was so glad that I had phoned that she kept me engaged for an hour, telling me all her troubles. It was rather like "Yes, but apart from that Mrs Lincoln, how did you enjoy the show?"

Years earlier, she had been madly in love with a stable lad who was considered infra dig by her wealthy though uneducated parents, who owned racehorses. They had intervened by dispatching her to foreign parts with threats of disinheritance and on the rebound she married another man and bore him one child. On a visit to her parents home a few years later, Roy was still on the scene and the spark of lust was rekindled. This resulted in many a roll in the literal hay, in the stables and, on one occasion the Dragon Lady herself discovered them, in flagrante delicto. Jean's mother, with remarkable loyalty to her daughter, telephoned the absent husband and apprised him of the goings on. Jean was sent home in disgrace, to a comfortable and well-off household where she was treated like a whore, according to her. Soon after, she fled the coop and returned to Wetherby with the child and with little or no support from her family, tried to live in a flat in Harrogate with Roy.

It did not work. Jean was unaccustomed to living on a shoestring and before too long, the little girl, Jane, was sent home to Frinton to live with her father and Jean and Roy continued their stormy relationship unencumbered for several years. With hindsight, I always wondered whether, if the parents had taken a different line and given the stable lad a decent job, say farm manager, and taken him into the bosom of the family, a lot of heartbreak might have been avoided. The whole story had a tragic ending. Within eight years, the relationship was over. Jean, after years of fighting her weight and bouncing from man to man, found true love.

Unfortunately, she also found a lump in her neck which grew and grew until it was finally diagnosed as Hodgkin's Disease or cancer of the lymph glands. This was not as treatable in 1970 as it today, and she died in 1972 aged thirty-eight. She was only a month older than I was. When she was first having a problem, she was living with me and she said to me, "If it is terminal, I just want to know, because I shall sell everything and go to the South of France and have a wild time until I die". They don't tell you though; they keep you hanging on in some sort of hope until it is too late.

Jean was treated with steroids and grew fatter and bald and all her plans with Richard, her new man, went out of the window. Not so much a wasted life as one ruined by the one person who should have supported her instead of trying to control her eldest daughters' life to satisfy her own standards, Mr Matthews had been a bricklayer originally so had progressed from lowly beginnings himself. They could have given Roy a chance but by that time they lived in a palatial house and had 'a position' in the community. It did not stop the locals from knowing that Jean was screwing the help.

Back to my own problems. I was allowed to keep the furniture, with the exception of a few items. The dining room suite, which had been purchased out of money which Jimmy had won at chemin de fer, eventually went to a new home. In addition, one gilt-framed mirror, which was a golf prize, and a picture of an Oriental beauty in garish colours by an artist named Tretchikoff, who was very popular at the time and also a golf prize, joined the meagre possessions that my husband claimed as his own. He was much better at golf than at marriage but, of course, he did spend a great deal of time practising that game and improving his handicap.

Until the divorce, my husband was responsible for the mortgage and all the utilities. I lived on toast and peanut butter until the boys in the flat cottoned on. Then they agreed to feed me if I cooked an evening meal for them. When the Great Dane went to a new home, my income went down by 20% and over the years, and I never received any increase. I counted myself fortunate if the pittance went into my bank at all. In 1970 he stopped paying altogether. Dani was ten years old, and I was too proud to take him to court or make any more fuss. We did not have the know-how or the Social Security arrangements that are available nowadays. I have been left deeply angry with any man who leaves his family without adequate support since then. Too often one hears the excuse for the failure to pay, "Let her boyfriend keep my kids in food and clothing: she doesn't need me to give up smoking boozing or golfing" or "she's got a job she doesn't need my money". That is not the point.

I did not have a job and little chance of finding one with a young family to look after during the school holidays and no means of transport. I got a cleaning job one morning a week but after three weeks I was told that I was too cultured to be asked to wash floors and what she wanted was a rough country type. I nearly cried: she paid me five shillings for two hours i.e. 12fi p an hour and that paid for two meals for Dani and me. I had no useful skills; all I could do was drive, and talk posh, and dance. None of these were big earners in a small village. I thought I might be able to use my verbal skills if I could get qualified and became an elocution teacher. I started to trek to Headingley on the service bus, about an hour each way, to take lessons from a dear man called Bill Robinson at the Leeds branch of the Guildhall School of Music and Drama. I passed all the performance tests with flying colours but the theory side of the teaching exams required an extensive knowledge of English poetry and drama, much of which I just learned parrot fashion.

My big handicap was the absence of wheels but I scraped together a few pounds and bought a second-hand Vespa, a fashionable little motor scooter which I was covered to ride under my regular driving licence and I took to the road with some trepidation. I found myself a job babysitting a young lady who had suffered a motor accident and whose speech, according to the mother, who had pots of cash, had become very rough after all that mixing with the nurses. I was employed to right this wrong but all we did was sit and talk and have tea. I think I was paid about £1 for the afternoon and so twice a week my income swelled. My treasured father brought me huge bags of greengroceries every Sunday morning, including sweets for the children, and cream to put on the apple pie I made on a Sunday. He used to take them out to visit my grandparents in Harehills Lane and they always came back with money in their pocket. None of them ever asked or expected a penny from me: they learned to budget in the same way as I did, and when their money was gone they had to go without.

I managed to make a few shillings a week, thanks to Julie Matthews and her family. I used their mini-van and filled it up with farm eggs from the Matthews' hens, then walked from door to door like a gypsy with my eggs in a basket. Fresh eggs were hard to get at the time but it was astonishing to experience the suspicion and caution that greeted me. I made sixpence a dozen. It took me all day to earn ten shillings (50p), but I was in no position to be choosy and sometimes Mrs Matthews gave me six eggs as well.

My old friend Pam came one night to visit with a view to moving in and sharing the running costs of the house with me. However, before we managed to put the plan into practice, her stepfather was diagnosed as having cancer and she stayed at home with her mother to help look after him. It was a strange twist of fate because a few years later she became the third Mrs Webster.

Somehow I managed to keep body and soul together and even bought a car, which was insured under the Woodland Garage policy, third-party only, and this gave me the freedom to take on other work. I contacted the local Education Authority and offered my services as a Keep Fit teacher for ladies classes. They sent a lengthy form asking for all my qualifications and as a result, I got two classes at three pounds a time, including travelling expenses. The problem was that the second class was 'Public Speaking', about which I knew nothing. They assumed that with Drama and Elocution credits to my name, speaking in public would fall within my remit. I could hardly admit that I was ill-equipped to teach this topic, after all it was three pounds I needed.

I went down to the Public Library and searched the shelves until I found what I required: 'Public Speaking' by Dale Carnegie and I took it home and perused it carefully, making notes as I went along. I had my first lecture prepared and I was on my way. My class gathered. There were a couple of area sales managers, a farmer, the head groundsman at Leeds United, a senior nurse unable to take promotion because that involved some lecturing and a dozen others. I started my spiel. Twenty minutes in to the class I had dried up and so I said, "Let's have a cup of coffee". That was my lucky break.

During the interval, my students starting arguing the pros and cons of supermarkets, which were in their infancy, as opposed to the corner shop. I grabbed opportunity with both hands and organised them into two teams to debate the issue. After the class, the first of a course of twelve, the sales managers took me out for a drink, mainly to pick my brain. I was a star! The next eleven weeks went without a hitch and for the first time I became aware that I had a gift for inspiring people to achieve more, I saw a look of real belief on their faces when I told them they could do it. What they would have thought if they had known that my first appearance as a public speaker had been the night of that first class I do not know. Probably, they would have concluded that if my bullshit worked for me, it would work for them too.

I also managed to secure an hour's work teaching ballroom dancing at an independent co-ed boarding school near Wetherby, and one afternoon being the Elocution teacher at a private girl's school. Bit-by-bit I was winning, but I needed something steadier. That came in the form of a job placing catalogues for a mail order company in households and inveigling the homemaker to run a credit club. I was moderately successful, putting in the minimum hours in order to fill my quota of 'starters'. I was paid a retainer, and commission, and petrol money, so it was fairly lucrative. I also acquired another lodger, Steve Pontefract, a sixteen-year old whose parents had moved but wanted their son to complete his 'O' levels at Tadcaster Grammar School. That was fine because he was only in the house Monday to Friday and when he left I acquired another one, this time a teacher.

It all helped to keep the wolf from the door but since in those days most folk looking for accommodation were male, it did not do my wild reputation any good. I am reminded that there is no smoke without fire by my eldest son, but I must point out one totally unjustified slur on my character. On one occasion, when my absent husband had been away on a 'golfing trip', I had been to the dentist to find a new incumbent in the surgery, a diminutive lady who was looking for somewhere to live. We had two flats available, so I invited her round to view. She arrived in a very snazzy sports car and finally left at 4:00 a.m. as daylight illuminated her departure. By nine o'clock it was all round the village that I had been entertaining a gentleman friend until dawn.

By this time both Dani and Brad were attending Saint Philomena's Convent in Wetherby, and making the journey on the bus, with Brad in charge, naturally. However, the time was coming for Brad to go to Ghyll Royd, not an arrangement that suited me, since I could not let my daughter travel to school on a service bus, alone. Furthermore, I felt that he was making good progress at the Convent, in spite of not seeing eye-to-eye with the sisters on occasions. Of course, like all children, mine brought their teaching and indoctrination home from school and, in the case of convent education, this has a distinctly religious bias.

One day, impatient and hassled by household chores, I was treated to a lecture from Bradley. I retorted that I had had a bellyful of platitudes as recited by the nuns. A few days later, he was assisting at school lunchtime by carrying a large container of custard from the school kitchen to the refectory. Not being the best co-ordinated of children, he dropped it. The assembled nuns were markedly unimpressed and one of them screamed threats of hell and damnation. Brad asserted his right to reply, and with his seven-year-old dignity intact, he replied, "I am sick and tired of all this Roman Catholic rubbish" and walked out. I wonder where he could have heard that phrase before.

At the start of the term before his eighth birthday, he started at Ghyll Royd and became not only one of the few boys to have run away but he held the record for the most extended period of freedom. I gather there had been some altercation with a teacher, and

Brad had trashed the latter's room. The said teacher was, in Russell's words, as bent as a nine-bob note, (not an expression known to the younger generation but substitute the word 'queer' for the word 'bent' and you will get the drift). Maybe he had approached Brad in a less than teacherly way.

Dani left the tender mercies of the brides of Christ and started a new school, in the village. Since this was only five minutes walk away, I decided that the time had come for me to get a decent job and make arrangements for my daughter to be looked after until I got home from work. Her father had made one attempt to remove her from me and send her to a school at Oakwood but I foiled that. However, he did have a private detective watching her arrive home from school while I was at work. On one occasion, two men in a car were seen speaking to her as she walked up the village and the neighbours reported this to the police. Nobody informed me. That was an illustration of their charity and care for the vulnerable. No one ever offered to let her go to their house after school and later on when a close neighbour overheard a "you show me yours and I'll show you mine" type conversation involving two young boys, it was reported to the police not to the mother. The snooper lived next door to one of the lads.

The first we knew about it was when a policewoman arrived at the door to question Dani and ask me if I wanted to press charges. I certainly did not, as far as I was concerned it was a matter to be sorted out between the parents involved and, in this case, that parent was the only one in the village who had given me the time of day. A remark of hers has always stuck with me, "A hymn of hate is being sung against you in this village," she told me one day.

Dani had developed a habit of rising early during the summer months and, donning her wellies on top of her pyjamas, then appearing at the bedside of this particular couple, not in the first flush of youth themselves, waking them up and saying she wanted breakfast. When telling me the tale, the lady in question, of impeccable pedigree herself, put her response to my daughter's plea for food succinctly. "I told her to fuck off," she said. Not even men said That Word in public, and I never said it in private.

The job that changed everything was a Civil Service post, that of Scientific Assistant at the National Lending Library for Science and technology at Boston Spa. One had to have five 'O' levels, including English and a science in order to qualify for the job. Thanks to my mother and the redoubtable Miss Raby, I was in.

Don had finally given up the flat next door and moved in with me and was working at an electronics company in Wetherby. We also had a part time lodger, who was on a sandwich course and only wanted accommodation for six months of the year. He was about four feet ten inches high and suffered from Diabetes. He drove a Daimler Dart and, when behind the wheel, he was invisible to the observers on the outside. For three years, Wilf returned to stay with us in East Keswick. He had a girlfriend during his stay one year, a young lady of rather odd appearance who later on, also moved in. She was at the Polytechnic, now known as Leeds Metropolitan University, studying Speech Pathology, but she failed her first year exams spectacularly and was not invited back for a second try. Within a short time the house was heaving with bodies, all paying their rent and sharing the tasks and my financial future was reasonably safe.

What was far less certain was my emotional security. Although we had maintained a working relationship for many years by this time and I totally hero worshipped him, my hero was still adamant that the future held nothing for us as a pair and to prove it had fallen madly in love with someone else. Don's academic career was in the doldrums, his switch to a combined Psychology and Statistics degree had proved to be a disaster when he discovered three weeks into the term that Maths was a compulsory subject and he had missed all the vital lectures. At the end of the year he got his marching orders and came to join me at the N.L.L. (the Nelly), with the intention of cutting his losses and returning to his first choice and doing an H.N.C. on a day-release course.

My former husband was in deep trouble having hit a pedestrian while driving up Easterly Road, no doubt under the influence of drink, and failing to stop. The victim died, but the post mortem revealed that he too had imbibed copious amounts of alcohol. The expected charge of manslaughter was commuted to careless driving, failing to stop, failing to report an accident etc. The result was a driving ban and I was suddenly quite popular as a chauffeuse, very nice too, because the Galaxy involved in the accident had gone and been replaced by an Aston Martin.

At night I might be driving an upmarket car but during the day I was still a lowly assistant at the N.L.L. where, after my initiation into the system, I had been posted to 'D Store' which housed all the one off publications or 'books'. The rest of the vast stock was in the form of periodicals, journals, and reports from all over the world. All loans were postal, and had to be requisitioned through a library or research establishment. An element of scientific knowledge was useful because the person making the request for a loan might abbreviate the title or mangle it in some way and if we idiots on the floor could not interpret, we needed some experts to run to for help. All the senior staff were science graduates and thus there was no promotion open to me or any other Scientific Assistant unless we acquired a relevant degree.

I loved the bookstore: amongst all the scientific dry tomes, it was possible to find real gems. All the books were purchased by title, since vetting every single one would have been a mammoth task and new issues would arrive in big boxes called coffins, having been labelled and officially welcomed to the library. A conveyor belt ran at shoulder level and the requested books were placed on this with the label torn off the order form. They then made their way round to a tip-off point where they were packed and despatched. One of the titles that found itself in my care was 'Birds of Britain'. Fair enough, ornithology is a legitimate science. However the birds in this book wore no feathers, in fact they wore precious little but very scanty knickers.

During the months of July and August, when the academic world was on vacation, there were some very quiet spells which offered wonderful opportunities to sit on a stool in between the racks of books and read. One book that caught my eye was the story of Elizabeth Garret Anderson, the first woman to graduate and be allowed to practise as a doctor. She was in her thirties when she decided to follow her chosen course of study and had received no formal education other than that provided to a clergyman's daughter. By reading avidly and studying privately, she gained a reasonable knowledge. Eventually, she was allowed to attend lectures but not to be present at post mortems or dissections. After years of struggle she won the day and there is a hospital named after her in London. Or was.

I was inspired; after all, I was only in my early thirties, with the benefit of six subjects at School Certificate level under my belt. I mentioned my idea to my immediate boss, who had followed a similar route herself. She immediately took me to the staff library where we found 'A' level syllabuses and past papers. Don had already tried to convince me that an academic leap was within my capabilities so he was immediately supportive. I could not face the thought of making the Nelly my life's work, while searching for someone to share my life and I was already concerned that when my children grew up and flew the nest, I would be alone and still a comparatively young woman.

During the run up to Christmas, I had watched television programmes about the loneliness of old people and one elderly lady complained bitterly that her sons never visited her. She struck me as being a miserable old beggar, and I was unsurprised that her kids did not want to be bothered. I could see myself getting to that stage, becoming a lonely, embittered old woman with no life of my own and emotionally dependent on my children so I decided to make a new life for myself. If you are fulfilled and useful, there is always going to be someone who needs you, even if your own family don't. So I set out on the great educational adventure.

My head of department, Betty Smith, was in her early forties and had been considered a little dim-witted as a child. She had suffered some lengthy illness, which necessitated her keeping to her bed for a year or so, but she seemed to be a slow learner. Not so, in fact. Eventually someone discovered that she was hard-of-hearing, and with a great deal of hard work she caught up. Betty had a degree in Librarianship, taken as an external course run by London University over a lengthy period and preceded by three 'A' levels, also done in her spare time. She must have been extremely bright because she did six weeks work for her Economics exam, cramming like mad, and still passed.

We considered my choices and concluded that I had precious few, since Maths and Sciences were out of the question. We decided on English Literature and Economic History, which I had never heard of before. I contacted the local College of Further Education and was informed that I could do a two-year course for each subject. This would have meant four years before I could apply to a University and they would not entertain any deviation from this. Thank you and goodbye, I said.

Time and tide waits for no man and certainly no woman, I was thirty three and time was at a premium. My alternative was to research the subjects and do it myself; after all I had managed to do a similar thing when I took School Cert. Didn't I? The store of books at my disposal was colossal, all the journals of the iron and steel industry, shipbuilding, agriculture, canals, coal mining, cotton, wool, but of course there was too much information and I ended up being over-informed. I studied the past question papers and concluded that I only needed to really know six topics really well. I could waffle through the rest, it was only required that one answered four of the sixteen questions so it was a reasonably good bet that the six most popular subjects would come up.

English was the subject with which I anticipated no difficulty. After all, I had quite an extensive knowledge as a result of my Drama and Elocution work. What I did not realise was that there is a way of answering the questions that only the teachers can tell you, and I did not have a teacher. At the end of a year, studying every night, lunchtime, and tea break, I managed to get a 'D' in History and an 'O' level pass in English. Another year of sweating then? All this was going on at the same time as I was working full-time, cooking for a houseful of lodgers, and being a part-time parent. My poor little girl must have had a very strange life. On Friday nights, I put down my books at ten o clock and went to a pub in the next village, to meet up with some of the 'Old Gang' from the past.

One of these, a boy I used to go to Junior school with, Tony Kristal, took me to a club in Leeds, one night and signed me in. I spent many a Friday night there until the early-hours dancing and nursing my one drink. There were usually quite a few of the crowd there and at least I had my own car, so I could leave when I wanted though occasionally, some chap would give me his best chat up line and ask if he could take me home. If he seemed reasonably intelligent, and not too unattractive, I might say yes as long as it was clearly understood that there was no commitment to any more than coffee and a little intelligent conversation. I am not trying to pretend that I lived a life of virtue but I was not into being picked up in a bar or nightclub.

I also still had Don to go home to, because even when we stopped sharing a bed we still shared a life. By this time, he was having a love affair with one of the two teenagers who had peeped over the gate at us when we first arrived in East Keswick. This was Penny, the older sister of young John, now in her twenties and also working at the Nelly. That romance continued for some years, eventually at a distance but it finally faded and they both found new loves. I was never jealous of Penny; probably I had given up any hope of being the woman in Don's life and was, at last, able to accept him as my closest friend.

I did get to enjoy a little of the social life that had been a part of my world during my marriage in the company of an unlikely escort, my ex-husband. When the worst of the anger had subsided, he took me and the children to Blackpool for the weekend. It might have been some sort of attempt at reconciliation, who knows. However a good time was had by all but of course I really did not care how he behaved. He was not my husband and I had someone else back at the ranch. Later on, we went on a late booking holiday with the three children. It was a cut-price cruise in the Mediterranean and we shared a six-berth cabin. On the last day some people we had spent a little time with, commented that we were the most happily married couple they had ever met. This seems to indicate that marriage is not very good for some relationships.

Jimmy suggested that we take the children to Paris for Christmas and then he retreated from our lives, having met a lady now known as Pamela One, who he married shortly afterwards. He had mentioned her to me in the past. She aspired to be greater than the sum of her parts, but Jimmy was impressed by her apparent education and arty tastes. His Best Man told me that the night before the marriage, the groom had confessed that he didn't know why he was marrying her, but he went through with it anyway.

Six months later, he was on the phone to me from a call box late one night and I met him out in the lane. We sat in the car. He never came into the house after he left, and he told me his tale of woe.
"She cries if we have a row. You used to threaten to throw a chip-pan full of hot fat over me. She goes to bed with her hair in rollers. You never did that."

"Anything else?" I asked.
"Yes, she's got no arse!"

He asked me if it was him, was he impossible to live with? I told him that this was indeed the case, but I felt that he could not afford to waste another nine years of his life and he might as well get out now. Three days later, he telephoned me at work to say Pamela had gone and he was taking me out for dinner that night. Unfortunately, on her departure, she took his gold toothpick, a gift from me. I would have liked it to go to one of my sons eventually.

We resumed our casual relationship. He never proposed any attempt at reconciliation, though it would not have been well received by me. I had found a very different way of life. One time when we were out, he told me that he had been seeing our old friend Pam, the hairdresser, for the odd night out. This was the same Pam who had planned to move in with me a few years earlier. His exact words were "She's lots of fun to go out with, but I couldn't fancy her if she was the last woman on earth". Shortly afterwards, she moved in with him, married him, and stayed with him until he died at the tragically early age of fifty four.

The second attempt at my English exam was looming and I had no idea how I was going to fare. I called in to see my father's cousin Joy, my childhood fairy godmother. As luck would have it, her younger son Tim was also re-sitting his 'A' level exams, having failed miserably the previous year and English was one of his subjects. He offered to give me a day of coaching and I snapped up the offer. It must have worked because this time I got a 'C' grade. Tim once more failed, and I have never seen him again since that day of tutoring. He dropped out and was a dreadful disappointment to his straight as a die parents. His older brother Christopher, who had been the wild one, signed up for a short service commission and became an officer and a gentleman for three years. He then went on to a lifetime job with Shell Oil and has never looked back.

I had planned on continuing my scholarship by applying to do a degree in Economic

History. However, in the meantime having talked to Wilf's girlfriend and I wondered if my talents would be better suited to a three-year Diploma in Speech Pathology which was available at what is now Leeds Metropolitan University. I talked about this option with a very senior member of staff at the N.L.L., Dr Parsons, who was one of the occupants of the office to which I had been transferred. He was an interesting chap, a total academic, who when queried about any topic would reply that he knew nothing about the subject, then spill out an almost encyclopaedic array of facts.

His advice was simple. With a degree in History, you are a History graduate, and so what are you going to do when you grow up? With the Diploma in Speech Pathology, you are a Speech Therapist and that is that. The die was cast, and I went along for an interview with the Principal, a Miss Margaret Jones, who would have taken me, even if I did not pass the English exam, because mature students were thin on the ground. In the event, all was well and the time to embark on a major change drew closer.

A year or so before, I had been moved from my comfortable niche in 'Book store' and given a rather interesting job working for a Chinese gentleman from Mauritius, who was in charge of acquiring missing parts of journals, some of which were very old indeed. I was despatched to 'C' store where the oldest publications were kept, and had to go through the shelves to note which month of which year was not in stock. A list was compiled and, with a covering letter, was sent to specialist booksellers around the world in the expectation that they would be able to supply some of the missing parts. When the replies came in, Foo-Kune decided who was making the best offer and the purchase would be made. Eventually the missing parts arrived in dusty boxes, and my job then was to check them in and then put them away on the appropriate shelf.

I found the work interesting and had a desk in an office with Foo-Kune, Dr Parsons, Dr Cross, and one other Scientific Assistant, Pete Atkin, who had probably been born at the Nelly. Mr Foo-Kune was a pleasant chap, whose sense of humour was quite different to the English one and we developed a way of life where I watched his face when he was telling a tale, and learned to laugh when I thought his expression warranted it. I tried to tell him amusing stories, but I don't think he got the point. When I left for good, he was away on holiday but he wrote a letter which was read out by another member of staff. Here is an extract, in his words: there are no spelling mistakes:

"I am very pleased for all the work you have done for the Second-Hand Purchase Section. You have been very efficient and you have tackle your work in large amount and have done so with great speed. I am sure all this will be shown on my chart of 'Expenses Versus Years' as a new peak for the year 1969/70. You have been very co-operative for which I am particularly pleased and grateful. Please give my (regards) love to your son Bradley who I admire so much. September 24th 1969, Wednesday 11:00 a.m."

That was the end of my Civil Service career and the beginning of a new life.

CHAPTER 11
"THE ONLY WAY IS UP

I suppose I must have felt a good deal of excitement on that first day of my college course, but maybe I was too busy to be aware of it. I lived some twelve miles from the University so, given the heavy traffic in the early morning, an early start was de rigeur. My journey took me round the outskirts of the city and I found a place to park in Blackman Lane, about five minutes walk from my destination. This street is now demolished to make way for urban renewal. I have always wondered where the name of that road came from. When I was a child, I imagined that the black men were coal miners or coal merchants. It never crossed my mind that it referred to gentlemen of a dark complexion but, I suppose, that was a possibility.

The houses in the area were grimy and blackened by the soot from the chimneys of factories built during the 19th century. All had doors opening straight on to the street and in 1969, were providing homes for the immigrant population, many of whom were black men and women from the day they were born rather than blackened by coal dust. Feeling full of cheer, and wearing a sensible tweedy suit and low heels, I set of to start a new career: that of full-time student. I was soon to discover how much fuller that time was to be than my experience of University undergraduates had led me to believe.

I located the room where registration was in process and found, not surprisingly, that I was old enough to be the mother of most of my fellow students. The exceptions were Gillian, a twenty-three year old ex-Army captain and Margaret, an attractive six-foot tall brunette of the same age, formerly in hospital administration. We had all given up well-paid employment to take on this course. At the time, after living on a grant for three years, as newly-qualified Speech therapists we would earn less than if we had stayed in our safe little jobs. We did not have any idea of the complexity of the subject, which we had elected to be our life's work. In common with the average 'man on the Clapham omnibus', we had some romantic idea that we were destined to become upmarket elocution teachers and could not imagine why the course was spread over three years.

I can tell you now that four years would not have been enough, and I am not talking about a course which entailed a few hours a week of formal lectures, a little practical work, and a great deal of time hanging out in the Student's Union bar. I discovered, on that day, that my week was to be programmed so that I would have thirty-six hours of lectures, one after another, including a day spent in clinics. There was to be no time for private study except the evenings, after I had cooked and done the essential cleaning and seen to my lodgers, not to mention giving any time to my daughter, who never complained.

The rest of my fellow students seemed very young and immature and why not, they were only eighteen after all, and they soon divided themselves up into like-minded groups, as people do. Gillian and Margaret chose me, naturally, I was only thirteen years their senior and like them, had some experience of a world outside the disco scene. We met our lecturers, who were all quite intimidating, because they knew something we didn't and we needed to find out what it was. They addressed us all very formally as "Miss ...." - in my case, Mrs Webster. Two of the younger purveyors of wisdom used to blush if I asked them a question. I believe that, on a scale of one to ten, their ability to intimidate me was about two whereas mine, to reverse the situation, was ten. I suppose that I had been around long enough to question most things: the other students were still blindly writing everything down without thinking.

We also met our anatomy lecturer, Doc Elliot, a friendly old man who declared that it might be better to keep your mouth shut and let others think you are a fool rather than open it and let them find out for certain that you are. We attended for two hours every Monday, lectures in the hallowed halls of the University proper, studying Phonetics with a couple of experts in this field. I was one of the few to enjoy the subject and eventually attained a Distinction in my second year exam. We had two Psychology lecturers. Colin, the senior of the two and Head of Department, was a likeable and able man and his assistant, Christine, no doubt knew her stuff but was totally devoid of any presentation skills. Her incompetence in this field of endeavour was so poor that, before many weeks of the first term had gone by, attendance at her lectures dwindled to a third or less of the twenty-two students. Since Psychology was an essential part of the course, and it was necessary to pass exams each year, three of us went to see Colin.

His handling of the matter was a lesson, which I have always remembered. He asked if we had spoken to Christine about it and we said, well, no, we are telling you. He countered this by asking if we were satisfied with his own performance and we voted yes. He then said that if you have a complaint or cause for comment, you should take that, in the first instant, to the person involved, and only after they have failed to put things right, should you consider going over their head. Wise words indeed, but of course a much tougher job than moaning to someone else.

It takes a good deal of courage to beard the lion especially when the lion is lacking the essential toughness associated with the breed. It had to be done and guess who was elected to be the bearers of the bad tidings. Of course, yours truly and her sidekicks, Gillian and Margaret.

The time for the lecture was upon us: we Three Musketeers sat alone in the classroom and in walked our quarry. She was astonished to find that her group had reduced to three but we quickly whisked her off to a small room and told her the blunt facts. Be dynamic, we said, be dramatic, be confident, wave your arms about, stand on the desk and do a dance. Do anything, just make us sit up and take notice. She was almost in tears. It must have been a terrible experience for her but we were as kind as we knew how to be. She went away and must have gone to see a witch doctor, because at the next lecture (and we were there in force) she breezed into the room and lo! ... she was dynamic, she was dramatic and only stopped short of dancing on the table. She kept it up for an hour and as she finished, we gave her a round of applause. On her way out of the room, she stopped at my desk and said, "Was that alright?" She never reverted to the old style and I hope that in later years she thinks of us with kindness.

The Principal was an untidy, overweight single lady, around the same age as I was, who had enjoyed a moderate success with a novel. Gillian attended a meeting of aspiring authors and Our Leader was there. In order to make conversation Gillian asked our revered head of department if her book was concerned with a topic she, the author, knew a good deal about. When the reply was affirmative, Gillian enquired what that subject was. "Sex" said the Principal and walked away. I have never read the tome but I believe it concerned a phallic transplant, quite avant-garde for the period.

Within a week or two, I had abandoned my sensible clothes and transformed myself into a student, wearing Mary Quant jeans, and kaftans. One of the latter was black and floor length, having enjoyed a previous existence as a blanket. It had been purchased in Spain when we were there with the children some years ago. I was in my element, treated as an agony aunt by the rest of my year, and surrounded by intelligent and handsome young men. I suppose there were attractive girls as well but I never noticed them. Before too long Gillian and Margaret moved in to East Keswick and we were able to collaborate on our studying. Unfortunately, Margaret met a boy who was into smoking pot and, I suspect, doing a little dabbling with LSD but before this became apparent, he too had moved in. Margaret underwent a personality change and things began to go missing from my cupboards and drawers. One of the oddest things to disappear was a number of eggs from the fridge and it got to the point where I had to search her room when she was out so that I could reclaim my clothes and jewellery. Eventually I asked them to leave, we were all saddened by the change in the kind sweet person we had known, and Dani particularly had been very attached to her. Margaret withdrew from the course and we never heard of her again.

The one lecturer from the Speech Therapy department for whom we all had a deep respect was Vivian Reeves whose speciality was the hearing impaired. She was a masterful exponent of the art of holding the audience's attention and did not suffer fools gladly She also knew her stuff and was a qualified and renowned Audiologist as well as a Speech Therapist. Unfortunately, she was only on the staff for the first year but during that time I was privileged to have a half-day of practical work with her each week which was a wonderful learning experience. When the year was over and I felt that a personal relationship was permissible, I invited her to dinner. We have remained friends, albeit at a long distance, ever since.

I had a hard time keeping up with the work that first year and fell a long way behind with the Psychology, largely due to the lack of interest generated by the aforementioned Christine. In addition, much of it seemed irrelevant to me and very dreary. The other horror-show lecture was Linguistics, which was a subject only recently, included in the syllabus. Our lecturer was bright eyed and bushy tailed, a real enthusiast who talked over our heads most of the time, so much so that I was in the habit of going to sleep during the lecture. On one occasion I seemed to drop myself deeply into the manure. During my nap, I had dreamed that I was appearing in a play called 'Daddy Longlegs', which had been filmed some years previously starring Fred Astaire and Leslie Caron. I awoke suddenly because the lecturer called my name.

"Daddy longlegs," I said loudly and was instantly horrified at my outburst.

"Yes," she said nodding approvingly and moving on to the person next to me. This student also said "Daddy Longlegs". It transpired that during my slumbers, the question of dialectical differences and regional variations had come up and the class had been asked what their local population called the spidery creature whose name had penetrated my dreams. Thank goodness there was no exam in this subject but, later in my professional life, linguistics became the greatest thing since sliced bread, it seemed, and I had to make the effort to come to terms with it.

One of the tasks we all had to take on was to try to appreciate the difficulties faced by a stammerer when in public in a situation where they had to ask for a drink in a bar or an item in a shop. We went in pairs on our mission, taking it in turns to be the afflicted, while our companion played the role of friend. It was fascinating to observe the reaction of the sales assistants. A lady in Boots the Chemist, was amazingly tolerant, waiting patiently and with no change in expression, while I went through the facial contortions accompanying a bad block, a total inability to get the sound out. We changed the type of dysfluency from shop to shop, a closed mouth for a 'b', 'p' or an 'm', and an open-mouthed block for a 'g' or a 'k'.

Apart from the embarrassment for both speaker and listener, the physical effort expended in this type of stammer is exhausting. It is sad that so many jokes are told about this unfortunate group of people. Stammering is no laughing matter and it is impossible to cure, only the stammerer can do that, with the advice and support of the therapist. Unfortunately, the one piece of assistance given by well-meaning companions is to tell the tongue-tied would-be speaker to take a deep breath and start again. This resulted in their dysfluent friends becoming ever more red-faced and unable to speak. A better technique would be the reverse: exhale, relax, and let the word slide out unnoticed.

The study of the voice itself I found tedious and technical because there are so many different muscles and cartilages to learn about. The mechanism of producing the musical sound we know as the human voice is so closely allied to the study of Physics that I used to go into panic mode as soon as the topic came up. The one useful detail that I picked up, was that tension in the upper chest and neck leads to poor voice quality, a common complaint among teachers and very irritating to the listener.

During my last year at the National Lending Library, My father's circumstances had taken rather a dramatic turn for the worse. The shop in the market had suffered a huge profit loss, in some part due to the increased popularity of supermarkets and no doubt due to a reduction in interest on the part of his partner, my uncle. The latter's wife, my Aunt Nan, now had two successful greengrocery shops on the parades of shops serving residential communities, and there was little need to keep the market stall running.

It was disposed of, marking the end of an era, and Johnnie went to work for his sister-in-law. It was not a successful arrangement. One day there was a small discrepancy in the cash float at the end of a busy day and she accused him of stealing a matter of a few pence. Hasty words were exchanged, and she told him that he was sacked. As he went to get in the van and drive away, she stopped him, and pointed out that the vehicle belonged to the business. He was forced to walk home without a coat on, and only his white linen work smock to keep out the rain. He was a dispirited, sixty-one year-old man with no job, no car, and no overcoat.

He rang me to tell me about it when I got home from work on the Friday night - by midnight I had found him another job! I went to The Nouveau for a quick drink and a dance. While I was there, I spoke to a young man I knew slightly, who mentioned that he had bought a greengrocery shop and was looking for someone to run it. I immediately telephoned my father and put Graham on the line. Johnnie went out and bought a vehicle the following day and he started work on Monday. There was only one fly in the ointment, as it turned out. Just like my Uncle before him, in his younger days, Graham also went out and spent the takings before the creditors had been paid. As a result, his financial backer, another friend from my school days, had to wind the business up. I last saw this charming and totally irresponsible young man in a shop in Filey. He had turned his hand, no pun intended, to pottery and soon disappeared again, possibly once more without paying the rent.

I asked at the National Lending Library to see if there might be a clerical post available for my father. Within a few days, a job as a porter/messenger came up. I felt that this was well below my father's abilities, but he applied and got the job. He loved it and everyone there loved him. He could hardly believe that he finished work at 4:30 p.m. on Friday and did not return until 8:00 a.m. on Monday, and that he had three weeks annual holiday plus Bank Holidays. He was used to working until 10:00 p.m. on Fridays delivering greengrocery orders, and until 7:00 p.m. on Saturdays, getting up at five in the morning every day in order to set up the huge stall while Clifford was doing the buying. Johnnie did the donkey-work while Clifford was being charming to the wealthy lady customers. These well-off ladies used to come in to choose their vegetables, as much for a flirtatious interlude as for the quality of the produce. I did once comment on the fact that the hard work seemed to all fall on my father's shoulders, but he replied that they both did what they were good at and that he would not want it any other way.

That Christmas of 1969 was the first time that my festive meal and the tree were not provided by my father and we had to fend for ourselves. Yuletide was looming and the cost of a suitable tree seemed extortionate. Don made a suggestion that was to become a part of the celebrations long after purchasing a real fir tree no longer presented a financial problem. When he was a child, money had been tight and the family were in the habit of making a sortie into the woods and cutting a large hawthorn branch. This was taken home and was later painted white as if covered with frost and decorated as every other tree at Christmas. Armed with suitable tools we made off toward the river, a jaunt well known to us during the summer months when the children and I would gather raspberries or blackberries. This time we returned with not only our 'tree', but trailing ivy and holly to drape around the house. I felt well satisfied with our afternoon: not only did the house look festive but we had shown that pleasure and fun did not have to come at great expense. It was to be thirty years before I actually paid for a Christmas tree again.

At that time I did not keep alcohol in the house because it was an unaffordable luxury. Occasionally Don would buy a bottle of stout and some cider and we had a drink known as a Black Velvet, a mixture of the two. We both seem to have developed an amazing capacity for vast quantities of booze since then. Just before Christmas, maybe on the 24th, I went to 'The Deer Park' on Street Lane at lunchtime to meet up with some of the old crowd. These included my good friend Tony Kristall, who always insisted that I had helped with his homework when we both attended Roundhay Talbot Road Juniors. It was the only chance I had for a little R&R. The children were generally visiting Granny Webster on a Saturday which left me free.

That Christmas Eve afternoon, the whole gang was going to the 'Mansion' in Roundhay Park for a last drink before we bade farewell and Merry Christmas. I went along at Tony's behest and as I left he came to the car with me and said I was to wait there until he returned. He went back inside and came back a few minutes later, signing that I should wind down the window. As I did, he handed me a half-bottle of Scotch, and five pounds. I was deeply touched.

It was not the first or last time he had shown his generosity. Once before he had pressed a fiver into my hand, and one day had been across the road on Street Lane parade and returned with steak and a joint of beef. There were no strings or conditions to his kindness, but I once had found myself without any money when I was leaving the Deer Park and asked Tony for a loan, which he gave without question. I repaid the money the following week and he told me some time later that I was the only person who had ever repaid a loan to him. Another time he was just leaving the Nouveau Club, to which he had introduced me and paid my membership fee, and he turned round to come to my side and discreetly pressed yet another five pounds into my hand, "Here you are kid, treat yourself".

Five pounds was a lot of money in 1969, but I went to see Elliot Nevies, an optician I used whenever new specs were needed. I told him that I was in the market for a change but, had limited funds. He produced some very dramatic frames, which were obviously expensive, and I regretfully told him that they were beyond my means. "How much can you spend?" he asked, and I told him about my windfall. "Five pounds is all they are," he lied, and he continued to show his generosity to me, and later on to David, for many years. Even after we left Leeds, we used to return to Elliot for our eye tests. Both of these kind men asked for nothing and were the only people to offer any help when I was struggling. Was it something that Jewish folk did and the rest did not? It wasn't the money; it was the knowledge that someone cared that made it important.

At this time, Father Christmas brought necessities like sweaters and pyjamas. The latter were essential for Brad, whose penchant for creeping out after lights-out and fetching furry animals such as the rabbit, or a family of gerbils, into his bed had resulted in large holes in his nightwear, not to mention their waste products. Fortunately, Grannie Webster and their father still bought toys but these had to be opened when the children visited them on Christmas Day, rather than being added to the few things that I had bought. I have conflicting feelings about this now; my grandparents always gave their gifts to my parents, so that the myth of a fat old man in a red suit, who visited under cover of the night, was continued. Of course, they did not have the pleasure of seeing my excitement and I am of the opinion that when children are little, the fairy-tale is more important than the reward to the benefactor.

I think that by the time Christmas arrived that year, my children had abandoned all illusions about Santa Claus, and on the 24th it snowed late on in the evening. We decided to put on our warm clothes and go down to the bottom of the village and wish everyone who was leaving the pub, the Duke of Wellington, a Merry Christmas. When we returned home I made tea and fruitcake and we sat round the fire. "Do you fancy opening some presents now?" I asked. Of course they did and consequently when we did finally retire for the night, we all slept peacefully until morning. A precedent was set for many years to come and continued long after they were grown up We all congregated on the night before Christmas, with wives, husbands, and children until I felt that maybe they might prefer to enjoy their own families and friends in their own way. When the time came, I initiated the change, since they probably would shirk that job for fear of hurting my feelings.

I was still trying to find myself the perfect man, an almost compulsive search to put someone in my life to make me feel like a whole person but it was getting more difficult as time went on. I now needed someone who could fulfil my intellectual needs as well as assuring me that I was sexually appealing and generally worth while and there is and always has been a dearth of single men in the right age group. Not that I was unused to consorting with younger men but hoping that one of these would be willing to accept responsibility for three children was going a bridge too far. Don was long lost to me, since he was going steady with Penny from down the lane, though we still tended to each other's housekeeping needs.

At thirteen, Brad was just one of the intellectual challenges that any prospective swain would have to meet. The other major problem was number-one son, who felt that his own emerging sexuality was vulnerable and who therefore viewed any suitor as a threat. Dani just wanted a Daddy and I wanted to give her one. My only romantic adventures during this time were a very casual relationship with Alan, a floor manager with Yorkshire TV which merely gave us both an occasional Saturday night out. On one of these nights, we went roaring up and down the lane on my three-wheeled tandem at midnight. There followed a short and passionate romance with a twenty-three year old business studies student, who flew off to Canada for the working part of his studies all too soon, and neither of these were destined to be permanent.

By the time the end of my first year as a student loomed up and the exams had come and gone, I felt that a holiday might be welcome and thanks to my frugality and the houseful of lodgers, I was in a position to afford it. With Gillian in tow, I went to a travel agent to see what was available to two poverty-stricken students and a ten-year-old child. The boys were still finishing their summer term at boarding school so I did not have to take them, otherwise it would have been out of the question. We found a vacancy in a Spanish resort unknown to me, but the hotel had a pool and the flight went from Manchester so we booked it. All three of us shared a room which was barely big enough for the beds but we managed to fit in. It was still a little early for the best of the weather on the Costa Brava and, on the first day that we were there, it rained slightly so we all went off on a jaunt. After dinner, Gill retired to bed to read, taking Dani with her, so I sat and sussed out the talent. There wasn't any that I could see so I followed them and had an early night.

The following day was clear and bright so we all enjoyed the sun, at one stage going up to a balcony area to make a change from the poolside. Unfortunately a crowd of young men who seemed to have come in a large group were playing with a ball up there, regardless of the hazard that this presented to the assembled company. I was unimpressed and at one point confiscated their ball and made my displeasure felt. This ability, I had no doubt acquired at my mother's knee. I certainly made no effort to be charming but, later that evening, I was joined at the bar where I was reading and having a pre-dinner drink, by two unprepossessing young men. One of these was short, chubby, and balding and his friend was pale, thin, and insignificant. Not my style darling, but since I was slowly revolving on my barstool, I made a witty remark and said "Do either of you want to go around with me for a while". It transpired that they were members of the large group that I had encountered earlier, a deputation from Stoke on Trent, who were at first-sitting at dinner, presumably to allow for a long night drinking sangria. Thank you and good-night! I was looking for something a little more upmarket.

After the repast, Gillian and Dani once more retired to the room and I went to the bar to have a nightcap. There were three very amply endowed ladies holding court at a table nearby and sporting elaborate hair styles which looked like huge mounds of horse dung carefully arranged on their heads. Their somewhat raucous voices suggested that they may have taken a ferry across the Mersey on several occasions. I personally felt that they would have been more at home in Southport than at their present destination but I suppose I did have the option to move to another table. I was reading a book, which had made quite a stir at the time, 'Catch 22'. This is an anti-war novel which had untold moments of humour if one had the intelligence to perceive them. It also contains allusions to historical and literary characters and the like, and is certainly not a trivial book. It is one which, when I re-read it for the fourth time thirty years later, struck me as being unfunny, merely tragic, and disclosing only that side of war.

My peace, such as it was, was disturbed by the arrival of the pale skinny young man of the revolving bar stool, who stopped by on his way to the ablutions to ask if I would care to join their party. I did not actually say that having my backside rubbed briskly with a rustic brick would be preferable, but I hoped that my expression when I gracefully declined the offer must have conveyed the right impression. Under normal circumstances, it would have achieved the right effect but the unfortunate young gentleman was either too dim or too drunk to get my drift, probably the latter. In the light of subsequent experience. I have since learned that alcohol has a tendency to induce a condition known as verbal diarrhoea in this particular individual.

Undeterred by my refusal to join, he came back to talk to me a while later, totally unaware that I had a ready supply of ugly pills ready and waiting for any unsuspecting would-be predator. It transpired that in spite of any appearance to the contrary, he had read the book in question more than once, although we were not laughing at the same things or at least not for the same reasons. After about half an hour, I began to wish he would take a verbal Diocalm or go back from whence he had come. I was looking for a brain surgeon who was handy with do-it-yourself tools, or even an engineer carrying The Times, but not some scrawny lad from Stoke.

I restrained myself from telling him to go away, or words to that effect, only to find myself being asked to accompany him to the following night's big occasion. This was to be a mind-bogglingly boring weekly event known as The Miss Solmar beauty contest, due to be held by the pool for the delectation of all guests of the Hotel Solmar. As a means of getting rid of him I gave it a 'maybe', fully confident that by the time morning came his hangover would have obliterated any memory of the night before. Not so.

When I came down to dinner the next night, he was there, resplendent in a suit no less, a smart shirt and tie, all dressed up for the ball. I, on the other hand had developed a nasty cold so I was even less my delightful self than usual, but I did not have the heart to tell him to leave me alone. I met him after dinner and was thoroughly unpleasant all evening which he seemed to find totally enchanting. Admittedly most of my acerbic wit was directed at the Spanish waiters, who understood only simple commands, so their sensibilities were not affected.

Before too long Miss Solmar was duly crowned and anointed, and the band stuck up a rousing melody. My little friend asked if I would care to join him in some gyrations on the dance floor. As a former exponent of the Terpsichorean art, I was filled with dread at the very thought of such an exercise but I bit the bullet and took my place facing him. It was a Jekyll and Hyde experience - a fairy-tale transformation. The Frog Prince come to life. And I hadn't even had to kiss him! My one prevailing thought was "Can he do that in a horizontal position?".

A little later we repaired en-masse to a nearby disco, and he and I were never more than centimetres apart for the next two hours. He was attentive, loving, and sexy, but not pushy and I went to bed much later, alone and with my virtue intact. That was not destined to last long. He and some of his companions were accommodated in an annexe, and since the rest were out carousing the whole night, we had the place to ourselves and Gill was happy doing the nurse-maid role back in the main body of the hotel. I was always in our room in time to catch a couple of hours sleep before breakfast. Significantly, Dani and he seemed to like each other. We spent the remainder of the holiday together, behaving like star-struck lovers and making plans for our future, even planning a name change since marriage was already on the agenda and his surname added to my first name made for a ludicrous combination. I had no intention of being called Shirley Turley.

By this time my cold was developing nicely and David, for this was the name of my Prince Charming, had obtained some antibiotics from one of his party, which I took regardless of the fact that they had not been prescribed for me. It transpired that these were largely Aureomycin. I got a significant allergic reaction to these after I got home.

The rest of the holiday passed in a haze of lust interspersed with the minimum of sleep. We visited Barcelona on a coach trip accompanied by Dani and Gill which I mention only because we witnessed a wedding in the cathedral in that city. This was an experience we never forgot, as much because of the sheer beauty of the interior and the music as because of the somehow symbolic nature of the occasion. Rather pathetic really, someone of my age getting so sloppy four days into a ludicrous holiday affair with a young man barely out of his teens. Calella de la Costa itself had little to commend it and I never entertained any desire to return, unlike the more northerly Calella de Pallafrugel which still calls me back after five holidays there.

The end of the holiday came and we bade farewell to David: one of those tragic moments when one wonders if the goodbye is forever. The scene was set to perfection, a late night departure in darkness, boarding an impersonal coach with tears welling up in our eyes, the stuff of a 1940s film with Bette Davis. I almost said "Don't let's ask for the moon, we have the stars already". I had had my fill of tragic goodbyes. I seemed to have spent my life on station platforms, airports and bus terminal en route to the rest of my life. It was 'Brief Encounter' and I was Celia Johnson, only better looking: I always wanted to be a 'fillum star'. Thank heavens it was the last time I ever had to play that particular role.

Naturally we had exchanged addresses but you know what happens in holiday romances, after a few days back at home the blood has cooled and realism kicks back in. We usually settle down within a short time and go back to faithful old Arthur or George or Mabel. Only I did not have that option. After a week or so there was no word from the potteries and I began to despair so I cooked up an elaborate plan which I put in to action with immediate effect and within 24 hours I was driving to Leeds City Station to meet a train. The fact that we were a totally mismatched couple in every way was no deterrent. He was twenty two, lacked formal education having being written off by a system which did little for the child who had reading difficulties regardless of their other talents.

His parents never expected any of their offspring to move out of the environment in which they had all been raised and, in spite of the paterfamilias being a man of some knowledge and intelligence, David was treated as some sort of unschooled waster. He had not an 'O' level to his name, not even in practical skills. If you were not in the top two streams it was assumed that the only work available was in the pottery or labouring in some trade and teachers had little interest. He had never lived in a house with a bathroom or an inside toilet and was going nowhere. I was on my way to degree status, owned my own large house (well, me and the Halifax), and I had been around the block a few times. Let us not disregard the small age difference, a mere fourteen years and three months and of course three children, the eldest of whom was less than nine years my paramour's junior. It was a totally unworkable situation.

Dani was delighted to see him again. He had been very kind to her during the holiday and what kept Mother happy, kept Dani happy. We had a long and largely horizontal, weekend, and then David returned to Stoke on Trent and his job. Unfortunately, his employer had been rather less than impressed by David's absence and did not welcome him back with open arms. Quite the reverse. The following weekend I went back to the station to greet my unemployed lover who brought all his worldly goods in one large suitcase, returnable.

He was nervous and deeply insecure, desperately eager to please, and anxious to be as helpful as possible. And he was unemployed, a formidable combination. When job interviews were imminent, the palms of his hands became wet with nervous perspiration, not helped by the anti-tuberculosis medication which he was still taking following a spell in a sanatorium. All in all we had a recipe for disaster. Within a short time I returned to my old job at the N.L.L. for the summer in order to supplement my grant. Eventually the D.S.S. agreed to pay David some unemployment benefit to which he added a few pounds by doing odd jobs around Bardsey, the next village. Finally he applied for a post with the Refuge insurance company which entailed collecting premiums on Life Insurance policies. He phoned me at work to ask if he could take the money for the bus fare from the telephone moneybox, borrowed a pair of Brad's shoes which were far too small, and went for the interview. He got the job and thereafter, having delivered me to work he would set off to do his rounds, knocking on doors in some of the seamier streets of Leeds, often not finishing until mid evening.

One of his previous jobs had been as an apprentice in the upholstery business and he soon set about refurbishing the two armchairs in the snug, very expertly, and the finished result was gratifying. Before too long he was doing jobs for other people, usually in our living room, which was hardly big enough for the three permanent residents, but we all seemed to manage. Money can't have been too tight because we went to the occasional dinner dance, and usually to the Bingley Arms at Bardsey for a late drink on a Friday, where he met 'the crowd'. They were as welcoming as all West Yorkshire natives, a far cry from their easterly neighbours, as we were to discover later.

David

Lust still figured large in our lives and often I would leave the bedroom in the very early hours in order to boost our flagging energy with tea and bacon sandwiches. Often, alone in the kitchen, I would wonder if it was all a dream. There was a small part of me that wanted to go back to find the bed empty so that I could return to the freedom which I had so hated, before David came into my life. We had already both changed our names by deed poll. Various alternatives had been considered, among them Chipping Sodbury, Brize Norton and similar upwardly mobile sounding names. Windsor was a familiar Leeds surname, a large bookmakers firm was Jim Windsor's, and the royal connection never struck us, so Windsor we became.

Don was still in residence and different though the two men were, they hit it off and we all got along fine. It was an odd situation, I suppose, but Don was probably relieved that I had found someone to care for me, and David never felt threatened by the presence of my long term 'ex' in our ménage. When he finally met my former husband, they also hit it off, and there was never any antagonism. Probably the only mild dissenter was number-one son, who no doubt felt that his nose had been pushed out, and his position as the heir to the throne had been usurped. Boys can get very territorial about their mother when the father is no longer around. They see themselves as the head of the family in the absence of the traditional patriarch.

It was a problem that only surfaced on rare occasions, but continued to do so until Russell formed an emotional relationship of his own. I have no idea how Brad felt about it. He has never discussed his inner-self with me and, at the time, there was no obvious problem. Given his awareness of his own intellectual superiority, he was unlikely to have felt threatened by someone with David's lack of formal education, but probably recognised the latter's ability to deal with the more practical side of life.

I had a heavy workload during that summer vacation; my poor showing in the Psychology stakes had brought a penalty of five essays to be completed before the commencement of the autumn term. Fortunately there was no shortage of reference books at my workplace and many found their way into my temporary library. In addition to this we had all been set an essay for Speech Pathology, my field of research was the idiosyncrasies of the speech and language development of twins. Once again, I was in the right place and a computer based search came up with all possible writings on the subject and the end result was a detailed rehash of my readings which gained me plaudits from our revered Head of Department, Miss J.

One evening, Vivian Reeves came to dinner, accompanied by her long-term gentleman friend, John, who was a well known and much admired expert in the field of Audiology. It was interesting that at no time did my rather timid David sound or seem intimidated by these two giants in their field, he was a perfect host and they were wonderful guests. Vivian was returning to her first love, the hearing-impaired, and we students lost a great lecturer and a warm and sensitive ally. She went to Wrexham and is there to this day, it is now twenty two years since we last met and regrettably our correspondence is limited to a long and informative letter from me and a short and almost illegible one from her, at Christmas. She has retired and is still single; I think that marriage would have put too many restrictions on her work.

Year two started in September 1970 and I was now an old hand, able to treat the new first-year students with an element of condescension. At least I now knew what I had got myself into; they still had all that to come. We found that we had another brand new lecturer to replace the irreplaceable Vivian. Her name was Chris Benstead and, in fairness to the good lady, I have to say she was excellent and she became very supportive to me later on. This second year was far more taxing than the previous one; there were more essays, more lectures, and more pressure in the clinical practice. The fact that the year-end exams were not purely internal, but formed Part One of our third-year finals, also put pressure on us all. Fortunately, I seemed to have come to grips with the Speech Pathology subjects and was getting some great marks for my work. Maybe this was due to the borrowed books from the N.L.L. from which I could crib, without fear of the staff who were marking the papers having a copy of the same tome in their possession. Most of the sources of my information were American publications and not generally available in this country.

My domestic life continued to improve and the transient population of The Laburnums settled down to a manageable number. This included the continued presence of Don who was now a part-time H.N.C. student returned to his first love, electronics, having abandoned his full-time aspirations. Eventually, he became a big noise in the Civil Aviation Authority working in Air Traffic Control, so proving that the all-hallowed degree was not the only way to the top. He was, and still is, a potent intellectual force and I shall always be grateful to the support he gave to me both emotionally and education-ally during my own wilderness years.

David and I managed to hold our relationship together against all expectations, a common remark at the time was "It'll never last" and this was a widely held view. His other and sister had not been well pleased at the outset and I can easily understand their viewpoint, but we made one or two visits to them and I think they eventually had to accept that I was not the scarlet woman they had imagined me to be. It's a good job they didn't live locally, because I am sure some kindly neighbour would have dished them the dirt on me and apprised them of the facts of my previous rather wild, existence.

The house and the mortgage were now legally mine, and we were keeping body and soul together entirely unsupported by any maintenance payments from Jimmy. These had stopped without notice when David entered my life. The boys school fees were still paid, but I received nothing for their keep during the school holidays, and not a penny for Dani. I discovered over thirty years later that my old friend Pam, who had now moved in with my former husband, was heavily subsidising the cost of educating my sons. I did not realise at the time that money was getting tight for Jimmie. However, he still went out drinking, and ate smoked salmon for Sunday brunch, while we were making do and eating the greens given to me by a rare friendly neighbour to feed the rabbit, for our own lunch. At least we did not have to eat the rabbit - that came later.

The biggest problem I had was keeping awake during tedious lectures; a lusty sex-life does not blend smoothly with the need to stay alert for an hour at a time in a classroom. One day as we filed out at the end of a lecture throughout which I had dozed sporadically, the Principal commented that maybe I should get more sleep. She was probably a little envious since her own long-term affair had ended and who can blame her? However, she had started relying on me to organise certain things as early as the end of the first year, she was a flapper and I was cool, calm and apparently in control. I learned later that it can be a mistake to let oneself get into the situation where the boss depends too much on a minion. Once they realise what a position they have got themselves into, in which the tail is wagging the dog, they can turn on you with disastrous results.

During this second year, I had been elected to do one of my clinical practice days at the Leeds General Infirmary and one of the major problems in the area was parking. I used my initiative and went down to the office at the L.G.I. wearing my white clinic coat and requested a parking disc. When asked what department I was in I truthfully said "Speech Therapy" and the permit was issued forthwith. Thereafter I parked every day in the hospital compound having befriended the car park attendant who used to let the dog out and take him for a walk round at lunchtime.

Sue Green and I had already served a two-week stint more or less unsupervised during the last two weeks of the vacation and as usual I had a good relationship with the domestic staff. Tea and coffee appeared as if by magic and our clinic coats were laundered. When our college principal made her first appearance, looking rather less than immaculate, my faithful retainer was not aware that this was my boss. Consequently, when coffee-time came and our newly-arrived leader asked if we had to pay, the reply was not very pleasing to her. "Well, this lady doesn't" said the tea-lady, pointing to me, "but I don't know about you". I tried to tactfully let the domestic help know that this was the Principal of the College, but she had chosen sides by this time.

On another occasion, a few weeks later, my superior told me that I should not fraternise with the non-professional helpers. When next held in conversation by Mrs Mopp, I excused myself, saying perhaps indiscreetly that I had been told not to spend clinic time talking to the staff. Mrs Mopp went straight to the Chief Speech Therapist and complained that the Dragon Lady had prohibited the nice young lady from talking to her. Unfortunately I got the fallout and was immediately transferred to a school for severely-learning-disabled children, under the supervision of the aforementioned Mrs Benstead. I started to wonder if I was getting myself into the right profession, but I felt that there was no going back and, as I said, my new clinical supervisor was very supportive. I remember her telling me that I had made a mistake in letting the boss depend on me too much. Sooner or later when these seniors realise that their authority has been diminished, there is a possibility that the devoted and efficient assistant will be rounded on and banished from the magic circle.

I never subscribed to the view that the cleaners, tea ladies, and car park attendants are lesser individuals and should be treated as inferior. These are the workers who grease the wheels and keep the machinery running smoothly and should be awarded the respect that they deserve. It has always worked for me. Years later, yet another superior was not happy to find that my clerical support staff called me by my first name and stated her point of view, that this sort of familiarity diminished my authority. I beg to differ, at that time my typing was done by a young woman who was considered difficult, rebellious and unruly, I only had to ask and Carol would do whatever I needed. It is a matter of how you ask and of having consideration for the member of staff concerned. Respect is earned and is not dependent on you having a title that states that you are superior.

The second academic year raced to its end and once again the exams were upon us, I was far from confident but in the event I passed everything, getting a distinction in the Phonetics exam. This was due, in part I suspect, to the fact that, as the penultimate candidate after five hours of interviewing trembling girls, I lifted the sagging spirits of the examiners when I walked in apparently brimming with confidence and shook both of them by the hand before sitting down to be grilled. I think that the written paper was easy in comparison to being face to face with the inquisitors but most of the others on the course had to re-sit. With the end-of-term came the prospect of another two-week block of clinical work and a return to the National Lending Library to earn some money. David had changed his job and was working in Wetherby at a firm supplying everything for the farming community. He was in his element and we have often thought that if we had not moved away, he would have ended up being the manager. I would have got a job somewhere in the West Riding and we might still live in the same house. We may even have the same circle of friends and go to the same pub for a drink on a Friday night.

I can't remember how it came about but a chap who lived in the village and had an antique shop in Wetherby, heard about David's ability to re-upholster and came to the house one night to ask if he would do a Victorian spoon-backed chair for him. This involved stripping the chair right down to the frame and starting again and we had no other place but the living room to perform the operation but there was money in it so David agreed. He did a wonderful job in red Dralon, a fashionable velvety fabric. The chair had a deep buttoned back which is quite challenging for the re-upholsterer. The finished chair made a good deal of money for the dealer so 'ere long another chair followed. This one collapsed as soon as the fabric was stripped off but David seemed to know what he was doing and he rebuilt the frame, re-stuffed, and re-covered it.

The next job was a large Chesterfield settee and, once we had that in the 12x13-foot living room, there wasn't much space for people. To add to the difficulty, there were repeated power-cuts. The lack of electricity was not allowed to hamper progress, however. We managed to carry on with the aid of two paraffin lamps and a few candles: me with my essays, David with his settee. This was a particularly interesting piece of furniture because it was stuffed mainly with grass, which we burned on the living-room fire. It had a drop-end, which is to say, one arm dropped down level with the seat, enabling a single occupant to lie out in comfort. I was always astonished at the skill and expertise employed in these very challenging jobs, and for years I have watched with admiration as David undertook deep buttoning and all manners of other complicated manoeuvres.

The finished job was always perfect and far superior to any anything in the shops. I knew that he had spent some of his early working life as an apprentice in the trade. A few years later, I was left speechless when, after having been entrusted with other people's treasured antiques and three-piece suites for years, he announced that before he came to join our impoverished household he had only ever re-covered tip-out dining chairs, a job that an enthusiastic amateur could tackle. As I started to write this section, I once again asked for confirmation of this fact and was assured that it was true; his only experience had been gained by watching what an expert did.

David is one of those amazingly gifted people who observes and is able to imitate what he has seen, using his native intelligence and ability to work out how to overcome problems in order to accomplish his objectives. The only person who has ever denigrated any of his success is himself, everyone else realises his real worth. He told me soon after our liaison got under way that I was the first person to ever tell him that he was good at something. I was not referring to his upholstery skills! These days, he displays his amazing talent when making the most beautiful furniture. People look at it, stroke it, and ask, "How does he do this?".

Among his other accomplishments, David seemed to be able to take on all manner of building and maintenance jobs during our time at The Laburnums. He tiled the kitchen, replaced several windows, not just the glass, the entire window frame. He created a wardrobe in our bedroom because we had moved back downstairs from the loft-room by this time, and redecorated most of the house. There seemed to be no end to his talents but this was only the beginning, the best was yet to come.

During that summer vacation, before the commencement of the final year, we made a trip to the coast, taking a large frame tent which I had bought second-hand, and two Great Danes, (one new, one second-hand), and three children. How we packed everything into a Ford Cortina, I do not know but we did. I had not visited Flamborough for years and we made several trips that August. On the way home on one occasion, we passed a derelict station with a large warehouse and three acres of land. I fell in love and announced that I was going to live here, back in the land of my forefathers.

The property was for sale and I lost no time in telephoning the agents the following day, the asking price was £7,000 so I offered £2,500. They seemed to consider this fair, so we went ahead with our dreams. There was already a house on the site that with major surgery could have been made inhabitable but it was the warehouse, which excited us. With hindsight, if we had bought the property and applied for Building Regulations to renovate the house, we could not have been turned down but at the time we were complete innocents. The local County Surveyor was helpful, but warned us that there had previously been several hopeful prospective purchasers, all of whose planning applications had been rejected on some pretext or another. His words were that these decisions had been 'political' and not of his making. In the meantime Fimber Station became our cause celèbre, and we planned all manner of detail, touches that we would incorporate into our finished dream house.

The warehouse was in an advanced state of dereliction. The roof had totally gone and trees were growing from the upper floor. Undeterred, we submitted a drawing of the expected finished appearance in order to obtain outline planning permission from the East Riding County Council. On one of our visits to Flamborough, we spoke to a local resident who was acquainted with the property. He commented that there would be quite a bit of work to do to make the place habitable. The windows needed replacing for instance. This was like raising the Titanic and commenting that the carpets could do with cleaning. How we could envisage such a mammoth operation is hard to envisage but fools rush in where angels fear to tread.

Time went by and no word came from the Planning Department but I was set on the idea of relocating and applied for a post with the East Riding Education Authority in the New Year and was offered a job provided I passed my finals. Having got that in the bag, I decided to rattle the cage of the ERCC Planning Department and telephoned them about our outline planning application.

"Oh hasn't anyone let you know, it has been rejected".
"Why is that" I queried.
"Too much coming and going at a busy roundabout" was the terse reply.

Years later the Council took the site over and developed it as a picnic site and play area: not too busy a roundabout for that then? Mr Moody had been right: the decision was indeed political.

However, as far as I was concerned, my move to the near-East was set in stone and I was not to be deterred. The weekend after I had received the bad news, I managed to obtain a newspaper from the area, 'The Driffield Times'. There were two possible houses in our price range. One was a fairly ordinary house at Wetwang, which did not stir us one iota, and the other was an elderly detached cottage of large proportions with a huge yard and outbuildings, which had formerly accommodated a chemical works. It required a great deal of hard work and money spending on it. The asking price was £3,750. I offered £3,500 but someone else was prepared to go the full nine yards.

I was not to be pushed so we returned the following weekend to have a close look at another property in the same village. This was a monolithic structure of Victorian design and comprised the former village school and the house that had formerly accommodated the schoolmaster. My comment at the time was "It is ghastly". We bought it! But not without the odd hiccup along the way, however.

The house in East Keswick was sold by putting an advertisement in the Yorkshire Evening Post. I wanted to avoid paying estate agents fees, a false economy as it turned out. The professionals would have raised at least another thousand pounds for the house. As it was, we were trampled in the rush and would-be buyers blocked my solicitor's telephone lines. The sale was agreed before teatime. A late viewer, who confessed he was merely window-shopping, stayed for a drink and strongly advised us to gazump, a new word to enter the language that year. This involved raising the price and letting the prospective purchasers progressively raise their offers. I felt that this was sharp practise and I refused to consider the idea. I am not quite so squeamish these days, but in fairness and in some explanation of my action or lack of it, I had not set out to bargain and had agreed to sell to the first viewer who had offered the full asking-price before he left the house. Regardless of the loss of up to two thousand pounds, I could not renège on a deal.

We could pay off the mortgage and buy the 'Old School' for cash and still have about eight hundred pounds to spare. We thought that this would see us through the massive project ahead of us. A holiday in Sicily was already booked for the Easter of 1972, a deliberate move designed to give me a complete rest away from the academic pressure for two weeks during the run up to my finals. Another of the students and her boyfriend Des, who was working and doing an H.N.C. in Building Studies, were joining us. We really needed Des because we wanted to hire a car to get to the airport and back and David was too young to drive a rental. He was not yet twenty-three.

We were anxious about leaving the sale and the purchase but my solicitor assured me that he was in control so we had an exceptional holiday. This was largely due to the local population, though Des was unflaggingly amusing and good-tempered. He still is as far as I know, but unfortunately, he now lives at the other end of the country so we have not seen him for years. However, on our return there were disastrous tidings. The solicitor told us that the vendor had reneged on the deal and agreed instead to sell to a local man. The estate agent was helpful but could do nothing though he told me that the owner considered himself a man of honour.

I found the vendor's telephone number and spent half-an-hour on the phone to him, using everything I had learned about manipulating behaviour with words over the years and at the end of the conversation I had won. What the man's motivation was I will never know: maybe he simply enjoyed playing power games and wanted to make us squirm. Oddly, because Driffield is or was a small market town where you cannot make a move without the entire population being aware, we have never encountered him in thirty-two years. It is almost as though having being beaten in his game, he self-destructed. He was a well-known character and his name has never come up in conversation, and I have never enquired about him.

Des did make a major contribution to the design of the house formerly known as 'The School'. One evening he was visiting us to make final arrangements for the holiday and he sat doodling, having taken note of the approximate measurements, and he came up with an innovative idea which would not have occurred to us. All we had thought of was a totally conventional design, which would have completely wasted a space with a good deal of potential. I could only think in terms of an ordinary living rooms downstairs, with bedrooms upstairs' design. I had not taken into consideration that this was not a building site with a large space; it already had features and character. There was one huge schoolroom that measured 45 feet by 18 feet, and about 17 feet high, and a smaller room 18 feet square. Des suggested a split-level ceiling with an open gallery running round, for the large room.

This meant that one bedroom and the bathroom and toilet would be suspended on rigid steel joists. One room would be taken off at the other end with a bedroom above and the centre was to be open to the existing ceiling height. The smaller room was to have a floor for a bedroom above it and little other alteration. In addition, there was a long, fairly new, kitchen block, and various cloakrooms.

The 'little house', as we have always called the schoolmaster's house, was fairly ordinary. It had a seven-foot wide kitchen, which included a walk in pantry at one end, with one power-point, and a Belfast sink supported on brick pillars and nothing else. Outside the back door, a yard with a six-foot high wall round it accommodated a former outside toilet, a coal-house, and another store. These structures were soon demolished to make way for a small walled area of flowerbeds. This part of the whole was integrated into the former girl's playground, which was separated from the boy's side by a wall between the toilets, a little further down the tarmac yard. The intention was that we would initially renovate the schoolmaster's house and then with somewhere reasonably comfortable to live, we could concentrate on the far bigger task of converting the school into our dream house. Eventually, the little house was intended to provide a retirement home for my father and he appeared to be happy with the plan.

In view of the fact that we intended to move to a more parochial and less permissive area, it seemed that the formality of marriage was a wise move. I had secured a job as a Speech Therapist in the Beverley area, dependent on my results in the forthcoming exams and to commence on September 1st 1972 . I felt that to be living-in-sin would be an unpopular career move, so a wedding was arranged for May 13th, exactly four weeks before our planned removal, and the end of the final year of my academic life. We had both already changed our names by Deed Poll, and I had been wearing the ring for almost two years, so it was a slightly unusual ceremony. Some friends collected the boys from Woodhouse Grove School in order that they could attend. In view of Brad's repeated phone calls to Jimmy to raise objections to returning to this seat of learning, it was surprising that they were still boarders. Many of the students from the course came and Don came up from his new home close to Stansted where he now worked, having flown the nest some months previously. Unfortunately, Johnnie had tickets for the Rugby Final at Wembley. Naturally, my mother lived too far away to make the trip, and so there were no family members in attendance.

We had ventured into home winemaking the previous year and we had a good supply of rose petal wine and some other potions for the celebrations. Joyce Heaton, my only good neighbour had made some vol-au-vents and everyone seemed to have a jolly time. The parents of David's friend, Paul, had travelled up from Stoke on Trent and we had handed over the master bedroom for their use. We slept on the floor in the spare room. At least David had someone there from his own environment, and they were lovely guests.

There was little time for relaxation. I immediately had to concentrate my attention on the forthcoming exams, and David spent his evenings packing crockery and similar items ready for the move, which was scheduled to take place the day after my last exam on June 17th 1972.

Our grandiose plans for our future home included a stately dining room, and I had already purchased a splendid Indian carpet and a seven-piece parlour suite. This was of Edwardian origins, and consisted of four dining chairs, two uneasy armchairs, and a chaise longue. This had set me back £25 in a junk shop and in view of the fact that the family, without visitors or friends numbered five, I bought a further set of similar chairs for a few dollars more. All were in need of attention from the master upholsterer, naturally. What we were short of now was a suitable table and I regretted turning down the offer of the one from my Granny Taylor's house. However help was at hand.

Young Johnnie Heaton, now all grown-up, popped in one night for a glass of home brew and offered a piece of information. Did I not remember that under a copious velour cover in their rumpus room, there was an Edwardian table of grand proportions beneath which many Heaton children and friends had played jolly make -believe games? No, I was unaware of its existence because it had always been completely covered but I was certainly interested and soon approached its owner regarding a possible deal. This proposition was received with interest, but no commitment, though I was hopeful that a satisfactory result would ensue.

Fate was to intervene in the form of a demand for payment of the gas bill at the Heaton establishment with a threat of imminent court action, a fact of which we apprised by John himself, who worked for the debt collection agency handling the debt. This prompted me to make a phone call to Joyce offering her a pathetic twenty pounds which was immediately accepted and the table was soon resting in our garage awaiting the move. A couple of nights later, Mike, the antique dealer, came to collect yet another chair and upon seeing the table he offered us fifty pounds for it. We refused and some years later we sold it at auction for eight hundred pounds.

We spent one or two weekends at the house at Kirkburn and Dani and I stayed there for a full week over Whitsuntide. I somehow managed under very primitive conditions while I spent as much time as I could, studying for the crucial exams starting on 12th June. David had the use of the pick-up mini van from the shop, and so we had a few chairs and bits of carpet in the house. We managed to cook with the camping gas stove, and I swept the house from the upstairs down with a yard brush, and burned scrap wood on an open fire. The living room was a joy, the wallpaper was peeling and the ceiling was black with mould, water ran down the staircase when it rained.

The natives all seemed friendly, though I realised later that they were merely curious. The residents of the East Riding are very suspicious of strangers, especially those from the West Riding. A long history of rape and pillage down the ages, from Vikings to Scots may be responsible for their caution, but if you were not born round here, you will never be allowed to join. It is an almost feudal society. My own interpretation was that unless you were raised with a bale of straw in your crib, there was no way your daughter would be allowed to marry their son and vice versa, not in the professional classes anyway.

To some extent things have changed. There has been a huge influx of invaders from the South looking for a cheaper place to buy property, but these outsiders stick together and now represent a large proportion of the population. The old guard remains guarded and keep themselves to themselves, almost like a well-to-do enclave. We were told by a patient of mine, himself an immigrant, that we may be accepted in twenty years or so, but I feel that it is when you first arrive in a strange place that a hand of friendship is really appreciated. Dani, at least, made two friends who did not hold her origins against her and they remained close until marriage took them to pastures new.

The time for the final exams arrived and I seemed to manage to struggle through the written papers though the practical gave some anxious moments. During this final year I had been doing my clinical work at St James's Hospital, and my patients included one or two odd characters. One of these, Jim Gallagher, was a former editor of the Yorkshire Evening News, suffering from the after effects of a cerebro-vascular accident or stroke. This had resulted in an almost total loss of his ability to communicate except for unaccountable breakthroughs when, as if a window had opened, he would suddenly say something coherent and relevant. If prompted with an opening line he could recite poems or Shakespeare or finish a well-known phrase.

One day, when I had been miming typing, he said "I used to play the piano, you know" and then the window closed again. Many years later I met his son, quite by accident, and he told me that Jim had always been a bit of a rogue and not only knew every landlady from Land's End to John o'Groats, but also knew the colour of their underwear.

Another of my gentlemen, also a stroke patient, had, not uncommonly in these cases, lost all inhibitions regarding cussing and blaspheming. In an era when four-letter words were unacceptable in a lady's company, he caused some consternation among the nursing auxiliaries. They did not understand the nature of his handicap, so when he told them to "F*** off" if they caused him to be less than delighted with their behaviour, they found his vocabulary disturbing. I regret to say, I derived considerable amusement from these hilarious incidents, but the other staff always departed in high dudgeon, which was probably why he did it.

For the occasion of my practical test, a group of similar patients had been selected to be given appointments so that I could be observed treating them and were forewarned that this was a very important day. They all arrived at the same time, ambulances not being as flexible as taxis. Those not in for the first session sat outside waiting while the examiners watched me go through my therapeutic routine with my first victim. When the two examiners left after about thirty minutes, I reasoned that the other student would also take up a similar length of time, so I stuck my head out of the door and said to the wait-ing group, "Come on in and have a cup of tea, they won't be back for ages".

Three more patients with varying degrees of post-traumatic speech and language loss trooped or were wheeled in and, just as I was pouring the brew, the door opened and the two examiners re-entered the clinic. "Oh shit", I thought, "caught in the act". The only thing to do was to use my initiative and bluff it out. "Come on in, you are just in the nick of time. Can you hold the fort a moment until I go for some more cups"? They seemed delighted with that notion and I then turned the tea break into a group therapy session using the crockery, biscuits, and visitors as therapeutic tools.

Later, after the patients had gone, there was a viva voce, which took all my flannelling skills to survive. However, they were both obviously willing me on and at one point when I was totally at a loss as to how to reply, I adopted an expression of wisdom and poised my face as if to speak, while hoping for a miracle. The miracle came. One weary exam-iner whose life must have been brightened by my relaxed approach smiled, said, "Yes of course, it is ...", supplying the answer. Amazingly, my practical exam earned a distinc-tion and I discovered many years later that I was described to my future employers as a human dynamo.

The very last ordeal was a two-hour neurology paper and as soon as that was over I bade my farewells and rushed home to pack the remaining boxes of our belongings.

CHAPTER 12
IN A FOREIGN LAND

The following morning, the removal van came, was filled to the gunnels and we all left to start a new life and a great adventure. Many times I have asked myself, how different would our lives have been if we had remained where we were? There may have been better career opportunities for both Dani and David, and certainly a better social life for us all. I think we truly believed that we were moving to a way of life away from the rat-race society of the city. At that time we did not envisage the less-desirable elements of our increasingly grasping world, ever invading the peace and quiet of the rural East Riding. I felt that I was giving us all a chance of a better life; at least we did not have to breathe in carbon monoxide fumes on the way to work.

It was not long before I got the full blast of the pig slurry used to spread organic goodness on the field. The perfume of this added interest to the clothes we were wearing, those on the washing line, our hair and, I am convinced, our breath. Unfortunately, we had failed to observe on our short visits that the local Squire ran a very productive pig farm whose forward-thinking methods did not preclude him from using an old tried-and-tested fertiliser.

We learned to live with it.

We started packing the removal van at an early hour and the job was still going on hours later, even the Luton-head was full, a first time for this company. We did have a large quantity of additional household goods because a number of items had already been amassed in readiness for our eventual move into the school when the conversion was complete.

It was teatime before we had finished unpacking at the other end. Unusually, I suppose, all the carpets except one had accompanied us because we needed some temporary floor coverings, in a house that was destined to become a building site we wanted carpet that owed us nothing. We gave the removers a beer, paid them the £25 plus a small bonus and they went on their way leaving us to revel in the joys of our new home. Fortunately, the pub down the village did a good line in take-away bar meals, and we had chairs to sit on, a table, a copious supply of home-brewed wine, and scrap wood to burn on the open fire. The black mildewed ceiling no longer worried us. We were warm, we were fed, and we had beds to sleep in. The fire heated the water and it was summer. We took the dogs for a stroll down the village and on the return we saw the huge building looming dark against the summer night sky. I never ceased to marvel at the fact that this was ours, lock, stock, and barrel. No loans, no mortgage, and the excitement of the task ahead to spur us on. Of course, there was also no job, no income, and not much expertise but I had great faith in David's ability to do everything. Poor man, what a responsibility.

It was a good job that the school building itself was dry and free from mould, because a great deal of our furniture and other possessions were stored in there for many months, in addition to steel girders, timber and animal feed. The place was vast and I had quite a job finding my way around. Mind you, it took me months to remember the way to the bathroom in the little two-bedroomed house that we occupied. The previous year, I had experienced a funny turn: what I believe to have been a transient ischaemic attack, and have had difficulty with my sense of direction since that time. I can still become totally disoriented in a completely familiar place, much to the astonishment of people who are unaware of my problem. Even going to the Ladies in a restaurant or pub presents me with difficulty, because I emerge and have no idea how to return to the rest of the party. Fortunately, I can always find my way to the bank.

The first week, David travelled back to Wetherby to work his notice and Dani and I were left dependent on sparse public transport. She started at her new school and arrived home the first teatime overjoyed that she had been judged brighter than the average and was accordingly in 4J. This was a step up from her previous school where her grade had depended on the say-so of the headmaster of the village school, who was not her biggest fan and who positively disliked me. The boost to her morale was a significant influence on her future academic achievements and she quickly settled in and made friends with her peers. We had a major animal tragedy that week but the full story is told elsewhere.

We were limited as to what work we could do on the house because, having applied for a renovation grant, we had to wait until permission came through from the County Council and they were swamped by applications. Unfortunately the local builders were taking full advantage of this scheme which awarded up to £1500 for each residence, and many local entrepreneurs had bought up derelict or down-at-heel property, in order to make a fat profit. This had a knock-on effect, because there were no joiners, bricklayers, plumbers, or electricians available for a little cash-in-hand overtime. Fortunately, we were able to bring our former odd-job brickie over from East Keswick for a week or two, and one of my former in-laws from Darlington stepped into the breach. The latter, Tommy, came down from the comfort of his own home for several days at a time and slept in a sleeping bag on the floor, building walls during the day.

The land surrounding the building required a large amount of attention. The grass was as high as an elephant's eye over the uneven area which had previously been the school gardens, and eight years of neglect had destroyed any semblance of a cultivated garden in the front of the schoolhouse. It was gloriously wild, and the first task was to bring the grass down to a reasonable height, a job we accomplished with a combination of paraffin and matches and an ancient scythe. Later on, this land was to provide a huge vegetable garden, nurtured and largely managed by Brad. It also made a lawn, which Brad rolled flat in the driving seat of a van. He was under-age for learning to drive but took the opportunity to do a little off-road practice on our future garden. To one side we constructed a large animal compound in which we kept the hens, ducks, rabbits, and geese, until they were big enough to eat. Gertie the goat had her own stall.

Inside the little house, the priority was to create a usable kitchen and we took a chance on the Inspectors being too busy to visit. David built cupboards from scratch because ready-made kitchens were in their infancy in those days. Des came to spend weekends with us and suggested that we knocked out the pantry and so enlarge the kitchen to a workable size. Actually I think we should have titled him Des the Destroyer, he appeared to delight in demolition and even brought tools with which to facilitate the task, for which we were very grateful. Janet, one of the former fourteen-year olds from early East Keswick days, also came with her husband, Harvey, and his electrical skills were utilised to good effect. It was fortunate that we had failed to appreciate the enormity of the project at the outset or we would never have had the nerve to take it on .

The bathroom was not included in the grantable work because it already boasted running water and the usual facilities but all the ceilings upstairs were very high and this alone gave the place of ablutions a very bleak feel. We decided to rectify this forthwith and I scoured demolition sites and yards for reclaimed materials, timber for the beams to support a lowered ceiling being the first requirement. We waited until after four-o-clock on a Friday to start any knocking and alteration so that we minimised the risk of an unscheduled visit from the powers that be. We need not have worried, they were far too busy watching the big boys to give any thought to minnows like us, no one came near until we asked them to pass the work so we could claim the grant money. Until that time finally arrived, we had arranged an overdraft and we managed not to exceed the set amount.

I started work on September 3rd. In my first month, after tax and other deductions, I made more on my travelling expenses than I drew in salary: my take-home pay was £52, and my expenses came to £54! This was reason enough for me never to take a day off sick; I needed those lunch and fuel allowances in order to feed the family. It became a way of life and I developed a reputation for being amazingly hardy: I rarely had time off sick. Apart from being a confirmed believer in my own ability to resist infection, I knew that patients were waiting and there was nobody who could fill in for me. It wasn't that sort of job.

David had registered at the local office of Social Security. To our surprise, a very nice man came to the house and declared that my twenty-four year old husband qualified as a married man with three children and as such was entitled to £13.00 a week. We insisted that we did not expect anything but he was adamant, and I have to say it was much appreciated. There were few jobs to be had, and the few ones that existed all involved travelling to Beverley. The wages offered just about equalled the Unemployment Benefit, and a large proportion of it would go in bus fares, if a bus were available. Getting about is not an easy task without a car when one lives in a village. At the time, it seemed more to the point for David to get on with the building jobs. If he had taken a job we would have needed to pay someone else to do the work, so it was six of one, and half a dozen of the other.

Most of our experts arrived to start work after six o-clock at night or during the weekend and we paid them in hard cash. Keith, was a plumber on South Dalton estate, how we managed to obtain his services I cannot recall, but he was on the job here by 8:00 a.m. on a Saturday and Sunday morning, up a ladder outside the bathroom, singing totally unrecognisable songs. We were still abed but because the pipe work to the ablutions was unfinished and not connected to any appliance inside the house, the ghostly serenade came to us down a length of plastic pipe. Keith filled another vital role later on. When we acquired the goat, I was not a natural milkmaid. There is a special technique for this operation when goats are concerned but the plumber was up to the job. He watched me struggling for a while then took over, giving me a short lesson in the finer points of dairy-maiding.

I must confess to becoming rather impatient with David, who spent a good deal of time watching the various experts carrying out their work instead of getting on with something he could do. His response to my remonstrations was to close one eye and tap the side of his nose with a straight forefinger. I learned later that this was meant to signal a message "I am watching and learning". Because of his amazing ability to learn by watching, we never need to call a builder, except from choice, and certainly not a joiner. We only occasionally enlist some assistance from my long-suffering son-in-law if the mysteries of wiring or plumbing become too much for David to deal with without guidance.

When I started my new job, the newly-appointed boss lady was on holiday and so I was presented with an armful of case notes and left to my own devices. It was a portent of things to come, in retrospect, and not an ideal way for a newly qualified and inexperienced therapist to start. On my first day in Driffield clinic, ten appointments had been made for me: one every half-hour and none of the children who arrived that day appeared to present with any speech or language problem that I had ever encountered before. I flannelled my way through somehow but of course a new set of ten were to arrive the following day in Bridlington. It was the same the day after, but the end of the week was easier because I went visiting schools.

On those days, I could work at my own pace, going to classrooms to collect the child in question. The biggest problems were teachers, who expected me to be teaching five year-olds to pronounce "th" correctly, or deal with regional accents. They had no real understanding of what my job was all about, and I was not awfully sure myself. Eventually I settled in to some sort of routine and the boss came to work in Bridlington once a week, to give some sort of support. Immediately after the last patient had left the clinic we each made a rapid getaway. She raced home to her school-aged children and I rushed to the builders merchants to fill up the boot with sand or bricks, then home to make a quick meal before I started mixing concrete, mortar or plaster. We worked until after ten o'clock each night and living conditions were primitive. I never knew what the state of the house would be when I arrived home at the end of the day.

At one time all the ground-floor walls were down to bare brick due to the extensive damp proof treatment and the upstairs reeked of woodworm killing chemicals. Dani moved out for several days and went to stay with some new friends in Driffield. I would like to put on record my sincere thanks to Chris Woodmansey and his family who were alone in offering the hand of friendship to us in the first weeks of our residence. Chris ran an old-established plumbing and decorating business in the town and came to give us a quotation for the installation of central heating. Before he left the house on that visit, he invited us to a party at his home, a flat above the shop, and he and his wife, Pat, remained good friends for many years. Their marriage reached a parting of the ways and Pat made a fresh start as a nurse. It has been a long time since we last saw her, but Chris stayed in our ken until he seemed to disappear from public view.

The boys had come home from school at the end of July and Brad immediately got stuck in to the hard physical work. Russell avoided any involvement in his tried-and-trusted fashion. This entailed either making so great a hash of what he had been asked to do, or playing the incompetent, so that we were glad to have him keep out of harms way. The boys made a friend, Alan Mather, who came along and mucked in, muck being the operative word. One of the tasks that he and Brad took on was cleaning out the roof void in the school prior to the woodworm treatment. This resulted in a heap of twigs, dirt, and nesting materials some five feet high in the big hall which was then loaded into a wheelbarrow and moved outside for disposal. I suspect that some of it was reclaimed by our feathered friends and recycled.

Thirty two years later, I was standing in Tesco's when a portly bearded and balding man came up to me wearing a quizzical look.

"Jumbo?" he asked. (this was the nickname bestowed on me thirty years previously by my children and used by all their friends at that time) "Yes", I replied, puzzled. It was Alan Mather, the first time I had seen him in many years. Thank Heavens I had not changed as much as he had.

We produced huge piles of bricks and rubble but could not afford the luxury of a skip to take it away so I dug some extremely large holes and filled these with the waste. Occasionally, one of these has arisen like a phoenix many years later, when gardening projects have decreed excavations. The largest of them reappeared only after we had vacated the school itself. Much of the rubble was bagged into plastic animal feed sacks and disposed of into private tips under cover of darkness. We probably spent as much on petrol doing this as it would have cost to hire a skip but we were hard-up novices and every penny mattered. I never took a trip in the car unless my employers were paying for the petrol. The supermarket was visited en-route from work and we did not go out socially.

Somehow, we managed to afford a camping holiday in Germany mainly for Russell's benefit, since he was taking the language at 'O' level. I don't think he spoke a word of the German tongue all the time we were there, and was his usual pain-in-the-neck the whole time we were away. The weather was not good and one night during the early hours, we awoke to find a stream running through the tent. David leapt up and went outside in the downpour to dig a trench round the outside of the encampment to divert the flow. I don't think that we have ever been camping since.

At the end of the summer vacation, Russell and Brad returned to Woodhouse Grove, where they were still pupils in spite of our repeated attempts to persuade Jimmy to let them leave and attend the local school. I was aware that his financial situation was unstable, and wanted Russell to be settled in another school in good time, before 'O' levels loomed on the horizon, but their father was adamant that they should continue at public school. I was of the opinion that Brad could survive and still achieve in a comprehensive, and that Russell needed the extra tuition offered by the smaller classes at private school. It seemed reasonable to cut the cost by withdrawing Brad but this was not to be.

We actually received approval of our grant application and the go ahead to commence work on November 14th 1972 although much had already been covertly achieved. One of the major jobs involved moving huge stone framed windows from around the building in order to build a new window at the front of the little house where the front elevation had to be preserved. The task was a huge one, the stone was fourteen inches thick, and none of the top ones could be shifted without mechanical aid. Our friendly neighbourhood squire rallied to the cause and came along with a tractor, once we had loosened the appropriate lumps sufficiently. He raised the bucket to the required height and the inside workers helped the masonry into the waiting receptacle, which was then lowered, to the ground.

It was frequently hair-raising work and potentially dangerous, how David escaped major injury is a miracle. The front door itself was coming out to make way for a window in order to give more light to the hallway, on the recommendation of the man in charge of awarding the grants. The largest, though not the heaviest single piece of stonework to be moved was the lintel over the door, which supported the brickwork above it. Our builder from East Keswick was in charge of this operation, which was performed without the assistance of Peter Hepworth and his tractor. John, the builder, insisted that we could manage with a block and tackle and somehow it worked. Replacing it to form the new window with smaller pieces which were thicker and heavier was far more nerve-racking and when one of the jacks gave way, we only just escaped severe injury. The original door lintel is now the top arch of the baronial hall style fireplace in the big house, "The Old School", as it is known.

On more than one occasion, I have arrived home from work to find that my kitchen units had been removed to allow access to the plumbing. On two occasions there was no floor in the living room. But one became accustomed to such minor inconveniences. When we first arrived we had used up all the part-tins of emulsion paint on the mildewed walls, achieving a colourful result which served until we reached a more advanced stage. By the time the boys came home for the Christmas holidays we had made the house reasonably habitable, having stayed up until two in the morning to wallpaper the small living room which was to be their bedroom. The night before Christmas Eve we were laying the living room carpet at midnight and still had only the open fire to heat the whole house. However we had the room festively decorated and a white-painted branch doing service as a tree.

The black-and-white television gave up the ghost on Christmas Day, and in those days we had no spares. Fortunately it was repairable after the holiday. It was a source of some annoyance to me that some of my patients whose parents had no visible means of support, and were therefore living on benefits, had colour television. I, the professional, had to manage with an ageing black-and-white set. However, I knew that one day things were going to improve, whereas they would always have to live in poor conditions. Their colour TV was a compensation for having little joy in their lives.

Before the school term was due to commence, a phone call from Jimmy put a sudden end to the boys' boarding school days, and I had to make rapid moves to arrange for them to start the new term as day-boys at the local comprehensive school. Russell was less than impressed with this, and it was certainly the worst possible time in his academic career for it to have come about. I was furious with his father for allowing it to happen because the whole fiasco could have been avoided if the move had been made a year earlier.

Brad fitted in with the new environment, in spite of being streets ahead of his peers and found the standards pathetically easy. On one occasion, having requested extra work, duly given, he asked if the finished piece was wanted before the school bus arrived to take him home, a matter of a few minutes later. I do not suppose his now-renowned sarcasm went unnoticed. He was immediately popular with his schoolmates and quickly lost his public school accent in order to fit in with the local populace. Later, he became the first student to be appointed to the board of governors, a considerable achievement in a society steeped in a tradition of not being allowed to join unless one was born in the area.

Russell, on the other hand, had no desire to join and viewed the whole business as strictly infra-dig. Unfortunately his own opinion of his abilities far exceeded reality, and with no effort at all he became wildly unpopular, at least with the staff. One day, he went drinking at lunchtime, with an adult friend, and was delivered home by a teacher, to whom he told the sad story that he drank too much because his ogre of a stepfather bullied him. We had to see the headmaster, who threatened expulsion if there was a recurrence of this and other unacceptable behaviour. Although both of the boys had previously done German, and Russell was taking it at 'O' level, Driffield School did not include it in their curriculum. In addition to this, the school was taking the examinations of a different board to the one used at Woodhouse Grove. In the event, Russell took one exam in one place, and then had to take the bus to Leeds so that he could sit another the next day at his former school.

This would have been taxing for someone of greater ability but for Russell, it was a disaster. He finished up with two passes in English and one in French and, understandably, declined the chance to return to school to re-sit. All credit is due to him; he paid for private tuition in Biology and went to Beverley night classes for Maths and passed both at the December session. In the meantime he took a horrible but well-paid job in a turkey-processing factory, where he earned a huge amount of money, having lied about his age. His failure must have been a dreadful blow to his pride and I really felt sorry for him, but he was so totally unlikeable that it was difficult to preserve a civil relationship. I truly hoped that someone would come and take him away, but that seemed like an unattainable dream.

Dani did well at her new school and was always given good reports. She was not a naturally brilliant student, but she worked hard and achieved results. She could have gone on to greater heights but did not have the motivation to study for an extended period.

In the meantime, we managed to complete the renovations to the little house we lived in, getting approval for the work and therefore the grant money by Easter 1973. The whole project had been designed to accommodate my father when the time came for him to retire but fate was to take a hand and he met a widow lady from Gloucester while on holiday in some far off sunspot. On his own home front, my grandmother had moved in with him and was in need of care, he could not abandon her and was thus unable to pursue his own life. However, he kept in touch with his fairly well provided for friend and the following year they went on holiday together. Very occasionally he went to Gloucester to spend a weekend with her, leaving Grannie in the care of Nan, my aunt, who, by this time had persuaded the old lady, now not in full possession of her marbles, to hand over all the family jewels.

These included 'Shirley's earrings', and the loss of these was devastating. Johnnie had suggested to me, some time before, that I should ask Granny for them. I simply could not do that: it struck me as too mercenary and grasping to try to relieve an old lady of her personal possessions when she was vulnerable. It would appear that I was alone in that philosophy.

It was not a question of value. I had always been assured that the earrings were to be mine, and if they had come from Woolworths, I would still have felt that my inheritance had been stolen. I will never see them again because I have been told that Nan had them made into a ring. I gather that the rest of Grannies jewellery was given to my aunt's sisters. These were the pieces that my mother had pawned in order to get the money to save the shop in the market. Granny asked Johnnie to bring her to see me one day as she wanted to give me her Canadian squirrel coat to compensate and she told me that she was afraid that if the authorities had found out that she was in possession of the jewellery, they might think that she was potty and lock her up. I cannot help wondering where she got that idea. I would have been glad to have become custodian of the earrings, but never got the chance.

A couple of years later, my father telephoned one night to ask me if we could go to Leeds to take away the family silver, before that too went the same way and we went after tea one evening. It had been a silver wedding anniversary gift from great uncle Fred Taylor to his wife, Theo, but now it is mine.

One night, Russell lay on the hearthrug in front of the fire, as we considered the possibilities regarding his future. At Woodhouse Grove, the Army as a career had been big on the agenda: as an officer and a gentleman, naturally. Russell fantasised about going into the Intelligence Corps, which we thought hilarious because he was not an expert at concealing anything. The jokes centred around a vision of my eldest son sleeping with a revolver under his pillow. Nonetheless, the following day a serious note crept into my ruminations. I telephoned the local Army Recruitment Office, told the sergeant in charge that I had a son, and asked if he would like to take him away. When I offered the inducement of said son having four 'O' levels, the man in the office asked if he would like to join the Intelligence Corps.

"Are you kidding me?" I questioned.

"Oh, he wouldn't" came the crestfallen reply.

"He'd love to" I said.

The following week we took Russell to Ashford, the training centre for the Corps and left him in the tender care of a massive Warrant Officer. Several hours later, we returned to collect my long-haired seventeen year old. He and the W.O. came marching across the parade ground to where we were waiting.

"He's in", said the big man.

"For nine years" countered Russell.

Someone had come to take him away. Maybe there is a God!

A few weeks later, I saw him on to the bus for York, where he would catch the London train. It was August and my feelings were mixed between relief that he had found some purpose and sadness that my first-born was flying the nest. By the time he came home for Christmas, he seemed to have matured and improved, albeit temporarily. He looked stunningly handsome in his uniform with its single stripe on the arm, an extra for every new recruit into the 'I' Corps. A few weeks later, we went to Ashford to see his passing out parade and were joined by his father and Pam. It was a proud day.

Little brother, Brad, had developed a passion of his own. This was of a slightly different sort and was a painfully shy, amply bosomed, brunette named Maggi. He also grew a luxuriant moustache, and long hair, to go with his sixth form status, having attained fairly spectacular results in his 'O' level exams. This was in spite of flatly refusing to do homework for those subjects which he considered irrelevant to his future.

This future was under discussion because during the summer vacation he had been working for our local bricklayer, Tim, a man of considerable knowledge on many subjects and not the run of the mill brickie. Brad felt that there was a career in building for him, but I pointed out that not everyone on a building site would appreciate his sense of humour. In addition I felt that his use of long words like "immediately" may well get him duffed up. He stated a desire to do a degree in Maths and potato growing and I suggested that he might care to give a long hard look at Civil Engineering, which seemed to me to combine academic ability with practical skill. The potatoes could be grown at the weekends. It obviously seemed to be a reasonable idea and one which held a certain appeal for him. He stayed on at school to do three 'A' levels, and continued to work for Tim during the holidays as well as doing huge amounts of gardening and odd jobs at home.

We had another Christmas in the little house. Johnnie came on the day itself, bringing Eileen, his former lady-friend for a drink. Her husband had expired and so had the big affair. Unfortunately she had suffered a heart attack and as a result, had developed gangrene in one leg which necessitated an amputation. She died shortly after, but her daughter kept in touch with my father until the end of his days, eventually returning a doll to me that I had been coerced into lending her fifty years before. Why did I want it? Because I vividly remember waking on Christmas Morning 1941, seeing the doll's face and beautiful long white gown, and naming her Gloria Jean in honour of a singing child film star of the period. She was part of my family.

We were on the verge of moving into the 'School' and during the Christmas holiday, Russell had been sleeping round there. The actual transfer of bodies was made on his birthday but most of the furniture stayed in-situ because the house was rented to a newly-wed teacher. There was still a great deal of work to be done but at least we had achieved a huge amount and we were 'in'. At last we could bring into use the huge dining table bought for a song from Mrs Heaton and use the chairs scrounged from junk shops, which David had reupholstered. However, that 29th December was not the first time that the room, in which these furnishings stood, had been used.

About a year and a half earlier, if memory serves me well, I had arranged that the quarterly meeting of the assembled Speech Therapists of East Yorkshire and Hull was over-confidently agreed to be held at 'The Old School'. The biggest push to be finished, in the history of our ventures, ensued. The formal Edwardian dining room was the last item on our agenda since it was not essential to our plans for moving in. However, it was the one area that could be completed regardless of the state of the rest of the house and it was decided that this would be the venue for the meeting at which my local paediatrician, Doctor Bogdan, was scheduled to give a presentation.

We were working until the early hours, day after day. Jack, the joiner, frequently reported for work at midnight and David employed his upholstery talents to re-cover eight dining chairs and the Parlour suite in a glowing yellow shadow velvet. We had a chap from Bridlington to strip the old stain off the floors in both the big room and the soon-to-be dining room. To save on expense, we had stripped only the area that would not be covered by carpet. When, an hour before our guests were due to arrive, I put the 12x15 ft. Indian carpet down, the old varnish was still visible. In a panic, I started to hand-scrape the offending area. After ten minutes of this, I suddenly realised that I had laid the carpet the wrong way round. It was pulled out from under the furniture and turned through 90 degrees. All was well.

There was no electricity, so the room was lit by paraffin lamps, and a huge arc lamp, powered from the little house, illuminated the way through the big room, which was still a building site. Our heating came from a portable gas fire. The expression on the faces of the guests as they entered this beautiful room from the brick-littered chaos, which led to it, was a joy to behold and the evening was a resounding success.

There were to be many other occasions when the enormous rooms were to be graced with admiring guests. The whole place became our dream house. Don came to visit, before and after and on one occasion, said, "When I look at this place, my faith in human endeavour is renewed".

Mr Franks, the building inspector said, "I never thought you could do it. Is it the way you imagined it would be?"

"Yes, exactly," I replied. Except for the fact that we had been forced to cut corners and to use inferior materials because of financial pressures.
These cuts were not made on structural jobs, but we had chipboard window ledges where we had wanted oak, and many other economies of a similar nature. More recent occupants have rectified these horrors but they have plenty of money and pay someone to do everything. We did it ourselves.

One time, we had just finished working in the big room after hours of hard graft. Tim Dulson, the builder was there and I had been mixing sand and cement backing for the walls of the big living room all evening since six-o-clock. David too was labouring for him and at 10:30 p.m. on a chilly March night, we were all outside having a rest. In spite of the cold, I was lying on the grass, resting my aching back and Tim said something that we have often recalled. "One day, people are going to pass here and wonder why some lucky bastards can afford to live in a place like this. They will never know the way you worked for it."
He who dares, wins.

CHAPTER 13
LIVING IN THE DREAM HOUSE

Immediately after Christmas 1974, it was all systems go for the move into what became known as 'The Big House'. As we vacated 'The Little House', a young couple, both teachers, moved in before the beds had the chance to get cold. The night of Russell's 18th birthday we had our first meal in our new residence and we used the huge dining room, all 324 square feet of it, magnificently furnished with Joyce Heaton's Edwardian table, which seated eighteen people in comfort at a later date. The wallpaper was an elegant ivory and lemon stripe; look-alike Edwardian wall lights with candle bulbs graced the walls. There was the seven-piece parlour suite, plus four additional similar chairs, all reupholstered by my brilliant husband. These all gave an authentic early-twentieth century appearance to the room. It was totally different to the rest of the house, which was far more rustic and country style.

One of the features of the room was the fireplace which was grey marble and tiles with yellow flowers on them in relief. This had been reclaimed from a shop in Norton whose owner was the father of one of my small patients at the local Junior school. He needed it removing from the shop and, since we had a home for it, David and Russell had travelled up there one morning and taken it out free of charge, all parties being delighted with the deal.

We made one enormous tactical mistake, however, much regretted in the coming years. When we first started work on the School itself, we had taken out the two solid fuel room heaters which had warmed the frozen hands of the student population in the past, and the chimney to the small classroom had been sealed. This was now our formal dining room, and the splendid fireplace with its brass fender and Tidy Betsy was therefore all show. In later years we would certainly have installed a wood-burning stove. Not that it was out of the question to rethink and re-do, but there were more important concerns at the time.

Naturally, all the locals were consumed with curiosity as to what the outsiders from the west, had done with their school so whenever the opportunity presented itself, we invited them in for a look round, One evening an elderly gentleman from a few houses away was the spur of the moment guest and as I walked in , with him bringing up the rear, I saw that Dani was seated at the table, reading. "Where's David "I asked. Without raising her head, she replied "He's upstairs having a crap," in her ladylike English, totally unaware of Mr Marson's presence. With some dignity, I said, "I have Mr Marson here with me." Appalled at her gaffe, she said "Oh, shit" and compounded the felony.

She was not the only member of the family to leave a lasting verbal impression on a member of the local community. We arranged to purchase some bantams from a former patient who lived at Southburn and one summer evening he arrived with the birds in a sack. They were alive of course. I called to Brad, who was about seventeen at the time and said loudly to him "Mr Walmesley has got the bantams." "I'm terribly sorry," he said to the gentleman holding the sack, "Is it very painful?"

Because Speech Therapists had eventually been awarded a substantial pay increase, which was paid some fifteen months in arrears, our finances had received a much-needed boost. We could now afford a carpet for the big room, and Heuga carpet tiles for the breakfast room. The unwelcome extra was the fact that, by the time the money was paid, it was a new tax year and the Chancellor had increased the basic rate to thirty percent. Even though the money had been earned in the previous tax year, I only received two-thirds of what I had been awarded. Imagine the uproar there would be today if taxes rose to that level.

On the work front, there were many rumbles at national level and it seemed that Speech Therapists would all change employers, and transfer to the National Health Service. In the meantime, some bright spark in Whitehall, had decided to alter all England's county boundaries much to the chagrin of the natives and at enormous expense to the local authorities. East Yorkshire was to be broken up and re-titled North Humberside, a name with all the charm and musicality of a reverberating expression of flatulence. We Yorkshire lads and lasses of all ages had always nursed a fierce pride in our heritage: once a Yorkshire lass gets her teeth into something, she doesn't let go until she gets what she wants. I was told that at my mother's knee. The Lincolnshire lad was now a South Humbersider, and I am sure he was as unhappy with his lot as the rest of us. Vast sums of money were spent on new stationery and logos, on new equipment and staff, and at the year-end, any money left in the county coffers was hurriedly spent so that it was not passed on to the new regime.

Within a short time, I no longer worked for the local authority; not even the new one. The Health Service and a totally new hierarchy had imposed itself. My immediate boss was still the same person but she was answerable to a Chief who was ensconced in an office in Grimsby. This did not suit my boss one bit and, because we in the old East Riding were fiercely loyal, we fell in quite happily with a hate campaign of amazing venom. This was all sub-rosa, naturally, though I am sure Miriam Hall, our new leader, was not unaware of our animosity.

In retrospect, an alliance with Miriam could have served me better. She was knowledgeable, experienced and very able to deal with authority, and as straight as a die. She certainly never used her sex appeal to win her way: she did not seem to possess any and because she was rather butch in her dress and hairstyle, we all assumed that she preferred female company, if you get my drift. We could have been totally incorrect but it suited our mindset at the time. Sorry, Miriam. On more than one occasion, she fought my corner in a couple of issues, and was supportive and fair. On the other side, I once had a steaming row with her over the phone in the clinic, in the presence of a patient, a fact which she ignored in her anger. Where is she now, I wonder?

Easter of 1975 saw Russell home for some pre-embarkation leave. He had graduated and was soon to be despatched to West Germany, for a tour of duty. He really did seem to have grown up. It was always such a joy when he came home on leave and he left his room immaculate when he left. I used to get home from work and go in to the downstairs bed-sitter that was his room; the total lack of the person who had lately occupied it always reduced me to tears. Mind you, the constant presence of that same person would no doubt have had a similar effect.

Brad and I had brought the wilderness outside to a state of order and vegetables kept us and some of our livestock well-fed. We needed them robust so that they grew big enough to eat as soon as possible. Money was still tight because after a few years working for a local business which supplied caravan accessories, David was once again job-seeking. In the years of creating our home, he had acquired many skills and before too long one of our friends asked him to do some work on their house. Tim Dulson, our builder, seemed to find work for him and so he drifted into being a self-employed Jack-of-all-Trades and remained so for the next twenty years.

Living in 'The School' was an amazing experience. The big living room was 32 feet long, and it was possible to work up a good head of steam when running from the bottom of the stairs to the kitchen. The wall of Dani's bedroom, suspended over the lounge on R.S.J.s , was covered with carpet tiles in a geometric pattern of two colours. I had quite a problem getting what I wanted because none of the carpet salesmen seemed to understand that they were selling carpet for a wall rather than a floor. In spite of my careful explanations of the proposed location, they could not stop assuring me of the hardwearing properties of their carpet. I did point out that I did not envisage that the area would receive a great deal of traffic but this information obviously did not register at a conscious level.

In the end, we bought some very thin rubber backed carpet tiles in Canterbury, whilst Russell was receiving his initiation into the potential joys of becoming an Intelligence Corpsman and stored them until we had somewhere to put them. Ultimately, they did wear well: the folk who bought the School from us took them down, and we reclaimed them. At first, we once again used them on a wall, then several years later, they were laid on the hall floor of a little house we had bought to renovate. I suppose the average person does not put carpet on a wall so the carpet salesmen have to be sympathised with.

There was an open staircase at one end of the lounge and the wall to one side was pine boarded as was the ceiling, all very different and avant-garde at the time. The wall was hung with brightly coloured woven rugs and an open gallery ran along above the fireplace which was a huge baronial stone surrounded aperture which we had created from the stone removed from the little house. A room of such great size cost a fortune to heat: it was 576 square feet but more than half was 17 feet high and, frankly, the cost of being warm in the winter was beyond our slender budget. We spent most of the time huddling in the relative warmth of the breakfast room and only sat in the big lounge on high days and holidays; it was at this time that our mistake of sealing the chimney in the smaller classroom became apparent.

Life rumbled along, we still had dogs, rabbits, ducks, hens and a cat, Brad still had Maggie and had actually become engaged to her. I did not approve because it was and is my opinion that seventeen is far too young to make this sort of commitment. I could not appreciate what he saw in her: she was always wilting and not the sort to roll up her sleeves and get on with things whereas Brad was very much the man-of-action. One time many years before, both he and I had been decorating the kitchen at East Keswick, he pasting wallpaper and I applying it to the walls. Time was getting on, it was certainly well past his bedtime so I suggested that we call a halt and resume the task in the morning. "There are only a few more lengths to put on, let's get it finished before we go to bed," he said, and so we did. He was about twelve at the time and has only just, thirty-three years later, started to slow down and not push himself to the limit over each task.

Brad's girlfriend, Maggie, was very shy and unsophisticated, she would sneak out of the door to go home after spending the day or the weekend here and not say "Goodbye, thank you for having me". It seemed like lack of good manners but I think it was a combination of an absence of home training and a paucity of confidence. She certainly changed in every way when she grew up. I cannot say that I liked her originally: she seemed vain and selfish, but Brad obviously adored her. By the time she was twenty-five, we loved her. She had worked like a slave on the house which they later built at Hutton and grown up into a considerate and thoughtful daughter-in-law. From the sixteen-year-old who wouldn't help with the washing-up if she had painted her nails that day, she transformed into a first class bricklayer's labourer, who heaved hundredweight bags of cement around and developed muscles to prove her ability. It's not how you start but how you finish that really counts.

We had the first of several superb parties just after Christmas, a combination of a birthday celebration for Russell and a housewarming party. There were 135 guests and I fed them all on jacket potatoes and home made meatloaf. The spuds had all been washed by being put through a rinse programme in the washing machine. In retrospect, I really don't know how I managed to cook that number but I did. Russell had brought his hi-fi system over from Germany and music filled the great room. Every guest contributed some booze and we had a bar which was manned by volunteers. You drank what you brought: if you brought spirits, the bottle went under the bar (a former Methodist Chapel altar front) and was served only to the donor. Generally the contribution was a bottle of wine or a seven-pint can of beer and, although the age range spanned at least five decades, we never had anyone drunk or incapable.

Neither did we have our bedrooms invaded by teenagers looking for a quiet place to fumble or pass out. I did all the catering for each party. Sometimes it was curry and rice, or stew or stuffed pancakes. We never had less than eighty to feed and I did it on a conveyor-belt system. I served from the worktop in the kitchen, the guests queued up, a few having been quietly informed that food was ready, and they were under orders to return the plates as soon as they had finished. A couple of volunteers washed up and returned the plates into service as others joined the end of the line. It was a magic formula and always worked perfectly. If the beer started to run out, someone went to the pub with a gallon demijohn which the landlord filled up. Halcyon days!

We invited everyone we knew and very few people refused our hospitality. We have often commented that the return invitations were rare which I find odd because if I accepted someone's food and the use of their home, I would feel duty-bound to return the politeness even if it was a chore.

We also entertained on a gracious scale in our Edwardian dining room, where we might have a dinner party for twelve to sixteen. All the ladies wore long dresses and the gentlemen wore jackets and ties. We brewed our own wine so it was not exorbitantly expensive to dine our friends: none of us expected to be offered spirits at that time and the important thing was to enjoy the company. Out of all the many friends of that time, only one couple remain in our circle, although they are now divorced, but we still maintain contact with both.

In 1976, two momentous events occurred. I saw an advertisement in a newspaper illustrating a truly splendid-looking car, and the reality lived up to the picture. As I was pulling in a substantial sum from my expense allowance, the purchase of a new car was a viable proposition. We tried out one Colt 'Celeste' in Leeds, and then again at the much closer Mitsubishi garage at Beeford. I succumbed to temptation and ordered one for delivery a few weeks later.

The second event was unrelated, yet closely linked. One of our Speech Therapists was an American girl, married to a Scot and she was playing host to her former Head of Department from Ithaca College in Upstate New York. He was in this country doing a sabbatical year and our department had laid on various events in order to demonstrate the British methods. This included spending the day with several therapists, on an individual basis, and I was chosen to give him a taste of Bridlington, since my clinic there was probably the most modern and well-equipped. This last, may I point out, largely due to the money that I had squeezed out of various local organisations, in exchange for being a fee-free speaker at their meetings?

Chuck Snyder liked me. He thought my approach was relaxed and realistic and we got along on a personal level, sharing a rather bitchy sense of humour. I suspect that this was, on his part, a reflection of his somewhat ambivalent sexuality. In spite of having sired five children, I later discovered that he was as much one of the girls as one of the boys.

As a farewell gesture to Chuck, we did what we were good at: we threw a party. He loved the house and announced that it was Adirondack American in style and as he offered an invitation to all the Speech Therapists to visit him in the States, he commented that he was positive that David and I would certainly take him up on the offer. The link with the car came when during the evening, the Mitsubishi dealer telephoned to say that the car had arrived. I told David the news that the Colt was ready for delivery and Chuck said, "Oh, you're buying a horse?". We explained that the Colt was a car and not a pony and as we bade him goodbye, we really did not expect to ever see him again, trips to America were not the commonplace thing in those days.

Some months later, David had a serious falling out with his boss which culminated in the keys to the premises being thrown on the desk as David walked out. Minutes later, as David stood at the bus stop, someone he knew drew up and offered him a lift home. This was unfortunate as the boss had regretted any hastiness, and gone to talk him into returning. On such coincidences life-changing events are decided. The moment had passed and there was no going back. We had always followed the principal that since I was the one with a decent and steady income, we would live on this and use anything David earned as extra. When he received his final salary cheque and holiday pay, we decided to do something special with it so I telephoned Chuck and said we were coming in January.

He had told us that he lived just outside New York. Now, if I tell someone that I live just outside Driffield, I mean four miles. We discovered that Chuck lived two hundred and fifty miles from The Big Apple. Naturally we did not appreciate this at the time, especially since he had declared that he would meet us at John F Kennedy Airport.

We had met a young couple from Banstead during a holiday in Yugoslavia, and they had already visited us and offered us a bed if ever we were flying from Gatwick. We set off on my birthday calling at Leeds en-route, in order to collect a suit that a traditional Jewish tailor was making for David. When we had gone for a fitting, we asked if it would be ready on January 13th as we were flying to America.
"What airport are you going from?" he asked.
"Gatwick", we answered.
He gave a Gallic shrug and looked doubtful. "What time is your flight?"

In the event, it was ready. I don't think that there had been any doubt in Jack's mind, it was an example of his humour and we were 90% sure that this was the case. We managed to reach Banstead that night in spite of running in to a fearful snowstorm and having to make several deviations. The following morning we boarded a Laker flight to New York. As we approached Kennedy Airport, the Captain announced that heavy snow had fallen on the city and we would have to circle, and stack, until the snow ploughs had cleared the runway. Exciting stuff!

When we finally landed and had braved the incredible sourness of the customs and passport officials we went through into the arrivals area, hoping to see our host awaiting our arrival. What we saw was a man with a board displaying our name. We approached him and he handed us a message. Would we please ring David Snyder at the number given below? After some hassle with a hard-bitten and unhelpful New York operator we got through to Chuck's brother on Long Island. Due to extreme weather conditions it was impossible to come to collect us but if we took the bus to Jamaica Station we could then take the Long Island Railroad to Bellmore where David would come to pick us up and we could stay the night. Alternatively, we could go straight to the Port Authority and take the Greyhound to Ithaca, overnight. We opted for a night's sleep close at hand and went out of the airport building to find the right bus stop. The snow was deep and crisp and even. Very deep.

The bus arrived and we boarded. "Where you guys from?" the driver asked.
"England", we replied.
"It sure as hell got to be better than this", he countered as he gave us a ticket.

After a short journey, he told us this was as far as we went on his bus, but that we now needed to wait for another going at right-angles. The city and its routes are based on a grid system, easy when you know how. We found ourselves standing in a doorway in Queens, where a few years earlier, the notorious killer known as the Black Panther had preyed on innocent young couples in parked cars, shooting them without motive. Eventually another hopeful passenger joined us but was uncommunicative, so it was with relief that we saw the approach of a bus with our destination marked on the front. Another ride and once again we were waiting, this time, for a train.

The joy of travel was not over and before long the train slowed to a halt. A voice came over the intercom, and announced to the driver that we had a malfunction on the doors. We had not previously encountered this phenomenon on a train. In England any sound other than the noise of the wheels on the track was the sotto voce communication between passengers who knew each other. It was years before we experienced jolly, reassuring messages from rail staff. Suddenly, a man in front of us shouted loudly to anyone who would listen: "Hey, they think Walt Disney is dead. He ain't, he's running the Long Island Railway". This was answered by another man further down the carriage and a debate ensued. It simply wasn't British but it did relieve the tension we were feeling at the time.

On our arrival at Bellmore, I found a payphone and let David Snyder know that we had landed. He asked us to wait in the waiting room, where a tramp was engaged with the task of trying to thread a needle in order to sew a button on his coat. Within ten minutes we were in the safety of our host's car and shortly after, we arrived at his home where his wife, Thelma made coffee and cake. At that point we found out that in America, coffee cake meant a cake to accompany the beverage rather than confectionery flavoured with coffee. Did this mean that lemon cake went with the hot drink usually only drunk when a cold or 'flu was afflicting the recipient, and chocolate cake went with cocoa, and so on? I don't think so.

We had never met David and Thelma before, but they had bodily removed their children from their beds to make room for us and eventually, at 4:00 a.m., we retired for what remained of the night. This couple was incredibly relaxed, patient, and tolerant and had two of the most hyper and frenetic children I have ever encountered. Not to mention the dog. We were awake by eight in the morning, our body clocks being in disarray and we were introduced to the concept of bacon and egg with cooked but cold bacon. The other amazing innovation in the kitchen was a microwave oven, the first one we had ever seen, but Thelma was a demonstrator and saleswoman of these devices and very experienced. After breakfast, David Snyder explained the options open to us with regard to our onward journey. These were: the Greyhound, a six- to eight-hour journey; or a flight from Kennedy to Triphammer, the airport for Ithaca, an hour away if it was a direct flight. We asked who was the carrier and were told that it was Allegheny Airlines.

"Are they safe?" I queried.
"Oh, sure, they haven't had an accident since --- let me see, last Thursday," was the reassuring reply.

We opted for the aeroplane and David Snyder took us to the airport since the weather had improved. Chuck's wife, Pauline, another total stranger, was there to meet us and took us to their amazing home where she poured us drinks in what appeared to be sundae glasses and announced that when our host returned from church with the assorted smaller Snyders, we were going out for dinner. Wonderful! What we really needed was a decent night's sleep, but these hospitable folk wanted to fill our hours with fun. Or did they want to parade their English visitors like prize livestock and marvel at our cultured speech.

Chuck came home from his Catholic deliberations, introduced the three hitherto unmet offspring, and told us that he was happy to pour the first drink but after that we were on our own. We had taken large quantities of Scotch with us but actually preferred the Bourbon which suited our host, since the latter was considerably cheaper. It was the size of the glasses that confounded us. They were big enough to accommodate a Knickerbocker Glory and lacked any elegance, finesse, or good taste. However they did bounce if they were dropped. As a gift, we had taken a set of six silver plated goblets which would hold a modest glass of wine, a marked contrast admittedly but whether they would ever get used I did not know.

The house was quite remarkable, built in 1860 by a well-known Methodist pioneer, Brigham Young; it was entirely wooden in construction, with two staircases and a spacious basement housing the heating furnace. There were only three bedrooms, each of huge proportions but quite unpractical. We occupied the master room with its seven-foot wide bed and I think Chuck and Pauline bunked in with the girls in a room which held two double beds. The three boys slept in large bunk beds in a room that had two sections as though it had been separate at one stage. Our room had a bathroom and there was an additional shower room in the other wing, and all the fittings appeared to be original. We were astonished that nothing had been updated. The downstairs washbasin was badly cracked, but we realised later that old is beautiful in a country with so little history, and shabbiness was no justification for replacement. The back staircase was covered in a synthetic carpet and sported a very stark metal handrail. I soon discovered that holding the latter when descending the stairs was a guarantee of a noticeable electric shock.

164

There were formal rooms furnished with a faded elegance but the most used area was the kitchen / breakfast room and a downmarket dining room, both equipped with wood-burning stoves and always warm and welcoming. We vowed to investigate the possibility of buying one of these in England. There was more snow than I had ever seen and the temperatures were lower than we had previously experienced. But, it was a dry, crisp, cold unlike the damp, penetrating, chill of the British winter. Fortunately there was a trunk full of rubber boots and warm coats in a variety of sizes available for when we ventured out for a walk around what had originally been a trading settlement in a heavily wooded area. At the back of the house, the garden, or yard, as they call it, was bordered by a river spanned by a waterfall which was spectacularly frozen over, with huge icicles forming a dramatic curtain. Even after many visits in all seasons and long years since the last time, the memory of that sight will remain with me always. How I would love to live in a beauty spot like that.

That first night, we dined at the home of Bob and Heidi Grant and had our first experience of Citizens' Band radio: I spoke to a driver and called myself Curly Shirley from England. Bob was a Physical Therapist and another guest, Walt Carlin, was an audiologist of considerable renown. All the people who we met during our stay were medically connected and qualified, or else academics and experts in their field. It was a somewhat rarefied atmosphere, and I was accepted as one of them. After dinner we went on to a party at a very different home, that of a younger upwardly-mobile couple who lived in a smaller, more modern, house. The wife showed me the baby's room and I asked where the baby was tonight, to be told that there was no baby yet. Perlease!

The whole week was planned and programmed. I was amazed to discover that Sunday dinner did not involve cooking a joint of meat, something I had never encountered before. We had spaghetti with meatballs, with the added interest of aniseed as a flavouring, another first. One of our visits that week was to a hospital clinic where Walt Carlin was the audiologist and we experienced what he referred to as "zapping a few babies". This entailed holding a device close to the ear of a new born, i.e. less than a couple of days old, and causing it to emit a noise. If the infant failed to respond by twitching or otherwise perceivably reacting, then it was obvious that some hearing loss was present and early action could be taken.

Every night we either dined at one of their friends or colleagues house, or they came to Chuck's The exception was the night that we all dined at the restaurant at the top of the Ithaca College staff building. In the late afternoon, I had been the guest lecturer to the faculty and given them the low-down on training and practice of British Speech Therapists, and consequently Chuck was able to entertain everyone at the department's expense. He was also able to claim for accommodating and entertaining us; otherwise I do not think the trip would have been on. He was notoriously tight-fisted, we later learned.

One of the audience that night was a man who ran a summer school for children with speech and language problems, and parents who could afford to pack them off for seven weeks residential care. It sounded fascinating, and Ed Badger invited me to go as a consultant at a pittance, but the experience could be invaluable. It was, but not for the right reasons. More later.

I was treated like visiting royalty all week. One of the dine-out nights was at Walt's house in the upmarket suburbs of Ithaca and, unusually, this was built of brick. When we arrived, with three feet of snow in the streets, we were amazed to find a barbecue alive and well on the patio. After starters, our host went out in the sub-zero temperatures to grill fillet steaks. It seemed like the ultimate insanity, but the meat was delicious. Jenny Carlin was also an audiologist who Walt had met when he was doing his training in Manchester, and she was a gracious and charming English woman.

He told us a story about his time in the damp and grey city. He had gone in search of a beefburger, and found a Wimpy Bar, where he forced down the accepted English version, being horrified at this travesty of a Big Mac. Later in the week, while waiting at a bus stop, he was surprised to see a single-decker bus draw up and discharge a considerable number of grubby and brawny men, wearing navy blue jackets which bore the legend WIMPY on the back. "My God, no wonder the beef burgers taste so bad, if these guys make them" he mused, being unaware of the existence of the building company who rejoiced in the same name as the snack bar chain.

Chuck seemed able to find time off from his duties to take us sightseeing and we visited Taylor's winery and the Steuben Glass company at Corning. This is the ancestral home of Pyrex, and there were many bargains available, if you did not have the problem of a transatlantic crossing by aeroplane to contend with. Another first was seeing ceramic hobs; unheard of in our neck of the woods, but one more thing I was determined to have in the future. That brought the total of 'must-haves' to three. A microwave oven, a wood-burning stove, and a ceramic hob. It had been a cheap flight to New York but the aftermath cost a lot of money!

When the time came for our return, the snow had cleared sufficiently for Chuck to drive us back to New York, a five hour trip since the top speed at which one can drive and remain inside legal limits was fifty miles an hour. Driving long distances in the States is tediously slow and boring because the scenery changes not at all in many miles, unlike the ever altering landscapes of this island home. We were duly delivered to Kennedy Airport and, after flight delays and a meal at a nearby restaurant at the expense of the airline, we took off for Gatwick and home. Once again, we stayed the night with our friends and the next morning when we went outside into the damp January day, temperature in the fifties, so not really seasonal. We were colder than we had been in the freezing-dry cold of Upstate New York, where we had plodded through deep snow, and never got our shoes wet.

On my return, I was in demand to tell all about the trip, few folk had ever crossed 'The

Pond' in those days, and we were considered very sophisticated and well-travelled. I discovered that I could get three weeks study leave which, together with my annual five weeks, gave me the necessary time to do six weeks at the Speech Camp and have a week at the end to holiday with David. He was to come out to stay with some other people we had met on our first visit, who lived in a converted warehouse down the road from Chuck's house. We wanted to avoid overstaying our welcome at any one venue.

I left on July 3rd in blazing heat, even the American newspapers showed headlines stating that Britain was having a heat wave. July 4th was Chuck's birthday and his sisters Roseanne and Mary Agnes were also at the house. This was my introduction to the concept of actually calling a person by two names; maybe it is a Catholic thing. Grandpa Snyder had been a shoemaker in Germany and the basement was full of lasts for shoes of all descriptions. Many of these ended up in the furnace and some found their way back to Europe, in my suitcases.

The following day, I was delivered to the camp and found myself in the depths of the forest with no means of escape. Contrary to my expectations, I was not given a sparsely-furnished room with few creature comforts and allocated a clinic room or office to carry out my therapeutic marvels. I was consigned to a wooden hut, to be shared with a delightful student and four children, one of whom wet the bed each night. There was a gap where the two sections of the pitched roof failed to meet through which the local wildlife dropped in to visit. The toilets and troughs for washing ourselves were a jolly walk in the forest away, and hot water was not on the menu; this made laundering wet sheets for our incontinent room-mate very difficult.

We slept in bunk beds three-high, and there were three drawers available for us to share. The showers had to be booked in advance, because they too were communal, and lacked any semblance of privacy. When the door opened, one entered this concreted room with showerheads protruding from a cement-rendered wall and ablutions were undertaken in full view of whoever entered, male or female. The whole place smacked of a prisoner-of-war camp without the benefit of Red Cross parcels. I felt that I had been reincarnated at my birth in 1934, from the spirit of a victim of the persecution of the Jews in Europe, and was now living a similar horror.

My place of work was a single-decker bus, and my client group was a mixture of ages and handicaps. Therapy was out of the question. This was a huge rip-off of parents able to pay to get their unfortunate offspring out of their way for six weeks. It was also a totally immoral misuse of student labour under the guise of giving them experience, and I was allowed no privilege or concession to recognise my status as a bona-fide Speech Therapist. We were on duty 14 hours a day and the conditions were appalling. It rained almost every day, we were wearing damp clothes, and before long the student Counsellors were going down with severe chest coughs. I decided that I had had enough and on the Saturday I phoned the Snyder residence to beg for succour. Pauline came for me and I packed my bag and left. Due to my reports to the big noise Speech Therapists in upstate New York, Ed Beaver was never again permitted to run his Internment Camp.

I ran for cover in Lansing, with the protection of the Snyder clan. I was asked by Alverda Farmer, a well-known therapist and lecturer, to talk to her students and I went to stay at her apartment for a few days. While I was there, she arranged transport to another hospital in the State for me and I was privileged to spend two days with one of the greats, Louis De Carlo. He invited me to work with him and do a PhD. in Audiology, but it seemed out of the question to abandon my husband, my children, and my home in England to pursue glory in America. I never did have much sense of adventure though I know David would not have hesitated to go, for a moment. I also spent some time with the president of The American Association of Speech Therapists, and gave him the inside information on the Camp of Horrors. I tried to justify the study leave and visited other clinics for the rest of the allotted time, seeing a different side of the work.

The last week before David and Dani came to join me, Chuck, Pauline, and four of the children went on holiday, leaving me in charge of Joe, aged seventeen, and the house. Easy. However, I had not bargained for a repressed adolescent filling the place with his friends all swilling beer and frolicking with their girlfriends. Joe didn't drink, not to the knowledge of his parents anyway, but that week the only way I could sleep without my conscience troubling me was to have an air-conditioning unit blasting noisily away all night. That way, I could neither hear nor see any evil.

On the day that the family returned, I ordered Joe to clear up all bottles and bottle tops and having cleaned the house throughout, I went for a shower. The phone rang and so, draped in a less than sufficient towel, I went into Joe's room to take the call. He seemed untroubled by my scanty dress but there was the sudden sound of the family car and I felt sure that this puritanical family would take a dim view of the cosy scene. I terminated the call in double quick time and took off to hide in the shower. As I departed, I spotted a beer bottle under one of the bunk beds. I retrieved it with great speed and buried in the depths of Joe's bed and appeared from the shower when I was certain that someone had reached the upper floor in time to see me doing so. Phew!

Dani travelled alone from Manchester to Kennedy, crossed to La Guardia, and just caught the last flight to Triphammer, the airport for Ithaca, where Pauline and I met her. David flew from points south and missed the connecting flight so he stayed over at the La Guardia Hilton and flew up the following morning. We all stayed with Dick and Patty at their converted warehouse. David paid for our keep by re-upholstering an old chair. During the first week, Chuck took us to the Steuben Glass factory again and to Niagara Falls. The second week we hired a car and we went touring, calling at the spot where the Civil War had begun, Gettysburg. We also went to Williamsburg, a rebuilt town in the style of the original Virginia settlers.

We had been invited to stay a few nights near Washington, at the home of Patty's parents and from this base we were able to see the sights in the Capitol. During our visit to

Arlington Cemetery, we witnessed the funeral of Gary Powers, the American U2 pilot who had been shot down and incarcerated by the Russians for allegedly spying on their country and later 'exchanged' for a Russian spy. He died many years later, and was buried, as a hero, in Washington.

At the end of our visit, Chuck and Pauline took us back to New York where we all stayed with David and Thelma. The Americans adopt a relaxed approach to accommodating numerous visitors and simply turn the children out of their beds to sleep on the floor, or they seem to have spare mattresses which can be produced at will. The other useful item is the sofa bed which might explain their cheery "Come and stay", an invitation extended to even the briefest of acquaintances. That weekend, six of us descended on the Snyder residence without causing any apparent disturbance, in spite of the fact that ten people needed sleeping quarters in a three-bedroomed house.

David Snyder took all the kids, their two and Elizabeth, Chuck's youngest, and Dani to Jones Beach on the Sunday and after a late lunch, chauffeured us to Kennedy to catch our flight home. I had been away for seven weeks and, for the last two, Brad had been in charge of the house and the animals all-alone. Naturally, everything was in perfect order on our return.

CHAPTER 14
AS TIME GOES BY

We made three further trips to the USA. The first one was over a year later, in September. On arrival at Lansing, Pauline announced that we were all making a weekend visit to the holiday home of Howard and Dorothy Dillingham in the Adirondack Mountains. Howard was a past President of Ithaca College, and Dorothy supplemented their more than adequate income by painting Impressionist pictures which she sold for a huge amount of money. She could turn out half-a-dozen a day, and I personally felt that a reasonably-disciplined chimpanzee could have done equally well.

Pauline had a deep desire for us to witness the leaves changing colour and I forced myself to keep from her the news that the leaves on our British trees also changed colour in the autumn. Winter can come very suddenly in upstate New York and apparently all the leaves may fall overnight if there is a frost. We drove the hundred or more miles to Old Forge through endless forests of the most spectacular natural phenomena I had ever seen. Pauline had been right - the browns and yellows of the British autumn could not compare to the sight of acres of maples sporting all shades of red and gold. We brought some examples home with us and my artistic daughter-in-law, Maggie, made them into a picture for me.

Howard and Dorothy lived, during their vacations, in a wooden cabin by the edge of one of the ironstone lakes, where their small boat could transport them from their own place to a neighbour's if they so wished. We took a slightly nerve wracking sortie with Chuck at the helm, David was happier with his feet on dry land. The living room had the obligatory wood burning stove and a grid in the floor through which issued hot air from the furnace in the basement. The bedrooms were simply-furnished with iron bedsteads covered with knitted blankets and in the bathroom we found a candle and a box of matches. I supposed that this was in case of a power-cut, but was informed that it was an air purifier. If one's ablutions included a major bowel movement, or even just a blast from a past meal, a lighted candle would burn off noxious odours within minutes. After the weekend, we returned to Lansing, until it was time to leave for New York in order to fly to Miami.

Three days were spent languishing in the hot sun before we embarked on a Norwegian Caribbean Lines boat for a three-day cruise to the Bahamas. Unfortunately, the extreme heat had affected me unexpectedly and my feet and ankles were badly swollen to the point at which I could only wear ancient Jesus sandals. This in turn meant that instead of dressing-up for dinner, I had to wear a trouser suit. So, feeling distinctly underdressed, we went down fort he repast. The mâitre de escorted us to our table which, to our dismay, was also occupied by four young and gleaming Americans from the Southern States. The gentlemen immediately leapt to their feet and effected introductions. "Hi there, I'm Ronnie Rabun and this is my wife, Phyllis". This by a sandy-haired fresh-complexioned young man, and referring to a slightly swarthier lady with bleached-blonde hair. "I'm Jerry Henderson and this here's ma wife Karen," contributed the other.

I suddenly became very British and restrained as I returned the introductions, and gave the Received Pronunciation of the Queen's English my full support. The English lady abroad is not to be treated lightly, even when wearing shabby sandals!

Before a morsel of food had passed my lips, Ronnie was plying me with questions about the state of the National Health Service, the Government, and the British economy. His pink face gleamed from the collar of his white tuxedo with lust for information and also for the opportunity to air his own knowledge. Jerry was more restrained in both manner and dress; a dark suit served him as the appropriate garb. Both girls were wearing large diamond rings and all were university graduates, not that this was exceptional in a country with a 'university' in every hick town, and where your plumber might well have a degree in something. At one point during the meal, Jerry turned to me and said in a distinct Southern drawl,

"Say, y'awl talk with a kind of fuuuunny accent."

I drew myself up and turned to him. In a passable impression of Dame Maggie Smith, or maybe it was Edith Evans, I replied with enormous dignity: "I must beg to point out to you, sir, that it is you and not I, who speaks with a funny accent."

It did not bode well for a happy trip, at least as far as mealtimes were concerned, but we bade them goodnight at the end of the meal and went on a tour of discovery. As on every cruise catering for the American market, there was an excess of food, the last meal of the day being a gargantuan buffet served at midnight, so we went for a look. In addition to a sumptuous feast, we saw our erstwhile dinner companions, wrapping large quantities of food in paper serviettes and secreting these parcels about their persons. They spotted us spotting them and, now far more relaxed, explained that their stash was for lunch on the following day when we were in port. They then expanded the story to tell us that they had just graduated and were desperately short of money, having all shared the same motel room en-route to the boat in order to economise. This was only days after Jerry and Karen got married, though the other two had tied the knot several weeks earlier.

The price of drinks on board was extortionate so we evolved a system where I carried a large handbag containing a bottle of Bacardi, which cost less for a litre in Nassau than it cost for one drink on board. We ladies retired to the nearest little-girls room with glasses of coca cola in our hand and filled them up with our own cheap booze, a technique which I turned into an art form as time went by. We were firm friends from there on and, at the end of our trip, they squashed us and our suitcase into their car and took us to the airport for our return flight to Kennedy.

Note 'suitcase' in the singular. This was because we had left the rest of our baggage with Chuck and Pauline, who were to meet us at David and Thelma's at the weekend. The home of these two charming people had become a regular stopping off place and David Snyder used to come and pick us up from the airport. One time, I telephoned him from home and the first thing he said was "Where are you?".

I told him I was at home in England. He replied: "Thank Heavens for that. I thought I had forgotten to come and pick you up from Kennedy and I'm on my second Martini."

We had developed a habit of carrying one suitcase inside another so that there was plenty of space for all our purchases on the return, because we used to go with Thelma to a wonderful store called Fortunoff's. Here, bed-linen, and towels, were at give-away prices, not to mention the low-priced 'Fruit of the Loom' tee shirts and socks. At the time the pound was strong against the dollar and we stocked up while the going was good.

We arrived home to less than salubrious accommodation. Several months earlier, a young man who was interested in buying our house had approached us, having heard, through the local grapevine, that we might consider selling. The fact that it was not on the market at the time had not deterred him. To cut a long story short, we sold to him for the princely sum of £25,500, but because he was unable to spend another £7,000, which would have secured the little house as well, we still had a roof over our heads. Unfortunately, that roof was over our tenant's head at the time and we had to get him out before we could move back in and start the planned extensions and improvements.

Happily our buyer had a wealthy and generous-hearted father, who offered us a 20% deposit in cash in order that we could buy another house for the tenant and finance the changes in ours. I bought, on sight, a terraced cottage in Driffield for £4,000 and moved Nick, our tenant, in there one weekend, promising him three months rent-free tenancy in return for him vacating our little house. He left the area before he started paying rent but I re-let immediately to a teacher who stayed for years, after which we sold for £11,500.

For the first time in our lives there was money to spare and one of the problems we had was how to invest this cash in the most effective way. At the time, the makers of M.G. cars was rumoured to be discontinuing producing this old favourite and it seemed that buying a sports model and mothballing it presented an reasonable opportunity to make some money. One Saturday afternoon, I took some time out from the garden and still wearing my old clothes, scruffy jeans and anorak, I sallied forth and walked in to the local M.G. showroom. Taking a speculative walk around a bright yellow low slung model, I tried it out for size and suitability, taking into consideration the fact that my ever-present back problem might make my entry and exit into the driving seat difficult if not impossible. From behind me, I heard the approach of footsteps and a male voice said the words he would live to rue.

"Now then my love and what can I do for you?"

He had undoubtedly appraised my costume and concluded that here was a bag lady with eyes bigger than her bank balance. I was not impressed by his terms of endearment or was it condescension?

I turned round and said to the unfortunate salesman:

"I think that the words for which you may be desperately searching are 'Can I help you, MADAM'. " At this point the sales manager appeared from his tiny office and dismissed the wretched salesman with the words "I will deal with this, thank you." In the event, I decided that the car was not designed for slipped disc sufferers, but the recipient of my verbal correction did not forget me and years later, having moved to the Ford dealer, he reminded me of the incident.

In the meantime, we were living on a building site: all the alterations we had effected four years earlier were re-done. The little house was originally intended for my father to occupy in his retirement, a plan abandoned when he married his well-off widow from Gloucestershire. We now made an entirely fresh start which involved almost every internal wall coming down and we were fortunate to be offered the loan of a 12-foot by 15-foot workman's shed in which to store our furniture. This was our lounge for five months. It had electricity, TV, fitted carpet and a bar, easy chairs to sit in and most of our crockery stacked up in boxes behind the chairs. I've seen worse holiday lodges.

We had demolished the former kitchen and, in its place, a large south-facing lounge was being erected on the site of both the kitchen and the walled garden. We were unable to lock up the house during this period. To reach our temporary sitting room, we left the former living room, soon-to-be new kitchen, and walked across the concrete base of the future lounge. Fortunately the weather was clement, but it was almost Christmas before we moved in. Meanwhile conditions were far from ideal. There was a lack of wall between our bedroom and the bathroom and some mornings we woke to see another family member washing at the washbasin. One Saturday, Dani was in the bath, when suddenly there was a major water leak and three men rallied to the cause. These gentlemen were the plumber, our friend Jack, and David, who all invaded the tiny bathroom to fix the problem while my daughter tried to maintain her sense of modesty with the aid of a face flannel.

The staircase had been ripped out and a ladder served to get us up and down, the problem of building the spiral staircase seemed insurmountable, at least to the experts. At last, I decided that if my gut feeling and my instructions were followed, the whole thing would work, and Tim, our favourite builder, was commissioned to erect a brick spiral with Westmoreland slate treads. It took a total of eight hours with David mixing mortar, me carrying in the bricks and Tim laying them as fast as we could supply him. The big problem was that after months of turning round, at the top of the stairs, in order to descend a ladder backwards, it took time to break the habit and I actually found myself coming down the new stairs in that fashion.

We had indulged our desire to have a wood-burning stove and one night we were huddling round this, with nothing on the floor except the boards, when Dani and her boyfriend arrived. They were guests at a party in the village hall, next-door-but-one. They told us that it seemed that one of the other guests, the grandmother of the party boy, had collapsed in a heap. As Paul put it "Granny Woods is tits up in t' village 'all". What he wanted was blankets, though had the good lady been truly 'tits up', she would have been beyond the assistance of blankets. Fortunately for her, there was a guest who had some medical experience and he gave mouth to mouth resuscitation until a real doctor arrived. She survived the experience, a stroke, and lived several more years.

Paul, my future son in law had a colourful vocabulary, and a less-than-restrained sense of humour; we had many entertaining times with him. Unfortunately, he and Dani eventually divorced, but we still see him occasionally and are on friendly terms. He is the father of my grandson, Robin, not to mention a houseful of girls from his second marriage. Poor Paul: farmers so need sons to follow in their tractor tracks, and the only one that he does have, has no desire to occupy a vacant John Deere.

In order to supply us with three bedrooms, the wall between bedroom two and the bathroom was taken out and a stud wall put up two feet into the larger room. This gave us the extra sleeping accommodation but left a deficiency in the bathroom department, to the tune of none. However, I had ascertained that by knocking off one of the three courses of bricks on the outside walls to gain four inches each side, I could squeeze a minuscule facility into an alcove on the landing. This was a major space saving achieve-ment: the whole room is a mere five feet six inches square and has the advantage that if one is suffering a stomach upset that necessitates evacuating from both ends simultane-ously, this can be easily achieved without moving from the throne of office. There was no space to open the door inwards and since the passage on the tiny landing was of the minimum dimensions, a sliding door was fitted. The kitchen was to be very large, 18 feet by 12 feet, and the design was somewhat revolutionary for us. It all worked well, though it was a time consuming task.

Once again, we were living in total chaos and I never knew what to expect when I arrived home from work. Every evening and all day at the weekend we worked on the renovations but at least this time we could afford to pay for some help.

With some of the profit from the sale of 'The Old School', we bought a somewhat derelict terraced house at Nafferton. Once our own home was in fairly good order, we started spending a good deal of our time pulling the second one to pieces and refurbishing it for resale. It was very spacious and it was no problem to achieve three bedrooms and bathroom upstairs. David built on a long kitchen and in addition to the dining room and lounge, there was an integral workshop, which we had hoped to convert to a garage. Planning permission for this was not forthcoming.

The smaller house next door also came on to the market and was snapped up by us for

Brad. We bought it for an incredible £1650 and loaned him the money, to be repaid when he could get a mortgage. He was already quite the expert in home improvements, having lived with us in our own houses and learned and contributed during that time. As always, he constantly worked beyond the limits tolerated by most folk. His skills had been enhanced by the fact that he had worked for builders and joiners during the school and university holidays, added to his philosophy that provided one read the instructions and applied a little native intelligence, most things could be achieved.

Having graduated with a BSc. from Leeds University and been offered a job with the Humberside County Council, he thought that it was time to make an honest woman of Maggie. A marriage was arranged, largely without any input from our side of the family. I can only imagine that the old habits held strong in this part of the world and the contribution, financial or otherwise, of the groom's family was unasked for.

Similarly, when the time came for my daughter to wed, the groom's family showed a marked lack of interest in everything except the menu. The second time around, Brad's soon to be in-laws did not ask for input, but we were not excluded from the arrangements. I find it rather strange: if you do not need a hand with the financing, at least make an effort to include the in-laws in the planning. We are all family, not the enemy. At Dani's second wedding we all sort of mucked in and sorted it, as she and Peter wanted it. I do not like being put in to a 'them and us' situation and that has happened too much recently, with the 'us' treated like second-class citizens.

We made another trip to the USA, a marathon of visits taking in Georgia, North Carolina, Kentucky, and upstate New York. We visited our cruise companions, Ronnie and Phyllis in Camilla and Karen and Jerry in Carolina. After spending five days with David and Margaret Smith, who had moved back to America and now had three children, we went by Greyhound to Pittsburgh, from where we flew to Syracuse and on to Lansing for a final stay with Chuck and Pauline. This marriage was in deep trouble and the atmosphere in the house was pulsating with antagonism. We completely lost touch with them after our return, my letters were not answered, and all attempts to contact them by telephone were unsuccessful.

Within weeks of our return, Dani and Paul were married at Huggate. The seating arrangements presented a small problem because there were so many divorced people to keep apart. Paul's mother would not sit at the family table, and I struggled to keep my own parents away from each other. In this last case I need not have worried. My father and his wife Connie had stayed overnight at our house and went up to the church with David while I went to the house to help Dani make her final preparations. My mother and Reg drove from Leeds, calling at York station to pick up Don and Elaine, As they arrived outside the church, Don saw that Johnnie was in the porch, talking to Brad and Russell who were acting as ushers and resplendent in their grey morning suits. Trying to avoid any untoward confrontation, Don engaged Dorothy and Reg in conversation with the object of keeping them in the car until Johnnie and his wife, Connie, went to their appointed pew. It did not work and my two long-divorced parents found themselves in the same place at the same time as each other for the first time in thirty-six years. Johnnie had lost some hair and put on a few pounds but he was still instantly recognisable. So, my mother, looking for all the world like the Queen Mother, in her big hat and fur stole, held out her hand and said, "Hello, Johnnie. How are you?".

Taking the offered hand, he replied, "I'm awfully sorry, I can't quite place you".

"You are joking", was her response.

"I seem to know your face, and I am sure I should know you, but I cannot remember your name", he said.

"Well, you certainly should. After all, you were married to me for fourteen years".

Fortunately, they found the incident faintly amusing and spent some time talking after the reception. Dorothy found the sight of Connie's granny vest, which became visible from time to time, hugely entertaining. Her explanation for her ex-husband's lack of recognition was fascinating. He would have been expecting to see a little white-haired old lady and not her still dark-haired self, looking smart and youthful. In that hat, I only just recognised her myself and that was on a double-take. The day went with a swing and no blood was spilt. Dani looked lovely and Paul promised to take care of her. Don't they all?

In the intervening years, Russell had served in the Intelligence Corps in Germany. As a result, he spoke the language like a native, thanks in part to his having what was referred to as a sleeping dictionary. This was the term applied to a steady girlfriend who was a native of the host country. In this case, the dictionary was a very attractive German girl named Astrid, who eventually became a slightly unbalanced liability. Maybe it was the result of years of coping with Russell; he seems to have some strange effect on his women or else has a penchant for taking up with potential head cases that are unable to deal with his lifestyle.

In Germany, he had developed a financially-beneficial sideline and started selling new cars to his fellow servicemen, eventually buying himself out of the services and selling cars from brochures on car parks. He was eminently successful at this and soon sent home enough money to purchase a property with a sitting tenant of advanced years. The snag was that the tenant, Mrs Franklin, had a daughter to whom the tenancy would legally pass, and so selling the house could be held up for a very long time. As ever, fate smiled on him, and the daughter upped and died of a heart attack. Russell was able to buy another nearby cottage into which Mrs Franklin moved, leaving him free to sell the original at a huge profit. He still lived in Celle, near Hanover, and had a house built there on the outskirts.

He and Astrid continued their somewhat tempestuous relationship, both throwing accusations of insanity at one another and to anyone else that would listen. By this time, Russell was in a Toyota dealership, but things went pear-shaped and he abandoned all and moved to Wegburg, putting Astrid out and the house on the market. He moved into a vast converted barn in the middle of a field and sold Mitsubishi cars for a commission. He came home for an extended Christmas holiday but, soon after his return, I had a phone call from a German hospital to inform me that he had had a heart attack.

With amazing speed, Brad and I arranged to go that night, and we rushed home from work, grabbed a bite to eat and left at 6:00 p.m. to drive to Felixstowe in order to catch the midnight boat to Zeebrugge. On arrival at the port, we waited in line to go through customs and when our turn came, we were asked for our documentation. I fished into my hurriedly packed bag for my passport, at that time a dark blue book, and handed it to the official. He was unimpressed and handed it back to me, asking if I could offer any improvement. Somewhat astonished at this request, I looked at the document, which I now held, and discovered that I had offered him an Anglia Building Society passbook. My heart sank. It would be impossible to obtain a British Visitors passport until the next day and I had no other proof of my identity with me. I rummaged frantically in my bag and to my utmost relief, found the passport at the bottom.

The following lunchtime, after a long drive through Belgium, and successfully following the directions, seeming to be constantly turning left at the church, we found the barn conversion. Russell was standing outside looking pale and wan, having been released from hospital on the promise that help was on its way. All the furniture that had been moved from Celle, and 27 boxes of linen, crockery, and clothing, were stacked around the house unopened. No doubt the thought of having this to unpack had triggered off the heart attack or, as it turned out, panic attack. As usual, Mother and Brad to the rescue. I washed and ironed thirty-one dirty shirts, innumerable socks and knickers, and cooked meals. The washing machine was in the basement and I descended and returned dozens of times each day. In spite of eating three cooked meals a day, I lost another 4lbs from an already fined-down body.

We drank prolifically. Booze was cheap over there and we started with a few Bourbon and Coke's before dinner, followed by a litre-and-a-half of vino collapso. Even without the alcohol, to which he was well-accustomed, Russell was in a bad way; he had totally lost his confidence and was unable to function. We went to see a neurologist and a heart specialist who could find nothing physically wrong with him and I soon speculated that he was experiencing what is known as a nervous breakdown. After a week, Brad had to return, so David drove his car to Felixstowe where he parked it and took the overnight ferry to Zeebrugge. We drove there early in the morning and met him. He handed Brad's car keys and directions for locating the vehicle to the owner. Brad got on the same boat from which David had disembarked, and David, Russell, and I drove back to Wegburg

During the next week, we moved the furniture around and went in search for wood to burn on the open fire. There was a derelict shed at the back of the property and, in the absence of better tools, David demolished it bit-by-bit using a spade. There was also a tree in a somewhat sorry state and the purchase of a Bushman saw enabled David to fell it and cut it into manageable pieces. A week later, we had to abandon Russell to his fate and come home. He stuck it out for a month and then there was a call from Tony, his boss, who was putting Russell on the boat with a car full of his possessions. Could we drive to Felixstowe and collect the voyager, who was not fit to drive the car himself. Once more unto the breach, dear friends. Another dash home from work and a hurried meal, another evening of driving to Felixstowe.

The Customs official gave him a hard time but he finally drove through and we bundled him into my car, David taking over the Colt, which Russell had brought with him. It was 11:00 p.m. and we drove straight home, thus covering almost five hundred miles since 6:00 p.m. and arriving home at three in the morning. I had to be at work next day but we couldn't go to bed without a couple of swift Scotches.

I suppose that this was the start of several nightmarish years, during which all my children experienced some emotional trauma, and I worried for England. Sleeping through the night became a thing of the past. Unfortunately, it is not only my own children who lay their troubles at my door, though I must say that Brad keeps his to himself as a rule. My son and daughters-in-law also hoped that I could sort out their lives for them, like some sort of Godmother who can make un-refuseable offers and take away their problems. To some extent it is still going on today and I would like to officially retire. In future, please tell me when the situation has been resolved or at least offer me solutions not problems.

After another few weeks it became clear that Russell was not fit to return. He was on a regime of happy pills and, when he was conscious, helped David at the house in Nafferton which was sold and needed finishing. Dani was pregnant at last, after a fairly traumatic time achieving that status. Not in terms of the required act, but in achieving the desired outcome. Frankly, it was all a bit much for me, a lady in her late forties but several years earlier, I had staunchly refused my doctor's deep need to put me on Vallium, for which I am truly grateful. Amen!

Russell's house in Celle was sold but the buyers were in no hurry to pay up which meant that he had no income.

Brad and Maggie had also sold their house and had to vacate it so they moved into the upstairs of the house that we were still working on and Brad gave a hand with the work. Russell decided that he could not return to his old way of life and we started considering the options, one of which was for him to try to secure a job as a car salesman. This meant that the car in which he had returned from Germany must be returned and the house in Wegburg cleared out and vacated. He was in no condition to make the trip alone so once more I packed a bag, this time ensuring that my passport was in the right place.

Another long drive to the port, another long crossing, and another long drive to the house in Wegburg, turning left at nearly every church en-route. Russell hoped to be able to pick up a second-hand car from the serviceman's NAAFI at the nearest Army establishment but, when we got there, the cupboard was bare. However, we dropped in to see a former business associate and discovered that it would be possible to buy a new Ford Escort very cheaply. I unpacked several thousand pounds from a money belt around my waist and wrote a cheque against my bank account in this country and we were in business.

Russell arranged for a removal firm to come for the contents of the house, promising them that there was barely enough furniture to furnish a modest apartment, and then promptly disappeared for the day, leaving me to pack and label everything. The removal men had confidently expected to be on the afternoon sailing, but that had long gone by the time they left Wegburg and I doubt that they would have even caught the night boat. As for us, we were desperate to get out before the bailiffs arrived and, with the car packed to the limit, we left for the last time. It was with relief that we boarded the boat, but there was no sleeping accommodation available and the reclining seats no longer reclined. Added to this, there was a school party on board, running amok in every part of the vessel. Fortunately, Russell had some happy pills in his wallet and we both passed a peaceful five hours in spite of the fact that the schoolchildren had been rioting about through the night, according to the lady seated behind us.

At this point, back at home, one spare bedroom was given over to my eldest son, and another to my younger one and his wife, who were about to move in. Luckily, they were heavily engaged with building their new house on a plot at Hutton, four miles away cross-country so, after having a hurried meal here, they were out all evening until bedtime. Remarkably, we never had a cross word: the Maggie-of-old had been replaced by a self-confident, able and hardworking woman who well-deserved the affection we felt for her. They finally moved out on December 16th but we had managed to get rid of Number One son well before that.

The experience of buying the car in Germany had given him a bright idea. Because the vehicle was purchased for export, it was duty-free, which dramatically dropped the price. One then paid VAT on the lower price on arrival in this country, making a substantial saving on UK prices. Within days, Russell had set up a business doing just that and advertising nationally. He organised an army of young men who went across the channel and brought back cars ordered by buyers looking for a good deal and who could pay cash. 'Importacar UK', as the venture was named, was hugely successful until the value of the pound against the German mark, and other currencies, made it unviable. By this time, Russell had become bored with cars and had aspirations in an entirely different field of endeavour.

Within weeks of being back in the district, the money from the sale of the house in Celle was in his pocket and he went house-hunting, restricting his spending to modest amounts. The first purchase was a two-bedroomed terraced house in the town, in need of total renovation. He used this as his office during the course of the destruction and renewal and even employed a secretary. His romance with Astrid blossomed anew, and she came over for a visit and an engagement ring. We never heard from her again, though I think Russell still speaks to her from time-to-time. He went on to buy properties wherever they became available, but the tales of his rise and fall, and rise and fall, and so on ad infinitum are legion. That should be his book, not mine. Suffice it to say that he has plumbed the depths in his search for fulfilment and managed to rise again.

Dani duly had her baby and, due to a marked lack of interest on the part of the other grandparents, I had unrestricted access to my first grandchild. I took advantage of my privileged position and found the experience world-changing. A good deal of folks did not approve of my involvement but, in the final analysis, the only person who suffered was my husband, I hope he feels that the price was worth the prize. My forfeit has been the loss of many sleepless nights, not only when Number One Grandson was spending weekends here but also worrying about his well-being and security when he was elsewhere. Not when he is with his mother of course but he has always had an unfortunate predilection for somewhat risky pastimes. Mountain biking, canoeing, rock climbing and surfing are less safe than knitting or doing jig saw puzzles. I vowed never to become so totally involved with another child again but the rewards have outweighed the agonising.

Conditions at work had deteriorated due to increased officialdom and the influx of a bevy of newly-qualified, degree-status, Speech Therapists. They had the advantage of a more up-to-date training, and I found myself struggling to keep up with their knowledge. I was happy doing what I did, working mainly with pre-school children in the clinic at Bridlington, but I found it lonely and isolating. The new girls had all kinds of modern ideas and my efforts to update my own knowledge did not appear to enhance my status. Everyone else seemed to be promoted and I felt inadequate and undervalued. I was constantly told that there was no funding for an upgrade for me, but it seemed that within weeks, one of the young Therapists was upgraded.

I asked for one day a week to be spent with a co-worker so that I could improve my technique and feel less isolated. A token arrangement was made. Later, I requested a transfer to the service for adult patients, which was initially approved but then refused on the grounds that I was too old to change. Things went from bad to worse and I felt that I received little or no support. I had a reputation for being able to deal with 'difficult' parents and teachers but it seemed that all of these were being steered my way and some failures were inevitable. I found myself going under and kept afloat only by telling myself that my income was essential and therefore I must survive.

I bought another terraced house in Driffield and renovation work got under way, with a view to Dani being able to use it if she failed to make a success of her marriage. In the meantime I rented the little house in Gibson Street to a young couple who have remained our friends ever since. The story of the intervening weeks or months is not mine to tell. Suffice it to say that Dani had arranged to rent a former farm worker's house further down the village, from our squire, Peter Hepworth. We knew nothing until she telephoned to say that she was bringing some furniture to put in this unheated cottage. It was bitterly cold and snowing, the house had been unoccupied for several months and there was no central heating, or carpets or curtains. We went into the loft in our house and found a carpet square and some curtains. David lit a fire, and Robin stayed here where he felt safe and where it was warm, until after the weekend. Maybe, after all, it was a good job that he had spent so much time with us.

Eventually, Mark and Wendy vacated the house in Gibson Street before their lease was up, in order that Dani could move in and once more she had some sort of home of her own. It was a hard time for us all, not least of all Robins father but before too long he found a new love, as did Dani and happy endings were on the agenda. His second marriage seems to have stayed the course and he has three lovely little girls. Happily, everyone is on amicable terms and bygones are just that.

Just as I thought it was safe to go back into the water another shark entered the scene. All my children were apparently in steady and secure situations. Brad's marriage to Maggie was a relationship that seemed as safe as Fort Knox. Russell had married a beautiful girl, Corina, who I still find lovely to look at and listen to. Her voice is soft and gentle and in her early forties she has lost none of her looks and figure. Dani had her Peter, to whom Robin was devoted, and he was just what Dani had always wanted and never had. As we left these last two, on Christmas Eve, I mentioned to David that everyone was settled and happy and at last I could relax. He made no comment.

Maggie had been unsettled for some time and it seemed that that she needed a total change and she certainly made a move as far as her job was concerned. Things were financially fine in their family. It was getting to the stage where two holidays a year, and maybe a second car, were not out of the question. Maggie then started to think that academia held some promise and talked about doing 'A' levels and a degree. Everyone was stunned when she left the newly-completed home, not least-of-all Brad, who had, as far as he and the rest of us could see, been the perfect husband. Maggie was approaching thirty and had been with the same man since she was sixteen. They had grown up together but not necessarily in the same direction. Folk change, their needs alter, and she needed something that she could not find in her marriage. Maybe she felt that she must try to make up for lost time and get a little excitement and romance into her life before it was too late. I can understand that.

Brad was devastated. And not just because he was in the throes of studying for his Civil Engineering Chartership exams.. We all missed her dreadfully, although we kept on touch for a long time until she moved to Scotland and remarried, at which point she put her whole past behind her and started afresh. She went on to great academic success and now has a University post, but is still childless, as she always said she would be.

Brad duly became a Chartered Member of the Institution of Civil Engineers and excelled in the exams, so he received a special mention. He is good at his job and a tower of strength whenever needed, so nothing has changed since he was four years old. Except his hair colour.

Dani managed to cope with her new life in spite of many difficulties, which are par for the course in a marriage break up. A shortage of money and funny 'phone calls added to feelings of insecurity and guilt, but these were eventually overcome.

My situation at work had deteriorated since my clinics had been altered and I was now spending several days a week in dark and depressing rooms which contrasted sharply with the bright airy accommodation I was used to in Bridlington. I would have liked to get out but I was the major wage earner and I felt trapped.

We were due to make another trip to America in late March but, some time before this, I had been ousted from my retreat in Bridlington to make way for the boss, who had left her husband. I now worked at the opposite end of the Health Authority district. Three of my days were spent in dingy rooms where the sunshine was never seen. There were two windows: one looked out on to a brick wall and the other's frame was painted black, with any view being obstructed by trees. It was all too much for someone already suffering from anxiety symptoms.

Several months earlier, I had arrived at the clinic in Bridlington, to find that not only had another therapist taken over my room and moved the furniture, but that she had also removed my pictures from the walls. I had nowhere to work and was forced to go round the building looking for an empty office. This was the clinic that I had equipped, to a large extent, with items bought with money that had been donated, and had been the result of my talks to various local charitable organisations. I did most of these in my own time, and at my own expense. Every year, before Christmas, some of the parents helped me to organise a coffee morning to raise funds so that we could buy extra toys and expensive items not provided by the Health Authority.

For some time I had felt less than appreciated, and there had been open criticism of my style of dress. The mothers of my small patients came to the clinic dressed in jeans and tee shirts so I wore trouser suits or semi-formal slacks. I had tried the 'just stepped out of Vogue magazine' look but both mothers and children clammed up, intimidated. I wanted to relate to my clients, not impress them. On one occasion, the boss lady came into the clinic at Bridlington and told me that Colonel N, our new Big Cheese, did not approve of trousers. I somewhat flippantly said that this was fine by me, and he did not have to wear them as far as I was concerned. Since I had been wearing trousers to work for fourteen years it seemed unreasonable to expect me to change at this point.

However, the matter was not allowed to drop and during a meeting of the entire staff, I was put under scrutiny and subjected to criticism. Fortunately, we had a fairly new member of staff who was also the local representative of the Union, and she stated in no uncertain terms that any attempt to force a change would amount to discrimination. I compromised by agreeing to wear a skirt for meetings and clinics where the Colonel may cross my path. "Is this a dagger I see before me, the handle toward my hand?" cried Lady Macbeth. I felt that I was seriously under threat.

One day, when I turned up to do my administrative work, the boss suggested that I should give up Speech Therapy and concentrate my energies on house renovation, I became increasingly anxious about my position. A few weeks before our trip to America, there was a defining incident.

There had been a severe fall of snow but as ever, I decided that the show must go on. I accordingly felt obligated to turn up for work on the off-chance that any of my patients were foolish enough to brave the weather and arrive at the clinic in Beverley. On that particular day I arrived, more-or-less on time, and was surprised when, a few minutes later, the first patient arrived. I was astonished to see him since the family lived on a farm well off-the-beaten-track, but the child's father had rolled out the Land Rover and kept the appointment. I expressed my surprise, adding that I had not anticipated that they would brave the extreme weather conditions. Later, in a letter of complaint, this reaction was reported by the mother of the child, who was not present at the time, as my annoyance that her son had turned up. Perhaps she assumed that I had made the hazardous journey to work to satisfy myself that I was capable of doing it, rather than to my somewhat old-fashioned dedication to duty. Suffice it to say that she penned a letter of complaint couched in the most venomous terms, but I was unaware of this until several weeks later.

The day after our return from America, a letter arrived summoning me to a disciplinary hearing. I never returned to work and spent several months suffering from 'stress'. It was a black period. I contacted the union with which Speech Therapists were associated, and they were all in favour of suing, getting me a backdated promotion and the attendant pay-rise. But, it meant that I would have to return to work. I decided to refuse their offer and, after giving a bravura performance as a confirmed head-case to an audience of one, a psychiatrist, I took early retirement on the grounds of insanity. Well, officially, ill-health.

At the end of our session together, the shrink said that it was with regret (I thought she was going to send me back in the firing line) that she must recommend that I did not return to my job. She added that she considered me a very talented lady and was certain that I would be a big success in whatever I decided to do in the future. I do not know what was in her mind. However, she was damned right. I was a huge success during my next career. I found my niche in life working with criminal nutcases!

The year of my absence from work was momentous in many ways. We had a wedding coming up but, before that happened, my first husband, who had long been married to Pamela, my old friend and hairdresser, had a stroke. They had moved out here to the East

Riding soon after Dani's first marriage, and were living at Huggate, having given up the garage in Leeds. He had been semi-retired since having lung cancer in 1978. Unfortunately for our daughter, he had not been supportive towards her when her marriage was in trouble, the only thing for which I was unable to forgive him. I had been mildly annoyed when he admitted to me, on one occasion when we met at the farm cottage where Dani and Paul lived, that at our divorce hearing he had confessed to twenty-four instances of adultery. He had made me give the grounds for the dissolution of the marriage, and I did so as the price I paid for my freedom. I did not imagine that he had lived a life of abstinence and sainthood but twenty-four adulterous liaisons?

Recently, an old friend from those bygone days said to Russell that I was a bit wild in my youth. This may well be true but not twenty-four cases wild. My wildest time was after the marriage had ended not during the course of it. However, I was prepared to forget all that, there is little point in agonising about the past and I had a good marriage in the present which compensated for all the bad times. When my ex-husband lay in his bed in the hospital, I went in to see him but I don't think that he recognised me. He came out of hospital, but soon after he fell into a coma, was re-admitted, and died just before his fifty-fifth birthday. Pam moved to Filey and I still keep in touch with her and her sister Pat, who was also a close friend in the past.

Jimmy was buried at Huggate. It was only when the will was read that anyone knew that he wanted to be cremated. Why do people let this happen? I cannot imagine David and I not being aware of each others wishes but I suppose that it is a part of the reluctance to face up to our mortality. When you make a will and discuss your funeral arrangements, you are admitting that you are going to die.

The best day of the year was Peter and Dani's wedding at the Register Office in Bridlington, followed by a family lunch party at The Bell in Driffield. It was a delight to see her so happy. Corina was expecting a baby and we all looked forward to another bundle of joy in the family. She does pregnancy and delivery in fine style, and did it on that first occasion just in time to be home for Christmas. Jake was undoubtedly one of the most gorgeous-looking babies ever seen. He had dark brown eyes and a permanently tanned complexion, it all added up to a child that everyone used to turn round to catch a second look at. He used to come and stay about once a month, so that his parents were free to go out, but my days of having a baby every weekend were over. Once in a while was enough for us both, but I suspect that this break for freedom might have been interpreted as a lack of interest. Not true, but it was time for David and I to have a life of our own.

I finally officially retired from the Health Service in the following January 1988, and celebrated by taking the whole family to a hotel for dinner and an overnight stay. It was time for a fresh beginning.

Before too long there would be another baby on the way, a long-awaited event for Dani and Peter. Perhaps now I would have a little girl to buy dollies for? Having said that, the boys always had dolls to play with, I do not hold with the mistaken idea that only girls should relate to other people and practice those communication skills on symbolic toys. If boys can play at driving cars and shooting villains, why can't they rehearse their relationships and housekeeping skills with dolls and dolls houses? Personally, I always much preferred the shooting and espionage games when I was with other playmates, but I also loved my family of dolls. I still have a collection and always make sure that Emily wears a cardigan during the winter. My own offspring think that I am slightly potty but my childhood was an extremely lonely one and my pretend children were all I had to keep me company.

From time-to-time I would buy toys from charity stalls and shops to use in my clinics, when I was working for the Health Service. One Friday evening, having purchased a scruffy and grubby doll with ginger hair at Cottingham market, I decided to give her a good clean up. Since I was planning on a soak in the bath myself, it seemed like a good idea to put my red-headed acquisition in the water at the same time, and give her a shampoo and scrub. David arrived home from work while I was so engaged, and he bounded up the stairs to see me. The door of the bathroom slid open, and he looked in to see a naked lady in her fifties, in the bath with a doll. He smiled a slow smile and said, "Don't worry, I won't tell the kids."

As a way of making a little extra money after my premature retirement, I answered an advertisement, which appealed for host families for French students during the summer vacation. A few weeks later I found myself waiting on York station for a foreigner of tender years. The intention was for him or her to attend our local school for two weeks to get a feeling for our education system. I found myself greeting a blue-chinned seventeen year-old, with whom I was saddled every day for three weeks. The following year, I had the supervisor instead, which was far easier. However, Luc was here for the event of the year.

On July 20th my granddaughter was born, to great rejoicing, particularly for Peter's parents, who had a family of five boys and several male grandchildren. For them it was the first girl in fifty years. Dani was only in hospital for a day or so and I left the visiting hours to Peter and his family. I had Robin and Luc to take care of and there would be plenty of time after they got home.

During my time with the Health Authority, I had trained as a Hypnotherapist in order to use this skill as an adjunct to accepted therapeutic techniques. I now used my training to supplement my retirement income and found this rewarding in every way. In addition, I was enrolled as an invigilator at local sittings of G.C.E. exams and, because all my qualifications were on the school file, I was asked to take a class in Dance and Drama at the local comprehensive school. Before too long, I was also roped in to teach a Keep Fit group, a class which I continued to run until I was sixty-nine years old. Fortunately, David had a fairly steady income, and we managed to cope financially in spite of the loss of my former salary.

As far as relaxation was concerned, I was having some enjoyment. Following his early retirement, my stepfather and mother had moved from Leeds and now lived in a bungalow in Beverley. We discovered Sequence Dancing and the three of us went two or three times a week. Reg threw his all into it, sending away for the scripts of the dances so that we could practice at home. Eventually, Dorothy had to abandon the new hobby as her mobility decreased, but Reg and I continued to go for some time until he decided he could not leave her alone for several hours at once.

One night I had a 'phone call from a strange-sounding gentleman who wanted me to visit him to offer hypnosis as a cure for his agoraphobia. I thought that he was too old for this to have any chance of success and I told him so. He insisted that we gave it a chance. However, he was living alone, having been separated from his wife for several years, and I was not prepared to visit him at home unless there was someone else in the house. He was agreeable to my taking a chaperone and in the event, Reg went with me and sat in on the sessions. It was a fortunate decision of mine to accept the assignment. When we arrived at the house for the first time, a large man with a grey complexion opened the door and we were ushered in to his sitting room. He told us his story.

He had served an apprenticeship to a chemist and taken a degree at London University during the Second World War. He had always suffered from a hearing loss but this was put right by a surgeon who was a customer at the pharmacy where my patient worked. The 32 year-old newly-hearing-perfect pharmacist went on to become a renowned research chemist and was instrumental in proving that Thalidomide was the cause of severely handicapped babies. He failed to persuade the company marketing the drug to withdraw it and incurred their displeasure by publishing his findings in The Lancet. It took ten years for the case to come to court and George was exonerated from any responsibility. In fact, he was applauded for his tenacity in proving the danger of the drug. However, the years had taken their toll.

He was guilt-ridden because he felt that if he had been able to prove his case sooner, many limbless children and their parents could have been spared. Our hero was awarded a Doctor of Science degree and became famous in certain circles. Working conditions at his company became impossible; they no longer wanted the man who had blown the whistle on a lucrative enterprise, so George moved to Hull and another major pharmaceutical company. Here, he invented Gaviscon and Lemsip, both household names today, and a drug called Immobilon, which is used to anaesthetise large animals when they need a short-term immobilisation. He also developed the antidote Revivon that will return the animal to normal if given within three minutes.

He travelled the world as an acknowledged expert in his field. Finally, he needed to wind down and so bought a chemist shop. Within a short time, he became unable to cope and meeting the customers proved a strain. He sold up and retired. His wife left him and he was forced to sell the large house where they lived in order to provide separate homes. His present residence was a tiny bungalow, heavily stained with nicotine. Dr George

Somers was now in a state of fear of the outside world, which even precluded him going out of the door to hang out his washing.

I held out no hope for his recovery but I did what he had requested and worked my magic on him. I made an appointment for the following week on the understanding that if he felt no improvement in his state of mind, he was to cancel the session and not waste his money. No such phone call was received and Reg and I turned up the next week.

A changed man opened the door to us. His complexion was fairly normal and he appeared to be brighter and more alert. Within a few weeks, George had stopped smoking, with no intervention from me, and was able to go to the shops. I dispensed with the services of my escort and the client went from strength to strength. He insisted that I kept visiting every week and though I told him that I was now unnecessarily taking his money, he was adamant. This relationship continued for years although I eventually cut down his dependence and my visits to once a month. He said that I had changed his life and he was kind and generous, not only to me but to my whole family.

One night, whilst David and I were on holiday in France, George dropped down dead in his bathroom. Ultimately, this event led to a major change in our future holiday plans. He left me a thousand pounds in his will. Although we used to jest about the possibility of a windfall enabling me to have a facelift, it seemed pointless to improve the face and leave the rest of me sagging. I decided to use the unexpected bonus to finance a special holiday and we settled on a riverboat trip through Russia. It was the start of our new holiday philosophy.

CHAPTER 15
THE CUCKOO'S NEST

During the years that I was seeing George and being a part-time teacher, I also took on another, very challenging role. One morning, David received a long manila envelope in the mail, his name hand written on the front. Upon opening it, he found inside nothing but a sheet of typing paper with a cutting from the York evening paper Sellotaped to it. This was quite obviously intended for me, since it was a job opportunity for a part-time Speech Therapist at a privately-owned semi-secure hospital for people who had committed an offence and were sectioned under the Mental Health Act. I did not really want the job but it struck me that extra money was not to be sniffed at, so I telephone the General Manager and arranged to go to a village on the outskirts of York to have a look at the set-up.

The administrative building was a gracious Georgian house built for Thomas Fairfax, a York merchant who rose to great heights in his day. Connected to this by corridors, locked at both ends, were the wards and living accommodation for the inmates, patients, or clients. At the time there were fourteen, and most of them were retarded, or emotionally-disturbed, or both. I later became convinced that this description might also fit some members of the staff.

What really influenced me to accept the post was the fact that a swimming pool was in the final stages of construction, so I officially applied for the job. There had been eight applicants, and only two were interviewed. I got the job, but no solid salary was on the table. When an offer was made, I wrote back to say that they were way out on the scale of financial reward, in the light of my experience etc., and therefore there was no way I would accept their offer. Frankly, I did not fancy the prospect of working with this client group, and had decided to price myself out of the running.

In my reply, I also pointed out that a permanent Speech Therapist was extraneous to their needs but, if asked, I would visit to do assessments as and when required. I quoted a fee of £55 per session, a ridiculously high figure at the time. Ian Fraser, the General Manager and a delightful man, was on the 'phone to me by 9:00 a.m. the following morning, accepting my terms and guaranteeing at least one day each week. He had made me an offer I could not refuse, and I started my new career in January 1990.

Everything about my new working environment was different from the regime to which I had been accustomed. My immediate first-line manager was a full figured Occupational Therapist who had the responsibility of organising the day-to-day lives of the client group. This was a major task and she had a deep understanding of their needs. Our top man was a renowned psychiatrist who at that time was the most highly paid consultant in his field in the country: a man who could be as hard-as-nails, and yet who was capable of great sympathy and understanding. He took no prisoners if you failed to deliver, and at my interview had questioned me relentlessly. As one of the interviewing panel, he asked me what I would do if I was alone in a room with a patient, whose behaviour took a turn for the worse, culminating in a chair being thrown at me. I gave this scenario some thought and then replied clearly and concisely "Duck".

A smile crossed his face, and he asked what would I do next. My response required a little thought but I said, "I don't know. But, whatever I did, it would be done slowly and with great calmness".

When he moved on, to take another job, we were all, patients and staff alike, devastated. I had endeared myself to him by producing reports on the clients, which were academic in content, to the point, and all-embracing. These were the result of my former superior's high standards and nit-picking, also owing a good deal to my extensive reading and plagiarism. I managed to steer a middle course between being down-to-earth and practical, and using sufficient technical terminology to impress other regimen with my erudition.

Our psychologist commented that he did not understand a good deal of what my reports said, but they read wonderfully. When describing one individual's dentition which was characterised by a pronounced anterior open bite (buckteeth, to the layman) I stole a line from 'The Lion in Winter', and said, "She smiles to excess but she chews with real distinction". Nobody recognised the quotation.

On the first day I was issued with a bunch of keys, which were attached to an extending chain clipped to my trouser waistband. Very few of the female staff wore skirts, when one works with rapists, and other sex offenders, trousers are a more sensible dress. Jackie, the Occupational Therapist, took me around and I assisted in cookery sessions, music groups, and quizzes. At all times, my priority was watching my back. By the time I made my second visit, I had a small caseload of real patients who had language problems.

One adult retardate who had limited comprehension and no expressive language at all. His only verbalisation was "da", and this served for everything. Earlier reports from his schools and institutions implied that he was able to enjoy subjects such as archaeology and geography. This was total rubbish, but it looked good on paper: the writers obviously felt that their efforts on his behalf had to be justified regardless of the truth. I just worked on improving his understanding at a very primitive level, and this did show minimal results.

It certainly did not justify the money and time that was spent on making small gains. He was twenty-seven years old, and had already learned all that he was capable of learning. One day, I arrived while he was at breakfast. He was sitting with a boiled egg in front of him, and with tears streaming down his face. I tried to find out the cause of his distress without success. Imagine that you are unable to communicate on any level that would enable you to tell another person that you are in pain, either mental or physical. Maybe someone was taking advantage of his incapacity to complain, and was abusing him in some way? In spite of the security, there were always incidents, and not only within the client population and not necessarily of a sexual nature.

It was unbelievable that such a large amount of items could go missing from a secure environment. Not merely typing paper, coffee, sugar, notepads, staplers etc. A large tent was taken from our department, as well as a microwave oven, and a video camera. The latter reappeared after two weeks. Someone going on holiday had obviously borrowed it, and the timing pointed to the perpetrators, about whom we had already voiced suspicions. These individuals arrived back at work at the same time that the video camera was found broken in the grounds, but proof was not available. The unqualified nursing assistants, were doing a job with no future at all. Unlike their State-Registered superiors, they had no training and little understanding of their charges' problems. From time-to-time there were incidents of an unpleasant nature, which resulted in immediate dismissal.

One of the very senior nursing staff on the administrative side had a major problem with his trousers. He seemed to be unable to keep his zipper fastened if there was a female around, and was not beyond locking the door of his office, or any other room, in order to have his wicked way with the unwilling lady. Eventually, he picked on the wrong one and she blew the whistle on him. She became applauded and he became unemployed.

One of the main perpetrators of the escaping 'crime' was a tall, very thin, albino young man that I'll call Alex. He had the privilege of ground freedom, and could work in the gardens or workshops, but he never breached those conditions. That would have no excitement. We used to jest that Alex could contract his bones like a mouse, and squeeze under doors, and certainly through tiny lavatory windows in a pub or café when on a trip. On one occasion, he disappeared from Blackpool Pleasure Beach. On another occasion he absconded from a churchyard, and was found hiding behind the washing on someone's line.

Alex had some problem with the bones in his feet, and I arrived one morning to find him on crutches having had the bones broken and reset. I told David, when I got home, that his escaping habit had been curtailed. My husband knew Alex, among many others, because he had been doing some joinery work at the hospital. David jokingly said, "Have they nailed his feet to the floor?" I explained, but a few days later, Alex took off again, on his crutches.

Another of our residents made the national news by spending several days on the roof. One more managed to reach Scarborough, where he enjoyed fish and chips, followed by an afternoon on the beach, and then walked into the police station where he asked to be taken home.

I was involved more directly in another incident involving a very disturbed young man.

He and another client asked me if I would take them for a walk round the grounds, and the ward manager gave permission. As we prepared to go, another male nurse asked me if I had a walkie-talkie, a precaution I rarely took since I was confident that I would come to no harm. He insisted that I took one with me, just in case. Nearing the end of our circuit of the grounds, Martin asked if we could go as far as the end of the drive.

I agreed, although I had a slight feeling of unease. We passed Bob, the gardener, and headed for the gateway. Across the road, an elderly lady was waiting for the bus and Martin suddenly broke into a run. I thought, for a split second that she had fallen and that my charge was rushing to her rescue but I soon realised that this was a break for freedom. I gather that the standard distress message was "Assistance needed", but this was frequently unnoticed among all the other unnecessary communications, so I said the first thing that came in to my head: "Mayday, Mayday. Front gate!".

It worked like magic. Within seconds, Bob leaped off his tractor and followed the runaway, assorted staff appeared as if by magic, including four in a car. Martin was quickly apprehended while John, the other member of our walking party, protested his innocence. Some time later, the latter managed to board the York to London train, only to be spotted by one of the consultant Psychiatrists en-route for a conference, on the same train. The police met him at Kings Cross.

Within a few weeks of my arrival, Jackie, my boss, was taken ill and was off work for several weeks, so I stepped into the breach. I found myself running music groups and quizzes. Some of these were off the top of my head, while others were based on pop music and involved me doing impressions of past pop idols. I must have been pretty good: they always guessed who I was doing.

One of my finest performances was a karaoke session in the music room when my escort was Mike, a Staff Nurse of very mild and tolerant disposition. Unfortunately, one member of the group decided he did not want to stay, and demanded that he be returned to the ward. This was not feasible since it was a large group and two members of staff were needed to attend in order to ensure security and safety. It might have been possible to radio for assistance but Mike was confident in his ability to placate the renegade, and went over to the door to calm him down, leaving his radio on the settee where he had been sitting next to another patient. Meanwhile, I carried on with the singsong, unaware that another member of the party had misappropriated the radio and switched it on. My rendition of 'Magic Moments' may have lacked finesse, but it certainly was not short on enthusiasm, and the assembled company showed their appreciation by joining in at the tops of their voices.

We were unaware of the fact that our performance was being broadcast to the entire establishment, and prevented any other communication through the system. The added extra was that the Mental Health Commission had a team visiting another patient who was deeply disturbed, and confined to a solitary room, and the strains of what was loosely described as music, reached their unwilling ears. After several minutes of blissful lack of awareness, we were disturbed by a red-faced and breathless nursing assistant, who was beating on the door and screaming, "Turn the f----ing radio off".

We were most put out. I was doing a sterling job in there, all on my own with a bunch of miscreants, while Mike played the peacemaker. When we opened the locked door, the messenger explained, and the missing radio was recovered and returned to its rightful owner. On my arrival back at the ward, Mark, the ward manager, who was generally very relaxed and a pleasure to work with, tried to castigate me. I argued that at least the visitors now had concrete evidence that we did not merely incarcerate our unfortunate charges. That it was now evident that we tried to bring a little light into their sorry lives. He made a valiant effort to look stern, then cracked out laughing. It was the same Mark who mocked my Mayday message. I retorted on that occasion that the result was immediate and effective.

One of my regular patients was Neville. He spoke with amazing speed, to the point of being unintelligible, and my remit was to slow him down. Unfortunately, he was then totally incapable of remembering what he was supposed to say. For instance, the session might start like this: "Now then Nev, I want you to say to me, my name is Neville Blank". "Right. My name is ---. My name is ---. My name is ---. Ooh, I've forgot", followed by a fit of giggles. He was just like an overgrown but not very bright six-year-old.

I started running discussion groups three times a week; my attendance had increased to that number of days. Generally, the same people came each time and at one time 'my boys' included two chaps who had terminated the lives of their nearest and dearest, and one who had narrowly escaped being guilty of the same crime. This last had attempted to kill his mother in a bid to free her of the devil. All were lovely fellows and we had some great times. One of the three, I'll call him Bill, was a well-informed and verbally-able expert in his own, technical, field and had been fairly wealthy. He eventually went to trial on a reduced charge of manslaughter and came out of it without a stain on his character but was confined to a mental hospital for a further period. He was later moved to another establishment and had full parole but he absconded because he was anxious about his children. At the time, as the law stood, if he had not been apprehended within thirty days, he was free. We were all silently cheering him on, but sixty-two minutes before the deadline, the police found him. Bill had been using his credit card to phone home, and at the moment of his being collared, he and some family were drinking champagne in celebration. They thought it was all over but they did not wait for the fat lady to sing.

The other one of my three musketeers was Harry who had intended to shoot himself in front of his lady. Unfortunately, she laughed and told him he did not have the nerve so he shot her instead. He was sent to our place because he was a suicide risk, but eventually returned to mainstream gaol and served a life sentence. I kept in touch with him throughout and he is now a free man again. We met him in York when he was in his last, open, prison and then, another time, I picked him up in Pocklington and brought him here for the day. As I write, he is living in a hostel and has a job. Hopefully, when his probationary period is over, he will be able to get a place of his own and start a new life.

These three deserve a special mention because they saved me from serious injury, if not worse, actually breaking the rules to do so. One morning, one of our weirder clients, Baz, came to the fringes of a group which I was hosting outside in the sunshine. He was always immaculately dressed and very well-mannered in spite of having features that were straight out of a scary movie, but he suffered from delusions. He was devoted to his mother and phoned her daily to get her to place bets on his behalf. On this occasion, he said to me "If anyone hurt my mother, I would kill them". I applauded his sentiments and carried on with my group, not attaching any great importance to the incident. In retrospect, I realise that the delusion of the day was that I had inflicted some injury on his parent.

After lunch, I gathered my next group together and unusually, we held the session on the ward, which was otherwise deserted with the exception of the Ward Manager, who was in his office. In retrospect, B was in a strange mood and probably should not have been unsupervised, but when he came over to join the party, I could hardly refuse. However, being slightly uneasy, I moved chairs so that I was sitting directly opposite him and I put one foot up on the seat. It is strange that warning bells sometimes ring in one's head, and I had a plan of action ready. I was acutely aware of his every move and when he suddenly came at me, I lifted my foot so that it hit him in the chest as he tried to get his hands around my throat. The next few seconds seemed like an eternity but very quickly one of my boys ran for help, and the other two, grabbed Baz, regardless of the fact that they were not supposed to intervene, only to fetch assistance. Unfortunately, my neck would have broken before assistance arrived. Bless you, fellows.

Baz eventually died in a bizarre fashion. He was in the bath, and visited at prescribed intervals, but he was found drowned, on his knees with his hands clasped behind his back and his head in the water. At the inquest a verdict of suicide was recorded. It was a happy release; I hope his adoring mother agreed. The parents of these tragic people bear a heavy cross; it must be impossible to not feel some responsibility for the disturbed mental state of their offspring.

There was one more patient later, who earned my lifelong gratitude. Barry was a later member of my discussion group. One day he asked me if I played badminton, to which I replied that I had never played anything and it was too late to start. His disagreement was forcefully expressed and he volunteered to teach me during the lunch hour. I feared the worst; my usual response to a flying object approaching me was to duck but I did not want to let him down when he was trying to help. To my astonishment, I managed to hit the shuttlecock and the game soon became a passion.

He went on to teach various other members of our staff and this was tremendously good for his morale. He eventually moved to a halfway house, and the first Christmas he sent a card that I shall always treasure, thanking both David and me for what we had done for him. Where is he now? I still play badminton, and I often wonder if he does.

David knew many of the 'clients', because early on in my time at Stockton-on-Forest, he had gone there to do a small job, which grew and grew. His first commission was to change the hanging side on a huge oak door, and he earned a large amount of money over the years. Some assignments were spin-offs, members of staff who had repairs and renovations to do, and who had been impressed with his efficiency, kept him gainfully employed.

Some of our residents were brighter than the average bear, and some from wealthy backgrounds. Mental illness is not exclusive to the criminal community or to those from less privileged background. One of our notable intellectuals was a former astrophysicist who had attempted to push his psychiatrist under a train. Another was an adored only-child of parents of mature years, who had attacked his father with an axe. The victim survived but the authorities took a dim view of this act of rebellion. We had several female residents, some of whom had a past characterised by enforced prostitution or paedophilia.

Self-harming was a typical trait. One young lady, in particular, became one of my regular customers. She certainly did not require Speech Therapy, but I had become a roving counsellor and whenever a particularly tough case, requiring a good deal of one-to-one input, came along, I was called upon to provide just that. This particular little body was about twenty-six but looked fifty. She was hunched and scarred, her face a mass of healed slashes and cuts, her arms and legs, likewise. As a child, her grandfather had subjected her to sexual abuse but when she tried to tell her mother about this, she was called a dirty little liar. Finally, her behaviour resulted in the authorities intervening and the mother abandoning all responsibility, so Sylvie was officially put in the care of her grandparents. That certainly facilitated Grandpa's role and the child was forced to stay put.

One morning, I arrived to be told, at the early hand-over meeting when incoming staff were brought up-to-date on the previous night's events, that Sylvie had swallowed a Ford Escort. My mind boggled! I couldn't possibly eat one in less than twenty-four hours! It transpired that it was only a Dinky car but even so! X-rays revealed that it was passing through, so the nursing staff dosed her with cascara and kept a close watch on her bowel movements until the vehicle emerged.

Before too long, she was at it again and ingested two torch batteries. Battery acid is not awfully good for the digestion but she did not show any ill effects immediately. I arrived to collect her from the ward and off we went for our cup of coffee and a cigarette. "Have the batteries come through yet, Sylv". I asked.

"No, not yet, Shirl," she answered, looking up at me from her hunched position at my side. I took a chance on her sense of humour.

"You know what they are going to do, don't you? They are going to get one of the nursing assistants to bonk you, and if his balls light up they'll know the batteries are still in there". Fortunately, she thought my comments were hilarious and eventually, the motions having been gone through, the crisis was passed.

One of our clients became nationally famous for his exploits. He had an amazing ability to pass himself off as a wealthy young man about town, and drove out of many up-market car showrooms with expensive vehicles. He was also good in the role of doctor or surgeon, and featured in a television program about his exploits, long after his departure from oue establishment. The interesting thing was that in a drama group, he was hopeless, finding it impossible to role-play to order.

My actual working day began when I walked on to the ward to receive the hand-over information, a necessity because it was essential to be acquainted with any incidents that may affect the behaviour of my charges. However, getting from the door to the office took some time, because a few patients, anxious to welcome me, invariably mobbed me. This greeting was often boisterous and excessively enthusiastic particularly in the case of Big Jack, a young criminal who pumped iron on a grand scale, with muscles to prove it. He would pick me up and swing me around burying his face in my neck and saying, "Cor Shirl, you smell f---ing lovely". This behaviour was strictly verboten but I managed to get away with it.

I felt that one of the troubles with my client group was that nobody had ever shown them any affection. I was much older than any other member of staff and, to some extent, I became a mother figure. Certainly, in my years in the National Health Service, the most enthusiastic welcome I ever received was a smile, and no one ever told me how good I smelled. The whole experience gave me a huge sense of worth; there was never a complaint about my ability, my report-writing, my clothes, or my hairstyle. I felt universally loved. Everyone should be so fortunate.

Eventually, as part of a scourge and cost-cutting exercise, my sessions were cut to a half-day a week. After two-and-a-half years of this, they decided to dispense with the services of their resident Speech Therapist. I had told them right from the start that my services were not necessary. They finally agreed, and in August 1997 I said goodbye for the last time. This was the end of my formal working life, and I could not have wished for a finer last act.

CHAPTER 16
FUR & FEATHERS

This chapter is all about animals. I warn you in advance so that, if you don't like livestock, you can pass rapidly on to the next chapter.

Because of my devotion to Reba, my Grandad Taylor's dog, or possibly due to the fact that I was a lonely only child, I always had a deep desire to have a pet. I spent a great deal of time with my dolls and treated them like real people, but much as I loved them, they never returned my affection, never snuggled up to me or made any comforting noises. My mother was not fond of animals, although her own father used to breed Yorkshire Terriers in the attic. I've often wondered how their ablutions and private functions were organised. Maybe this was the reason for Mummy's lack of affection for dogs or the mess they made. I suspect that the responsibility incurred in the ownership of animals was another point against it. However, why I do not know, she eventually capitulated, and a Red Cocker Spaniel, with a kennel name Konk of Scarcroft, came into my life.

It was, for me, love-at-first-sight. However, in retrospect, Mother was probably right. Dogs should not be left alone in a house all day to entertain themselves, especially not Cockers. Konky's idea of entertainment was to chew up the kitchen mat, or rip the net curtains from end to end. This was not an endearing habit in wartime, when replacement of these items was more than just a financial problem. He also suffered some irritation on his scalp, which made him scratch his head raw, and it seemed impossible to clear this up. About thirteen months after his arrival, as if by magic, he disappeared. One morning I got up to find him gone. The weather was bitterly cold, but for weeks I walked the streets before and after school calling for him, tears streaming down my face. The theory put forward was that he had been stolen, since dogs were in short supply at the time (this was 1945).

Thirty-five years later, my son Brad had an unbelievably destructive dog that nearly broke his heart with her antics, and I said out loud to myself "If I had a dog like that, who destroyed my home, I'd either lose it or have it put down". I suddenly realised that maybe this was the explanation for Konky's disappearance. As I said, the mystery has never been solved and it was pointless asking my mother, who would never have allowed the truth to tarnish her image and my father seemed to know nothing when I asked him, albeit 55 years later.

We did have a budgie called Peter, but I could not find a meaningful relationship with him and at one time three goldfish swam around a glass bowl but it is hard to communicate with a goldfish on any level. It was to be fifteen years until I had a real pet again and by that time I had three children who occupied most of my affection and communication skills.

During the last months of my first marriage, we had adopted a huge sand-coloured Great Dane, whose owner was no longer able to cope. No wonder, when he occupied the settee there was no way you could get him off. Two adults could just manage to tip-up the sofa and persuade Richard that vacating was the order of the day. However, in the early hours of the morning when my husband went to answer the call of nature, Richard would occupy the bed and defy anyone to deprive him of the position. Jimmy shouted at him, while covering his sensitive naked parts like a footballer, all to no avail. Only if I got out of bed would Richard move.

Richard weighed an estimated fifteen stones: there's no arguing with a dog that size. Eventually, after a press photograph reached Cleveland, a gentleman contacted me to say that he believed Richard to be a dog he had lost years before. Facts did not bear this out, but by that time divorce was looming on my horizon, and I duly delivered the dog to the North-East. Last seen, he was hauling an old man through the streets of Middlesborough.

The people who rented the ground floor flat in the house next door, who were named Anne and Tony Booth, had a raison d'etre. Their main interest in life was the Great Danes they owned and kept in the tiny living room of the flat. The dogs were both Harlequins, that is, black and white. The male went by the name of Cassius and bitch was called Paris, the idea being to breed them and make a good profit. Unfortunately, this was not to be.

Cass had a very calm nature until riled, in common with most of his breed but these dogs are immensely powerful and can cause havoc in a field of sheep, pigs or calves, even by merely playing rough and snapping at lower legs as they would with another dog. The terror that they strike in the other animal can cause profound shock and a farmer does not hang about to see if it is all a game. Unfortunately, they escaped one day and went on a jolly race around a field of livestock. In this case, it was their owner, Tony, who pulled the trigger, hoping to put a shot in their back legs and bring them down then get them to a vet. Both dogs died of shock and it was a miracle that Tony did not turn the gun on himself.

Fortunately they had acquired a mis-marked bitch, Donna, who survived the incident and who went on to produce one live pup some years later. In the meantime, the Dane population increased to as many as seven. Some were only passing through, but then Anne and Tony bought a real showstopper, Corky, who had been a star of a dog food advert. He was destined to play a large part in our lives.

My adult passion with dogs began with Corky, who was only a lodger while his folks were in Tokyo for two years. He was a big chap, thirty-six inches to the shoulder topped by a massive head. For me, that started a love affair with Great Danes that lasts to this day, though ownership is now financially unviable. Corky was gentle and obedient, stately and spectacular looking, a black and white Harlequin that, were you to buy one in 2004, would cost fifteen hundred to two thousand pounds. We always hoped that his owners would stay in Japan forever, but they came home and reclaimed him. Dani was desolate and spent the evening before his departure sitting in the kitchen with him, in floods of tears.

Shortly after this I ventured into Siamese cats with Charlie, a large blue-point who looked as if he was made of nylon, and Mai Ling, a seal-point who put it about a bit and presented us with a litter of undoubted bastards, Charlie having met his end under a truck. We managed to find homes for all of them except the grey, which we kept, and who used to curl up with the new Danes, of whom more later. They were very fond of the cats and would not have willingly hurt them. Unfortunately they did not realise that a dog weighing several stones should not lie on a very small pussycat, and I came in one day to find the kitten mortally crushed.

The Danes in question were Sacha, known as Arthur, who was an adoptidog and Sheba, whom we bought when she was eight weeks old. She was utterly lovable and grew to enormous proportions very quickly. We have always nursed the puppies on our knee during the evening, to pre-empt any piddling on the floor. When they start to wriggle you stand up and carry them outside to perform their ablutions, thus preventing the formation of bad habits. Great Danes do not appreciate their own enormity and still want to sit on your knee when they are fully grown and weigh several stones. This can present major difficulties.

Arthur was a merle. That is, grey with black patches; basically a mis-marked Harlequin. He was something of a problem from the start, and we resorted to the use of an 'animal coaxer' to discipline him. This is a long stick with a battery-operated probe on the end which administers a minor but effective electric shock to the miscreant. Unfortunately, the first week we lived in Kirkburn, Arthur and Sheba escaped one day, and went for a jolly romp in a field with some prize heifers. Naturally the farmer protected his livestock in the time-honoured way, and the only one open to him if his cattle were to remain safe, and Sheba was shot. Unfortunately it was Arthur who was the problem, but he took off and made it home. We tried unsuccessfully to give him away, but he was always brought back within a few days. Is it true that only the good die young? Sheba certainly did.

A word about adopted animals. If someone is willing to give their dog away, there is invariably a good reason, and we have had quite a lot of experience in this field. If the owners are about to or have already departed this earth, then that is a good reason. Otherwise act with extreme caution. The beast in question may be un-biddable, un-trainable, un-lovely in temperament, or otherwise difficult. We have had them all. One of our failures was a bloodhound named Henry. These are very large dogs and, after a few days, Henry started to get mildly unpleasant if anyone walked past his feeding bowl. His mildness quickly grew into downright aggression, and he was promptly returned to sender.

Shortly after we moved to Kirkburn, a gentleman by the name of Arthur Collins-Browne also took up residence in a house further down the village. His house was one that we had viewed and rejected when we were looking for a home in this area. He acquired two dogs: both of which were Pointers. Not long after that, he borrowed a shotgun from the landlord of the village pub and, leaving the dogs at home, he drove his very expensive car into the countryside and shot himself through the mouth. This did nothing for his dentition, and even less for his general health, and he was already beyond human intervention when he was found. The dogs survived this event, and within hours the jungle telegraph was appealing for adoptive parents for the two dogs. Not a lot of folks would take on a pair of orphaned dogs, but because of our strange temperament we did not see it as a great problem. We already had a Jack Russell bitch who took up little space, so what the hell?

One of the two seemed to be hard of hearing and retarded, but otherwise inoffensive. Her one failing was that she would regularly disappear at night and leave us to drive around the country lanes looking for her. She eventually returned at seven-thirty in the morning in the care of an elderly neighbour, Mr King. He lived in a farm worker's cottage, next door to the late Collins-Brown. What we later learned was that the dog was in the habit of arriving at their door late at night, and being invited in, then fed on chicken and chocolate biscuits until it was too late to send her home. Trixie, as she was called, was a very elegant liver and white Pennine pointer and her kennel-mate was a Continental variety, characterised by a broader head. The latter's name, on arrival chez-Windsor, was Darkie. We re-named her as Tarka ; the nearest I could get to a name acoustically similar to her own.

Since the dogs had formerly lived next-door to a couple by the name of King, late at night Trixie sought comfort there. Mrs King, the lady of the house, childless herself, had apparently been the Nanny to the ill-fated Collins-Brown fifty years before, and seemed to think that Trixie had embodied the soul of her deceased master and come home to Nanny. They both, that is Mrs King and Trixie, became a real liability and one had to go. Fortunately, an agricultural college student working in the village fell in love with her. The dog, not Mrs King. Her parents, farmers themselves, came and took Trixie away to greener pastures, all of which they owned. They telephoned a few weeks later to report that all was well and another dog story came to a close. Tarka stayed with us for many years and was quite a character.

When we had the ducks, hens, and geese, Tarka used to hide round a corner, leaning forward periodically to see where they were. At some point she would rush out and round them up but never touched them. She was a remarkable dog, the only animal I have ever seen who would fall over, having fallen asleep standing up. We always have hearths at least a foot high to lift the fireplace up above the level of a sleeping Great Dane, and Tarka liked to stand on the hearth and doze. On at least two occasions she literally fell off, landing on the floor as her legs surrendered to the lure of Morpheus. At other times, her hindquarters slowly sank lower and lower, until the animal hydraulics kicked in and she temporarily regained full alert.

The Jack Russell, named Möshe, as in Dayan, as in Israel (alright: look him up in an encyclopaedia) was a little wonder. Very devoted to Brad, she would climb ladders to get to him. Not that he lived up a ladder, but we were heavily committed to construction work by then, and Brad liked to be in at the deep end. One day when David and I had gone across the main road to get some timber, we left the dogs in the house. It was unlocked, of course: at that time we never locked the doors. We had not appreciated that Tarka could and would push open the door. Tarka made it to the other side, while Möshe didn't.

When we had first arrived in Kirkburn, there was a large backyard, which had formerly been the girl's playground. The building, the school and the house separated this side of the whole from the boy's playground. A high wall divided the two sets of toilets. At playtime, there was a strict 'no fraternisation rule. The boys' yard had a urinal with no door; probably big enough for three or four at a time and the back-splash was slate. If memory serves me, I'm pretty sure that the slate now forms part of the floor of the woodshed, but the outbuilding itself eventually became home to Gertie the goat.

I first met Gertie while visiting a little girl patient at home, and espied her grazing in a garden down the road. I refer to the goat of course; the child was really fairly normal. The small girl whose family owned the goat, chanced to visit the house, whilst I was there, not that I was aware of the relationship at the time. When I asked, "Who owns the goat?", fortune had dictated that I was in the right place at the right time or that she was. "Do you want to sell her?", was the next question and five minutes later her mother arrived to see if I was serious. Five pounds changed hands and Gertie jumped in the back of my Hillman Estate car.

"She'll be fine in the car", I was assured. "Just get her out quickly at the other end, because she has a tendency to pee as soon as the car stops." When I arrived home, having lost some documentation to Gertie's appetite en-route, I dared not stop the car and spent some anxious minutes reversing in and out of the drive, while tooting frantically on the horn in the hope that David would come and detrain the passenger before the call of nature became too urgent. In the event, this was achieved without mishap, and Gertie became one of us, along with hens, ducks, geese, rabbits, and a pig. Ah, the good life!

We finally managed to get her 'tupped' and, after giving birth to her kid, Georgina, Brad and I used to have to milk her twice a day. She was not impressed with the idea, having come to it rather late in life. She was five when we got her, and regularly used to put her foot in the bucket during the milking, which was carried out in the open, and in a corner to render escape less likely. The kid had the disconcerting habit of running at my back when I was kneeling at the udder, mounting it (not in the biblical sense), running up to my shoulders and then at the wall, and going round like a wall of death motorcyclist, finally landing back on terra-firma to gather herself for a repeat performance. Just what you want at eight in the morning! Or worse, in the early hours after a night out, when a top-up milking enabled me to stay in bed a little longer in the morning

Gertie and the kid met their end suddenly and in a somewhat sinister way. I came home from work to find them both poorly. There is a saying in the goat community "There is no such thing as a sick goat. You either have a live one, or a dead one". The babe was gone within an hour. I called the vet who came and administered a shot of anti-biotic and left another one for later. David was away so Brad and I had to do the job. But, in the morning, Gertie had given up the ghost and I had to ring the knackers' yard to come and collect the carcass. After that, I lost heart. The consensus was that they had been poisoned, whether accidentally or by person or persons unknown, we have never found out.

We were very self-sufficient at that time. We bred the ducks, geese, and rabbits for the table (David had the chore of killing, I did the gutting etc.) Brad and I were in charge of gardening and grew nothing that couldn't be eaten either by the people or the animals. I had to lie to Dani and Brad about the rabbits we ate: it usually arrived at the table already off the bone and was referred to as chicken. The ducks were Muscovies, and they and the geese ran around the garden, while Tarka, the Pointer, stood guard and rounded them up every now and then. She used to hide, standing round a corner with her nose just out, until she was ready to make her move. She never harmed anything but she loved the game.

Pansy also came by Hillman Avenger. We had spent the evening dining with some people we hardly knew, in Howden. I had met the wife one day, only because she was walking a huge Great Dane and I had stopped the car to speak to her. It transpired that her husband was a pig farmer and for some reason she invited us to dinner with them. Just as we were leaving their house, around midnight, the husband asked if we wanted a wreakling, i.e. a runt. He had a tea chest we could put her in for the journey so we said "Why not?".

I'll tell you why not. By the time we arrived home some forty minutes later, this pig must have shat for Yorkshire, and the smell was horrendous. We had all the windows open and were smoking furiously in the hope of killing the appalling stink, though all to no avail. On arriving home at 1:00 a.m. we had to find a berth for Pansy the Pig, who we later renamed Malone, because at the time the two Ronnies, a comedy duo, were doing a series of sketches about a fat private detective called Piggy Malone.

Later, we made a movable sty in the school playing field, long before it became our garden, by erecting an enclosure made out of old doors supported by stacks of breeze-blocks. One day I was leaning in to feed Pansy Malone and the doors collapsed. Naturally I fell in and Pansy escaped, but she was eventually recaptured. On another occasion, Brad arrived home from school to find her in the old Methodist chapel across the road, and duly got her home by grabbing her back legs and 'wheel-barrowing' her across the road and into her sty. Pansy was the only real problem animal we ever had: she used to eat everything in sight, including our chicks. We all hated her and eating her was a joy, though getting her to market was a tale and a half.

The idea is to get a sack, throw in some pig-nuts and, when the pig follows, you tie the neck of the sack and ticketty-boo. Unfortunately, when the time came for her to go to market, Pansy came out at the other end of the sack and took off. I eventually had to 'wheel-barrow' her and escorted her to her sty, to await David coming to collect her later in the day, with a van, to take her to meet her maker. It must be easy to appreciate that no tears were shed over her passing to the great pigsty in the sky. The pork was wonderful.

The rabbit thing started at the instigation of my boss's husband, Jack, who had a broad Yorkshire accent and who reassured us about every new venture with the words "I'll show you how to go on", spoken from the lateral extremities of his mouth. He gave us our first rabbit, a New Zealand White of substantial proportions, by the name of Arthur's Dad. Later we also acquired Arthur, from a different source and, in the meantime, at least two breeding does. One of these was called Hermione, a sable, and the other a beautiful grey chinchilla whose name escapes me at present.

One of my jobs was to collect vast quantities of greens including dandelion leaves, and waste from the local greengrocers, to supplement their diet of shop-bought rabbit food. Well, not exactly shop, but from local mills supplying animal feed, along with pig-weaner for the ducks, dog food and pig nuts, all by the hundredweight. That Hillman Avenger certainly earned its keep. When it wasn't hauling animals or the food for them, it was carrying bricks, sand, cement, timber, or glass. I became an expert at loading it and tying red flags on the end of protruding loads.

I always tried to think of interesting names for the livestock, though we never named the ones we were going to eat. However, we did sometimes eat the ones we had named: Gilbert the goose was a classic example. We had three to rear and Gilbert was the biggest so he had been earmarked by the landlord of the pub in the village. Come the killing day, Gilbert was of huge proportions and too big for their needs so we had to eat him / her ourselves. And very nice too.

The ducks were called José, Dorita, and José's Friend, but the chickens were too numerous to name. Sometimes the hens would escape into the field and no eggs were available for us. But Tarka invariably came to the rescue, as her Pointer instincts kicked in, and she would root them out and stand there with her tail quivering, one foot raised, so that we could go and collect the crop.

The cats are many, and often forgettable with a couple of exceptions. Pushkin, an adopticat was afraid of nothing: not man, nor Great Dane, nor No. 43 bus, a fact which no doubt led to his sudden end. He had an astonishing capacity for despatching the local wildlife. On one occasion, Brad saw him carrying something in his mouth up onto the roof of the single-storey kitchen. Fifteen minutes later, he was sure that he had seen the same thing. In the next hour, when Brad thought he was seeing things when Pushkin appeared to repeat the mission a further three times, Brad went up to the roof to find out what had been going on, he found five dead young rabbits, all lined up in the gutter!

Mother, another stray cat who graced us with six kittens not long after moving in, hence her somewhat unusual name, was a long-stayer who had to be put to sleep or suffer surgery and worse. We kept one of her kittens and he was a real star who would help himself to poppy and sesame seed biscuits out of our mouths, but he soon went missing too.

It remains the dogs that are the real heartbreakers when they go. Each time we swear we can't go through it again but we always do! One of the most enduring was Ambrose, a feisty Jack Russell who lived to a great age, and who finally succumbed to a series of strokes over a couple of days at the age of thirteen. During his lifetime we had acquired another Dane. Cass was a brindle and very handsome. He was very much a part my eldest grandson's childhood, and was as good-naturedly clumsy as all Danes. Robin, then only two years old, would walk in and cover his face to protect himself from Cass's wagging tail. He was once knocked flying, simply because the dog had turned round and bumped against him. Cass stood about 36 inches to the shoulder and on one occasion, as he walked past the high directors' chair on which Robin was standing, the child launched himself on to Cass's back. Fortunately, I was close by and able to come to the rescue before the dog swung round to see what was slowing him down, and unseated his rider.

Maybe our greatest love, in the dog world was Dexter, a tiny red Cocker spaniel, who had survived flooding at his breeder's kennels in the winter that we bought him. He was pathetically small and we hardly dare leave him alone, so David or I took him to work with us so that we could feed him at four-hourly intervals. He was our baby and our love. One Saturday when he was about six, Robin and I took his family Labrador and Dex for a country walk across the fields. Suddenly, Dex was gone and I saw some steps a little way ahead. "What's up there?" I asked.

"It's the bypass", was the reply and the rest is silence. We were totally destroyed by his death, and vowed that we could not cope with this sort of loss again, but the house was so still and we found it difficult to talk. After thirteen days, I bought a Hull Daily Mail and turned straight to the pets column. Someone wanted to re-home a nine-month old black Cocker, and I phoned as soon as I got home. Two hours later, Winston came to live with us and saved our sanity. A year later, Disraeli joined him and nearly sent us back to the madhouse. All dogs are a huge responsibility, they are a tie, an expense, a hazard to one's life and limb, and they make untold mess and dirt. They are always there and no matter how much you curse them and shout at their mis-doings, they unfailingly come sidling back if there is the smallest chance of gaining your attention and affection. I could never willingly be without a dog, and as I write tears stream down my face for Dex.

The other day, I went to the car park at Beverley Leisure Centre and encountered a lady walking three great Danes. That's what I want for Christmas, please, Santa.

CHAPTER 17
AROUND THE WORLD

Once more, if adventure and travel is not your bag, you could skip this one. However, in many cases, it is the people one meets, and their peculiarities, that make the trips memorable rather than the scenery. Let's face it, we can read about places in conventional travel books. To a major extent, this is about me and where I have been and if you are not interested, how come you are reading this?

The very first time my feet left my island home was for a very brief trip. In 1938 I went to Yeadon Airport with my parents and took a short flight in a tiny yellow aeroplane. I think that the cost was five shillings each, but I went free-of-charge. We were not in the air long enough for me to throw up, an accomplishment which I had down to a fine art on car journeys but, in fact, I never have done so on an aeroplane. However, there was an occasion, during my pregnancy with Dani, when I had to thrust the infant Brad into the arms of the stewardess and bolt for the heads, since upchucking seemed imminent.

The unpleasantness known as The Second World War seriously interfered with any possibility of foreign travel for several years, though it never had been a part of working-class life. After the hostilities had ended, there were two possible holiday destinations outside these shores. Switzerland had been a neutral country, and this became a favoured destination for those who could afford it. The Channel Islands had been occupied by the savage hordes but the tiny islands were still British and the weather, influenced as it is by the Gulf Stream, was usually better than on the mainland.

It was to Jersey that my father and I flew in 1948 for two weeks in the sun. When we arrived at the fairly modest hotel, the manageress greeted us as Mr and Mrs Taylor, naturally, since we had booked a twin room. Johnnie disenchanted her by saying that I was not his wife, and her jaw dropped immediately. She soon engineered the said mandible back into place, as her adult guest added that I was his daughter. It was a mistake that was frequently made, since he looked ten years younger than his actual age, and I looked several years older than mine.

Jersey became a favourite holiday destination over the years, not just for me but also for my mother and Reg, until foreign travel became commonplace. Nowadays, it is cheaper to go somewhere more exotic, and the Channel Isles have become a luxury. The stories of my adventures on a motorbike have already been chronicled, and the experience was quite extraordinary for the period. Apart from the trip to Jersey with Johnnie in 1948, this had been my first experience of 'abroad'.

I went on holiday to Jersey and to Majorca all on my own, because Jimmy could never save a cent and so holidays together were out of the question. This was before the days of package deals and on the trip to the Balearics, I stayed en-pension with some very nice fellow guests. I also had a brief but passionate foreign 'affaire' with the son of the Palma Chief of Police, and finally saw the Caves of Drach, about which I had been informed while listening to a long ago radio programme. Years later, Spain became the cheapest place to go although Jimmy and I had discovered it long before the gold rush.

We had managed to have some holidays during the middle years of our marriage. When I only had Russell to worry about, I went off to Bridlington with a friend of Jimmy's. That is to say in his care. He was a sales representative and transported Russell and me to Bridlington, booked me into the commercial hotel he used when he was in that part of the country, and we met up at night for a drink in the bar. I expect my husband found some way of entertaining himself in my absence. In general, there was little money to spare for holidays.

Every year until Dani was born, we used to go to the Motor Show in London, leaving the boys in the care of Jimmy's mother. I went down to Maidstone to stay with my own mother for a week occasionally, on the train with a two-year old and a baby in a carrycot. One particular time, we travelled first class due to the crowded nature of the train and the other occupant of the compartment was a gentleman hiding from us behind The Times. I was pregnant, so Russell sidled up to the man and confided, "My Mummy has a baby in her tummy". This revelation did not impress the reluctant recipient of the information. Shortly after, the train shunted in preparation for take off and made that strange noise, possibly only known to those who have travelled by steam, and sounding like poorly-controlled flatulence. With a look of delight, Russell turned to me and said "Ooh Mummy, you just burped through your bottom." There was a quiet snigger from the depths of The Times.

Eventually, we had a real holiday, just the two of us, leaving the entire savage horde at home in the care of two, far too young, nannies, who I later discovered had been entertaining the male population of Wetherby and district in our absence. We had a variety of household helps, largely as a result of me having being incapacitated with a slipped disc, and therefore prevented from carrying out my housewifely duties.

However, these nannies did allow us to go on holiday without the children. Our first trip was to Spain which we discovered long before the gold-rush, when we drove all the way from Leeds in an elegant white Jaguar of the day, a mark 8, registration TKU 7. We made an overnight stop in Maidstone and the following day crossed the channel to Calais or Boulogne, where we boarded the train, car and all. We sped through the night to Lyons, occupying a first-class sleeper en-route. That in itself was rather splendid: a small private compartment equipped with tiny but adequate private facilities, and breakfast served before our arrival at our disembarkation point.

Finally, we unloaded the car from the train and set off on our southward journey making an overnight stop at a tiny French harbour on the Mediterranean coast, by the name of Port Bou. The next morning our travels were resumed and, passing Tossa and

Lloret de Mar, we settled on one of Derek's suggested hotels, The Reina Elisenda, at San Felieu de Gulxols and rested our heads there. This one cost two pounds a night, including dinner and breakfast, and was very upmarket. Of course all the hotels Derek stayed in were: he generally left without going through the formality of paying the bill. There was an in-house hairdresser's salon, which I visited, and one of the hairdressers was leaving in order to join his aunt who ran a small hotel south of Barcelona at Castelldefells. "See you there" I promised.

A couple of days later we reached Barcelona and, after failing find a room at The Avenida Palace, again recommended by our old friend Derek, we managed to get a room at The Ritz. Did I say a room? The concierge at The Avenida had effected the reservation on our behalf, assuming that we were loaded with cash. Within fifteen minutes, we found ourselves in a suite of enormous proportions, which included a sitting room and a bathroom big enough to hold twenty people. It had two of everything, plus a Roman bath with steps going down into it, and big enough for a family of four to bathe together. It was totally spectacular, as was the bill, which I still have in my possession, but in those days one could buy much more with one's money. The total, with breakfast, was 1,750 pesetas, equivalent to about £10 in English money. Then, not now.

Fortunately we did not dine in the hotel but went downtown. In those days, the system of paying the bar bill on departure was the norm in bars, and we inadvertently left one such establishment without settling the bill. Ten minutes later, we remembered our omission and returned to square up, to be met with smiles all round. Imagine that happening now. On our return to the hotel, we sat down for a nightcap in the lounge and after a few moments, Jimmy wriggled in his chair and thrust his hand down the side of his seat, bringing it out clutching a wallet stuffed with dollars. In an unguarded moment of reflex honesty, he called a passing waiter and handed over the booty. I repeat, imagine that happening now.

The next morning we checked out, having spent a restless night listening to the traffic and, later on in the day, we went to the bullfight. From there, we travelled to the establishment run by the aunt of my coiffeur in San Felieu, both English, to find the latter sitting outside nursing a Sangria. We stayed a week there in Castelldefels for the princely sum of £1.00 a night half-board, and met some lunatic London boys and a few Spanish film stars. One of the boys, Tony, was a real joker and one day he came on to the beach wearing his swimming trunks and a bowler hat, carrying a briefcase. He approached a couple sitting close to us and introduced himself to them thus, "Good Morning. Thank you for travelling with us. I am Jock Strapp, from Strapp Tours and I've just come to see if you are enjoying your holiday". After some moments of protestation from the pair, he left and moved on to another unsuspecting couple. When we finally left, we had an extra passenger, the young hairdresser, who we eventually dropped off in Dover.

We met up with the boys again when we made our annual visit to the Motor Show and had a night out with them in London. They took us to a club, The Establishment, where we saw some unheard-of performers who later became famous: namely Peter Cook, Dudley Moore, Jonathan Miller, and Alan Bennett. The trip to Spain was repeated the following year accompanied by the children and portable nanny, the daughter of a friend. Heading for the south coast and the Newhaven ferry, it soon became obvious that keeping three children entertained was going to present a challenge. Just before a we reached Doncaster, Dani started asking "Are we nearly there?" These days, Castelldefels is a thriving resort, and many of the small places we visited at that time, where there was little but a beach bar, are now completely built-up.

As we became more affluent and more adventurous, a cruise in First Class on the P&O boat Orcades was quite an experience. Our cabin was just big enough to get dressed in, one at a time, and there were no en-suite bathrooms. If a bath was required, the cabin steward ran the water and cleaned up afterwards. However, one dressed for dinner and waiters were always at one's elbow, two to a table. If someone took out a cigarette, the waiter was there with a lighter. On this trip, we were scheduled to make a stop in Malta, and the Chief Barman asked us if we could do him a favour. He asked us to visit Saccone and Speed, a wine and spirits wholesaler in Valletta and order a case each of gin, whisky, and brandy to be delivered to us on the boat.

Jimmy happily agreed, and the goods duly arrived before we sailed. The barman was clearly all set to make a substantial profit. We paid twelve shillings a litre for the gin, as I remember - that is 60p in today's money. At the time, gin was around two pounds a bottle in England and the total duty-free allowance was half a bottle per person. The Master at Arms came to pay us a visit to remind us about this, and we just managed to squeeze him into our diminutive accommodation. In his West Yorkshire accent, my husband explained: "Don't worry about it, son, we are having a party in the cabin". Shortly after, a steward came with some sack wheels and removed the offending booze and we got a bottle of Scotch for our trouble.

The following year we did a one-class trip on The Mauritania, on which I became friendly with the world famous entertainer and harmonica virtuoso, Larry Adler. He gave me a piece of invaluable advice, to be myself and to follow my own star rather than being what other people expected of me. I am still trying to do just that. Unfortunately, if I dig my heels in because I do not want to do what has been proposed, my offspring tell me that I am getting difficult in my old age. I presume they mean that I am doing what I want to do rather than what they think I should want to do.

Our last holiday together was after the divorce. We took the children on a very cheap Mediterranean cruise, and gained the reputation of being a sublimely happily-married couple. It was easy: if Jimmy objected to something or complained in any way, my response was to tell him to get off my case, since he was not married to me.

Just before I was due to start my academic career, I had decided to take the children on holiday, and we prepared for a great adventure. The plan was to drive through France to the Basque coast of Spain and camp wherever we landed. I had bought a two-man pup tent from a policeman friend that we had all got to know when the neighbours called the law out to the parties, and two sleeping bags were purchased. We packed large amounts of tinned goods, a small amount of clothes, a borrowed tent as a spare and, with a confidence only known to the ignorant, we set off. My car was an elderly Riley 4/72 with real leather seats, and a real tin exhaust pipe which fell off a few miles after I caught it on the ramp when driving off the ferry. Russell was almost thirteen and totally incompetent, Brad was eleven and organised the tent in double-quick time, and Dani was nine and wanted chips making with powdered potato. The second tent proved to be useless, and Brad spent four weeks sleeping in the car next to the tent.

One night, after going to Guernica and to the caves at Santamaminé, we were returning to where we had been staying west of San Sebastian, when we were caught in a frightful storm. I could not see to drive so we pulled off the road on the way down a mountain. I got the Russell and Dani plastered on red wine and bread so that they would sleep without complaining, and we all spent the night in the car. We were relieved to arrive back at our base camp and stayed there until we were due to set off for home.

When we were a hundred miles or so into our return journey, the car sprung a leak on the top hose. We went to a garage in Bordeaux where they fitted a replacement, but I think that the mechanic had experienced a slip of the screwdriver because a few miles further on the problem started again. I stopped a charming German couple in a Mercedes to ask if they knew of a BMC dealer in the area and they guided us to a huge main dealership out by the airport. This was closed, naturally, because it was Saturday teatime. I was at my wit's end, with three children in the car, nowhere to sleep, and the car reluctant to go any further.

The caretaker lived in a bungalow at the front of the showroom and assured me that first thing Monday morning all would be well. I turned to his wife and asked if she knew anywhere we could camp for a couple of nights, within a mile or so. "Madame, vous pouvez camper içi", she said. I immediately wept in gratitude, and they helped us to make our camp at the end of their garden. Dani and Russell were taken to sleep in the house, and Brad and I stayed in the tent. There was a night watchman on duty in the showroom, and he unlocked the doors when we needed to use the ablutions in the executive suite. It was bliss, hot water, and real toilets.

The following day, the couple went to visit their daughter and we rested, did the washing, ate fresh tomatoes from the garden and, when they came home, we had hot chocolate in their sitting room. The next day, the car was fixed by noon and we set off once more. Our last night was spent in sleeping bags on the beach at Calais, and the following day we arrived back in Maidstone, still with money left out of the hundred pounds I had taken with me. After a few days with my mother to recover, we went home to East Keswick, the children to their respective schools and me to work my notice at the library.

My most memorable holiday has to be the one on which I met my lovely David, but that has been documented elsewhere as have our American adventures. However, we did have a rather unusual vacation in Sicily, immediately before my final exams for the Diploma in Speech Pathology. As mentioned elsewhere, it seemed sensible to have a real rest before the final push to graduate, so we booked a very cheap holiday indeed. Maybe it was so priced because the hotel was not finished when we arrived. Des and Sue from the Poly joined us on that trip. Yes, the same Des who had played a large part in designing the layout of our future home.

On the first evening, David and I set off on a recconnaissance trip to locate the nearest booze shop, which we found about half a mile up a fairly deserted road. It was a café-cum-bar with some outside seats, but hardly up-market. We went inside and started to look round the well-stocked shelves. No sooner had we pointed at a bottle that caught our attention than the owner, Vitor, pulled out a collapsible card table and two chairs. Within half a minute, we each had a glass of amber liquid in a tumbler placed in front of us. Vitor spoke no English. We spoke no Italian and no Sicilian. So we smiled and resolved to purchase a bottle of local plonk and beat a rapid retreat. The road to hell is paved with good intentions.

The first mistake was made when I innocently pointed to the shelves of booze. Like a greyhound out of the slips, Vitor was on his feet and asking "Biquieri?". Since I failed to understand, I assumed that this was the name of the golden nectar. I smiled approvingly; after all, in this country you could get your throat cut for disagreeing. Like a shot, our host was pouring again and too late, I appreciated that what he had been asking was "Would you care for a beakerful?".

One of the locals had entered the bar by this time and stood looking at us with benevolence, I hoped. We smiled. Within minutes several more locals joined our audience. Everyone smiled and nodded. I said to David "We can't beat this mob, we'd better see if we can join them". With a limited amount of common language, fraternisation is possible, if difficult, but with no Italian other than "macaroni", "spaghetti" and "Honi Soit Qui Mal Y Pense", the task seemed insurmountable.

I took the initiative, and pointed to myself and stated my name, and then did a repeat performance of the pantomime indicating David. It was a little like 'Open Sesame' or 'Abracadabra.' The entire company drew up chairs and introduced themselves. More large beakers of wine arrived, along with the village Customs Officer, and the policeman, both wearing guns. Somehow, with a blend of French and Spanish added to signs, gestures and a little intuition we got along. Then the star of the show entered.

Big Frank was tall, elegant and a smooth operator. He thought. He wore a brown' well-tailored suit, polished shoes, and a fawn gabardine coat with epaulettes, draped Sinatra-style around his shoulders. He came over to shake hands with us and announced "I no speaka da English. I only speaka da American". We said, that was fine, and that we could speaka da American too. At least we now had a translator.

Eventually we said we must go and asked for the bill with some trepidation. A good deal of vino had been consumed but, apparently, someone else must have paid because our account came to less than two drinks at home. We left, much the worse for zibibo, and set out to walk back to the hotel. Reeling down the road and laughing like drains, we were somewhat surprised when a battered estate car screamed to a halt just ahead of us. The driver called to us from the window of the vehicle. "Saracen Sands?" he asked. This was the name of our hotel.

"Si, si", I replied, and he threw open the door of his jalopy. Like idiots, we got in and he took off at an alarming pace. It was at that juncture that I recalled that only two weeks earlier, a young British couple had been abducted in Sicily, the girl raped, and the man beaten up.

The hotel was situated at the bottom of the road down which we were walking and immediately past the hotel there was a T-junction. If you failed to turn either left or right or stop, you would require an amphibious vehicle because there was only sand and sea ahead. Our driver seemed disinclined to carry out any of these manoeuvres, and I was convinced that abduction was a distinct possibility. As we drew level with the entrance to the hotel, Juan Fangio stepped on the brakes, did a wheelie-turn and, much to our relief, came to a halt in front of the main entrance to the hotel. Weakly, we climbed out. A tall, suited, man appeared and spoke to the driver in Italian. A few words were exchanged. Then, in frightfully upper-crust English, we were asked, "I say, were you lorst? He thought you were lorst and brought you home". Lost? We thought we were goners.

We never walked back from Vitor's bar. Either we went back by police car driven by a very inebriated Sergio, or one of the other regulars would stop and give us a lift. One night, having washed my hair and covered my pin curls with a wig before leaving the hotel, we were staggering back for dinner along the tree-lined path, when a low-flying branch plucked off my coiffure and Dino screamed to a halt simultaneously. He was momentarily horrified; he thought I had been beheaded.

Frank came to our hotel for a drink one night, and became enamoured of a very pretty peaches-and-cream English girl, who was on holiday with her boyfriend, the son of a Conservative MP. The Sicilian was desperate for us to fix up a date and arranged that if we could swing it, he would take us all to Palermo. His father-in-law had a ceramics shop in the village and we bumped into Frank there. Nobody spoke English. They did not even "speaka da American", so Frank could speak freely about his plans for a night on the town with Patricia in Palermo. We stood around in the shop drinking local brandy brought in on a tray, in glasses of course. "I see you tonight, you fix it with Patricia. We go to Palermo. Don't tell my vife.", he said while we all smiled, including his 'vife'.

The date never came off. We had advised the lady in question to make herself scarce and fortunately we did not incur Frank's wrath. He and his father-in-law were Mafiosi, the pottery shop was a sideline, and Papa owned the brickworks nearby. Frank owned a furniture shop of considerable size, and aspired to include David in the business somehow. The locals and their hospitality made this a truly memorable holiday.

The unfinished aspect of the hotel involved the presence of innumerable workmen, some of whom were chiselling floor tiles off the terrace immediately over our room. Work commenced at seven a.m. This did not impress us so, after a day or two, I started complaining by telephone to reception. This turned out to be a fruitless exercise but suddenly all went quiet, due, I discovered, to the fact that it was Easter Italian style. After the festivities, the noise resumed so I left a note at Reception and went to bed. The following morning the silence was golden but when we arrived for breakfast everyone was asking, "Who is in room 234?". We were, and that is how I had signed the note, which said: "When the man comes on to the roof tomorrow morning to commence chiselling off the tiles, I shall not complain to the management. I shall personally go up there and throw him off the said roof. Is this perfectly clear? Room 234." It transpired that the manager himself had been awaiting the worker's arrival and moved him on to another job.

This was our honeymoon; it seemed to go well so we thought we'd get married after our return.

France became our favourite destination because of the ease of getting there and the convenience of packing the cases and not having to wonder if they would arrive at the same time and in the same country as their owners. The visits have been too numerous to remember, but have included many very brief visits, solely for filling the petrol tank of the car with cheap diesel fuel, and the car's interior with cheap French wine. On one occasion we even removed the rear seat so that the weight saved would make room for another two bottles.

We toured the chateaux of the Loire, the battlefields of World War One, and the D Day landing beaches, and always found splendid chambres d'hôtes which we re-visited time and again. On many of these trips we were accompanied by Robin, who apparently never tires of art galleries, museums and old ruins. We have made many expeditions to Normandy and visited every WW2 museum, and several vast cemeteries. Of these, the one that is guaranteed to reduce me to tears is the small one for the Americans who fell in Brittany, situated at St James. We found a wonderful chambre d'hôte in the farming country near Sartilly, run by a delightful couple with whom we made friends. André and I conversed in a mixture of languages and then translated for our respective spouses, but sadly after many happy visits, they have now retired and moved.

On the other side of the country, our favourite pied à terre has to be a little house in the Valley of the Somme, decorated on the outside with huge brightly-coloured metal butterflies. On first sight I thought that they were gross but, over the years, they grew on me and I now have similar ones on our front wall at home. When we left this particular residence at the finish of the first holiday there, I said, "Well, we won't be coming back here again." Never say never; we have already been four times. The last one was when we took Reg with us to try to locate the memorials to his two uncles who had been killed during the final months of the conflict. Seeing all those graves and reading the huge memorials is a deeply moving experience.

There is another place about which I have said those same derogatory words, and which became a favourite for us. Calella de Palafrugell is a small resort a few miles down the road from Tossa de Mar, and it is high on my list of places to see again before my end is nigh, although we have already been there five times. It is largely undiscovered by the British holidaymaker, mainly because there is no high-rise development, and little in the way of commercial entertainment. There is but one disco, and only a few hotels. We have driven all the way on the last three occasions, taking two or three days to make the trip. The last time we made no prior booking, relying on the local letting agency having somewhere suitable when we arrived. I hope that when we finally return, we do not find that commerce has taken over.

The big break came when a patient of mine died and made a bequest to me in his will. A thousand pounds seemed a huge amount of money and although I had promised myself a facelift, in the event, we decided to embark on a great adventure and go to Russia. It was in the heyday of Glasnost and foreign money was Tsar. We flew from London to St. Petersburg where, after a harrowing time getting through the Customs and Security process, we boarded a coach that had seen much better days. The brown plastic upholstery was ripped, and the windscreen broken, but since we had not expected luxury, we were undismayed. It was a little unnerving when the coach driver was unable to find the vessel which was to take us down the river to Moscow, but finally it was located and we boarded.

This was not a cruise liner. The sheets were patched and the towels threadbare. The curtains covering the huge window were made of cheap and nasty nylon, and the bathroom was nothing if not primitive. Any attempt to describe this particular facility requires a great feat of imagination on the part of the reader, but I will give it a shot.

The entire structure was made of plastic and came as a package; they must have been manufactured in bulk and then slotted in wherever needed. The problem was that conversation from any of the body's orifices was clearly audible to the passengers in the adjoining cabin, and when our neighbours were using their smallest room, the light from next door illuminated our bathroom as well. These compartments measured around four feet in each direction and housed a toilet across from a sink. We discovered that a rather rubbery, orange, curtain drew across the toilet and screened it from the remaining area when one took a shower. The shower-head was taken from its resting-place in the basin and hooked up to the wall, and the entire compartment then served as a shower cabinet. There was no plug for the basin, so a piece of tinfoil pressed into the space where it should have been held the water long enough to rinse out knickers and socks.

Which reminds me! A week or two past, I read in the travel section of The Telegraph on Saturday, an article by one of their correspondents which dealt with the tiresome business of keeping a fresh and constant supply of clothing destined for one's nether regions. With great excitement she related that her problem was now solved since, she had discovered disposable knickers at Mothercare. Does her husband or other male companion have to languish in the same pair for a fortnight? Perhaps he uses some of hers. All I pack for a two-week holiday is three pairs each because I discovered, long before disposable pants or Travelwash, that shampoo, shower gel or common soap was perfectly adequate for the piffling job of freshening scanties. When washed and well wrung-out, the items should then be laid out on a towel, rolled up, and stamped upon. It works well enough for us and the cost is negligible. I have to say that the sight of holidaymakers hauling enormous suitcases to the check-in irritates me. The older the passenger, the larger the luggage looms. It amazes me that the elderly owners do not have a heart attack before they have been allocated a seat number.

However, back in the USSR, the food was almost inedible except for the bread, and the worst thing of all was the slices of salted cold rice pudding served at breakfast on several occasions. St Petersburg has a three-month growing season and fresh vegetables are not available unless grown in a greenhouse. There are tomatoes, cucumbers, potatoes, cabbage, and beetroot.

Both here and in Moscow, children ran ahead of us from one historic site to another, begging for dollars and speaking excellent English in order to do so. There are spectacularly flamboyant old buildings in both cities and the Kremlin itself is among these, while St Basil's Cathedral is like an illustration from a book of fairy stories, made of barley sugar and Blackpool rock. Every morning, straight after breakfast, we were herded on to a coach and taken to places of interest, then back to the boat for lunch and off again within an hour. Occasionally we would arrive back at the dock to find no trace of our boat. Had we been abandoned? Finally we would locate it two boat-widths away, necessitating boarding and crossing the first two in order to reach ours.

On one such occasion, in desperate need of the toilet, I rushed ahead and requested our key, going post-haste to the cabin and relieving myself. In the bathroom, naturally, but on coming out of this smallest of small rooms, I realised that this was not our cabin. It was not even our boat. Fortunately the rightful occupants were not in residence at the time, so I returned the key and took off before I was arrested and sent to the Gulag.

The following year, we repeated the experience of river-cruising and went from Kiev to the Black Sea on a similar, but marginally more comfortable, vessel with catering done by a Swiss hotel management company which was a definite improvement. On our first evening, still moored in Kiev, I could feel movement and my bunk appeared to be going up and down as though we were sailing. I thought no more of it but the following day, I had the same experience and finally discovered the cause. My narrow cot was hinged to the wall so that it could be lifted during the day to make more space, and apparently the same applied to the adjoining cabin. A portly gentleman, that I had already nicknamed Carlton-Browne of the Foreign Office, occupied this one. When he sat down, my bed went up and when he stood up, mine went down. I was sleeping closer to him than to David.

The girls in Yalta were amazingly gorgeous, parading in short flimsy dresses with their hair done up in chiffon scarves, and our courier told us that, because they had little in their lives that was luxurious, they always went out and presented the best that they had to the world.

In Odessa, we went to the Opera House, a relic of 19th century decadence on a small scale. There we watched an all-male ballet company dancing Giselle, among other more modern ballets. The tallest men danced the female roles, en pointe and wearing tutus: it was amazing and never to be forgotten.

The joy of river-cruising is that, in the absence of any entertainment, one can sit in the cabin watching the banks going past, the locals standing watching and waving. When passing through the locks, they would pass food parcels and clean clothes to crew members who were obviously part of the family.

When Robin was fifteen, we took him ostensibly free-of-charge on a cruise to Norway, and into the Arctic Circle where we witnessed the phenomena of sun at midnight. It was a horrendously rough crossing both ways, and I was not enamoured with Page and Moy's administration department so this was another occasion when I have said "Never again". However, like childbirth, one soon forgets the pain and we subsequently travelled with them again several times.

We usually pay for the cheapest available cabin, even if it is practically in steerage. I never see the point of paying for a superior cabin just for the privilege of having a window. There is nothing to see except the sea or the dockside. The service, food, and entertainment are the same and the ports-of-call are identical. The cheapskates like me still get escorted ashore in a launch and do not have to swim for it.

Of these cruises, probably our favourite trip was around the coast of Italy during which we shared a table with a very pleasant couple from Sussex with whom we are still in contact circa 2004. On one trip on The Ocean Majesty, we were invited to dine with the Captain on his Welcome Night. It was rather splendid getting the star treatment and all the free booze. Two years later, on the same boat, the Captain of the lugger was again our old friend Christos Karabagias, who had entertained us so royally the previous year. I bumped into him a couple of hours before the Captain's Welcome Dinner on the second night out, and reminded him that we had had the pleasure of dining at his table on the previous occasion. Nudge, nudge. "What's your cabin number?" he asked.

"J95", I told him.

Later, when we officially shook hands, he spoke to his sidekick in Greek and the latter leaned forward and said to David: "What's your cabin number?". Two nights later we met him again as he was going ashore in St. Petersburg and exchanged some pleasantries. "What's your cabin number?" he asked, so, barely suppressing my laughter, I asked if he was going to drop in for a drink. Sure enough, on the penultimate evening, an invitation to dine at his table for the farewell dinner came through the door, so we wined at his or Page and Moy's expense once more. On this holiday we seemed to find a great number of rather odd characters and these are more entertaining in retrospect than some of the ports-of-call.

In the reception lounge of the Harwich Port Authority, I first espied Mrs Gummidge. This is not her real name, you understand. She was wearing an aged plaid wool suit over a sweater, the sleeves of which hung well below the sleeves of the jacket To accessorise with this she wore long apricot-tinted socks sliding lower with every step to meet her large brown men's loafers. Her facial features were interestingly different, the eyes pale and watery and the lower jaw micrognathic. Her bottom teeth sloped backwards at an extremely sharp angle and the upper set were hell-bent in pursuing an entirely different direction. Her wardrobe was certainly interesting. Another outfit consisted of a mid-calf-length Harris Tweed skirt, which had obviously survived many revolutions in the washing machine. All of her clothes including several long, long-sleeved cardigans, were resisting any attempt to iron them.

The wearer was of exceptional height, maybe approaching six feet. For her appearance in the passenger talent show choir, she wore a sweatshirt, grey jogging pants tight at the ankle, and a black skirt. On the last morning, while waiting to disembark, she came to sit nearby and engaged me in conversation. She used to teach English and Scripture at Leeds Girls High School donkeys years ago, but suffered with mental illness and has been an in-patient in many psychiatric hospitals in one of which she met her husband. She had left him at home because he was suddenly called to have an operation for glaucoma. She neither knew nor seemed to care who was looking after him. At the last minute, she asked for my address. What could I say? Somehow, "No, sorry, I already have a list of border-line nutcases to write to, of my own choosing, without adding any more" didn't seem appropriate, so I handed it over. I am yet to receive a letter, so fingers crossed it may never happen.

We also had The Bag Lady, who had long grey hair swept up into a ponytail, but with long clumps at the front which were intentionally free. She always wore an anorak and smoked incessantly, sitting on deck in the same corner. The most colourful character on the style-front was the Rhinestone Cowboy, a mannish lady of indeterminate years somewhere between fifty and seventy, at a guess, travelling with two female companions. She had very short butch hair, enormous false eyelashes, and a selection of sequinned and spangled jogging suits to suit every occasion. However she made a concession for the Captain's Welcome and Farewell Dinners, and wore amazing floaty chiffon creations that prompted me to wonder if it was a fellow in drag. All her outfits were supplemented with baubles bangles and beads of every type.

Usually, by the time we finish dinner at night it is ten o clock, and we are seldom long out of bed. On the last cruise we did before writing this, we had noisy neighbours on all sides who seemed not to realise that their conversations and flatulence were clearly audible through the thin cabin walls. The one's at our back clearly had a problem remembering where they had put anything, and used to open every drawer in a frantic search, slamming each one hard enough to make our wall shake. Eventually, we join in and start speaking loudly in an attempt to demonstrate the thinness of the walls.

It is nice to be recognised by the crew and dining room staff, and on the Ocean Majesty we have had the same table on all three voyages. Sitting at a large table is a chancy business; your fellow travellers could all be ghastly. On the other hand if you sit at a table for four and they are awful, you have nowhere else to turn. Fortunately, the only time we have risked this, on the Princess Danae, our companions were splendid, and we are still in touch.

We eventually decided that our financial status would allow us to venture further afield and we booked a holiday in Sri Lanka, which entailed a tour followed by a week at the beach. The hotels on tour were stupendous and the guide extremely erudite and informative. The local people were charming and friendly. Unfortunately, I inadvertently threw away David's return air ticket and we had to pay again. £617 for a single. God Bless Visa. We eventually got the money back from the holiday insurance.

Our next long-haul was to South Africa travelling under the wing of the Saga organisation. We flew from Leeds / Bradford Airport to Cape Town, via Amsterdam, in April 2003. It was a long flight, but it was overnight and within the same time zone.

KLM managed to leave our luggage in Amsterdam, but at least they knew where it was and let us know before we went through the nerve-racking wait at the carousel. They gave us two really super toiletries bags containing T-shirts, socks and tights, as well as all the usual stuff. Not needed in fact, since I always carry such items in my hand luggage. I've always been convinced that my bags would fail to arrive one day, so maybe now I can relax and hope that lightning will not strike twice in my suitcases. Unfortunately I can't use the toilet bags for Christmas presents because the zips have KLM on them!

I can certainly recommend Saga for everything except the preponderance of geriatrics on the cast list, although, chronologically at least, I must include myself among their number. The hotel was unostentatious and comfortable, the staff pleasant, and the natives friendly. The big problem was the food, which was varied, plentiful, and impossible to resist. The bar was open, free-of-charge, from 11:00 a.m. until 11:00 p.m. and there was entertainment of various kinds on many evenings. One of the performers was Gerry and his Pacemaker, an ageing gentleman of dark complexion who crooned and played the keyboard, and very good he was too. The first time he came, he played Let's Twist Again, and numerous old folks leapt to their feet and gave it big licks, including yours truly. After the evening was over, when he was packing his bags for home, I asked why he did not play more upbeat music since it brought a favourable response. Gerry replied that he had suffered a heart attack a couple of years back and playing fast music raised his blood pressure. Hence he got his nickname.

On another spectacular night, we were graced by a demonstration of Ballroom Dancing by two young local couples. The boys were black from head to toe except for their wing collars and white bow ties, and the girls possibly of Asian extraction and stunningly lovely, and all as talented as they were charming. After the show they came to dance with the audience, which was super for me having been a professional ballroom teacher. We had a demonstration of reflexology, a talk on diamonds, a craft fair, and other jolly entertainment. The most memorable was a group of elderly ladies who, all dressed in pink, sang and played songs which were popular in the 1930s and 1940s. If there was a dry eye in the room, it certainly was not mine. Unfortunately, on the other nights there was nothing to do after nine o'clock at night, and it was a pity to forgo all that free booze, so we spent a lot of time trying to make conversation with the bar staff. This was somewhat limited, since the TV in the bar was permanently on, featuring nothing except local soaps of execrable standard which were avidly watched by the said bartenders, and since we were the only smokers, we had to stay in the bar or go to bed.

There was yet another Fred and Ginger on the guest list, unmarried and occupying separate rooms. He was totally unintelligible, and she had not changed her hairstyle since 1950, but at every opportunity they leaped on to the dance-floor. He had even brought his patent leather dance shoes with him for this very activity.

We met a couple who were doing an extended trip, having already visited the eastern Cape. She was a former hairdresser and her lively and erudite companion was an eighty-two year old accountant. The lady was fifty-nine, her companion was eighty-two. They also had separate rooms. However she did tell us that there was a smokers' lounge at Cape Town airport, and we located it on the return journey. It was absolutely sumptuous, with Internet facilities, a coffee bar, big settees, and chess sets and other games laid out. It was certainly an improvement on the non-smoking facilities. At Johannesburg, a clerical gentleman boarded and duly took his seat. We saw him again at Schiphol; he approached us as we were standing at a small, high, round table provided for smokers.

"I'm going to be wicked", he said.

"You're going to have a cigarette", I replied. It's a long period of deprivation. I asked him why he wore his crucifix in his breast pocket and he said it was because he was a Bishop. He was half Jewish and called David and was at the time the Roman Catholic Bishop of Liverpool, which brings my score of bishops with whom I have been on first name terms to three. Amazing for an old atheist like me.

At the present time, I am grateful that the funds are finally available to do the travelling that we have long wanted to do, and I have no further responsibilities as far as my elderly relations are concerned. I now only have the dogs!

This year, 2004, we have yet to do our cruise thing. We are to explore The Red Sea and Cairo; hopefully our captain will invite us to dine with him yet again. We have a very exclusive cruise down the Adriatic coast of the former Yugoslavia, planned for next April and still want to go to China and Japan. I feel strongly that these long haul trips need to be taken before some physical incapacity hits us. Being fit and healthy today does not mean that I will be the same tomorrow, in spite of my ancestors' track record.

I have learned one invaluable lesson and I was not a fast study in this area. Never, never, go on a coach holiday that involves early morning starts followed by an endless journey to the South Coast for a cross-channel ferry.

CHAPTER 18
WHERE HAVE ALL THE FLOWERS GONE

My father, Johnnie, became widowed after seventeen years of marriage to Connie and came over to Driffield to live near to us. After a couple of years living alone in a flat, he became unable to cope and decided to go into a care home. This was something of a relief to me, as he had been prone to falling and ringing up at very inconvenient times, like five thirty in the morning, to say that he was on the floor and could not get up. I don't know who he would have telephoned if he had still been at Stockport, but maybe I made a mistake in bringing him here. At least he had friends there whereas, after he moved, he never went out, or joined any clubs, or made any new friends. This was odd in a way, because he was quite a gregarious chap and had no trouble striking up a conversation with total strangers, but he seemed content with his own company.

Every Sunday we collected him and he joined us for the day, watched old films on the television, and read the papers, staying the night as long as he was able to get up the stairs. When that became more difficult, we took him home after the evening meal. Later on, this routine was abandoned and Dani used to go round with a Sunday dinner on a plate for him to put in the microwave oven. On one visit, she could not get any reply and resorted to opening the letterbox and shouting. There was a strong smell of burning and smoke poured out. Panic-stricken, she 'phoned us to go with a key and within ten minutes we all burst in, much to Johnnie's astonishment. He had overdone something in the microwave oven and the smell was the result.

His speech had become increasingly unintelligible; the medics attributed this to mild Parkinson's Disease, which was a possibility. For many years I had noted that he walked on a wide base, had a tendency to shuffle, and displayed a marked tremor of his hands, both signs of a cerebeller dysfunction but he remained happy and good-natured. He had a particularly bad fall one night and hit his back on a corner. He pulled his emergency cord and, when the ambulance men arrived, they judged from his speech that he had had a stroke and whipped him into hospital. This was the beginning of the end because he was catheterised and never regained normal bladder function.

When I was planning a trip to Italy with Robin, Johnnie and I viewed a few care homes so that he could be safe while I was away, and he chose one in Driffield. He really enjoyed his week there, and after my return, he decided to move in permanently. He had enjoyed the company and the security and when Dani and I took him a week later, he walked in as though he was going home, never giving us a backward glance. Eventually, he got bored, but before too long he was unable to make any decisions for himself or remember quite simple facts. The flat where he had lived was owned by the trustees of his late wife's will, so all I had to do was get rid of the furniture. The sale of the apartment was not up to me, and this was just as well because prices had dropped and it remained unsold until after his death.

Dani and her family were very good to him and visited him regularly. Shortly after he went in to the residential home, she got a job there, so she saw him on a more regular basis. One day he said to me that he remembered his grandmother, Ma, who lived to be about 97, saying to him: "You can live too long, Johnnie". He too was ready to go. Unfortunately, his body outlasted his mind, and he became increasingly befuddled. One day when I went, he asked if we could hire a car so that we could go and visit his mother. Another time he told me that he could not remember the name of his first wife, my mother, or what had happened to her. He had no recollection of the visits that she and Reg had made to him while he was in the flat. Neither did he remember Connie's name although he had a photograph of her beside his bed. God bless him: he was such a nice man, full of generosity and fun.

One Sunday, a couple of years earlier when he was at our house, I had asked about his funeral and he had said that a cardboard box would be fine, blue if possible. In the event it was white, but draped in a floating dark blue cloth which allowed the white to show through. He was ready to go a year earlier and, if it had been possible, I would have helped him. They shoot horses, don't they?

On December 11th 1998 he quietly died and we cremated him in a cardboard coffin, as arranged. Later in the year, when the weather was better, we took his ashes to Flamborough so that he could join his ancestors and I walked over the rocks and poured them into a pool, to be taken away by the tide.

We talk about him still and remember him with love.

It was odd that both my parents ended up living close to me after being so far away for many years. Reg and Dorothy had moved up to Leeds in 1974, when promotion decreed a change of location. Dorothy had been retired from her job as Registrar of Births, Deaths, and Marriages for several years but, unwilling to do the coffee-morning rounds, had very soon taken on part-time secretarial work, at which she excelled. The move north put an end to this but, before long, she had become a general factotum at her hairdressing salon, unpaid. Reg took early retirement from his job as Superintendent in charge of hiring and firing at the Zurich Insurance office in Leeds when he was 63, and they soon started to look around for a bungalow in the West Riding. Prices were high in the area, but far lower in the east of the county. It seemed like a good idea to have them within easy reach so that if illness or incapacity struck, I was close enough to be with them in less than half an hour.

Over the years, these two had become fairly affluent and, while insisting that it was all Reg's money, Dorothy made a habit of passing me envelopes stuffed with banknotes. Sometimes they would arrive at our house for an unannounced visit and on the way in, she would distract Reg's attention long enough for her to slip what we came to refer to as a 'flying blue envelope' into a convenient drawer. Over the years, hundreds of pounds must have come my way, but there was no way they would countenance any gift that would avoid Inheritance Tax. They never even had a tax-free savings account, until I persuaded Reg to open an ISA after my mother's death.

They had worked hard for their savings, but seemed to have a mental block when it came to long-term planning and practicality. They had a fear of handing anything over to me, because one of their friends had given her house to her children and then, apparently, been unable to have any say in its disposal. I was appalled that they had so little trust in me, but they always treated me as if I was some half-witted child, in spite of the fact that when they needed to borrow fifty thousand pounds to buy another house, I immediately offered the money.

I took it upon myself to go house-hunting on their behalf and came up with two detached bungalows in Beverley, one of which they predictably fell in love with and bought. It was light, spacious, and totally lacking in style or character. It had the most ghastly, garish, carpets imaginable. The worst of these was still there in December 2004. The others were quickly replaced with more loud patterns of their own choosing. They were delighted with Beverley and used to go for jolly drives to Bridlington where they sat in a cliff-top car park eating a sandwich lunch. Thank goodness that they liked it, or it would have been all my fault.

I was free to accompany them on jaunts. We discovered Sequence Dancing, which Reg took very seriously and various venues were found. Dorothy was still quite agile and so he was danced off his feet, partnering us both. When my father came to live here, they started visiting him and taking Red Cross parcels of whisky, and salmon fishcakes, my mother enjoying playing Lady Bountiful to her erstwhile husband.

After he went into care, they never went to see him again. Dorothy said she couldn't bear going to places like that! I refrained from saying that I was more concerned with how he felt, suddenly becoming persona non grata, but I was very angry. She never knew that he finally went to meet his maker in a cardboard box, because I told them I did not want anyone outside the immediate family at the funeral. I don't think that they would have gone, but if they could not visit him in a care home, I was not about to let them show up at his funeral.

Eventually, Dorothy became house-bound, and suffered a great deal of pain from arthritis, so for a while my stepfather and I went dancing without her until he decided that she should not be left alone for long periods, at which time my dancing days came to an end. By this time, playing badminton had become my cause célèbre. I called in to see them afterwards, and started giving a hand with the spring cleaning and within a short time I was co-opted into becoming the official cleaning lady, a job I really did not want. In spite of allegedly poor eyesight, my mother could spot a speck of dust at twenty paces and the entire house was bottomed twice weekly.

I hated the job with venom but it supplemented my pension and the money was useful when David was 'between jobs'. She loved the position of control and became increasingly demanding and condescending, as she grew older. Strangely enough, for a mother who had put such importance on my education, she was resentful of the fact that I knew more about something than she did and snide comments about my abilities were commonplace. I was always expected to be a good little girl, do as I was told, and not argue with her. This is not easy for a sixty-five year-old career girl, who has managed to have a successful life, and who is not short of a bob or two.

Criticism of my children and my grandchildren abounded. They were nothing like as good as I had been, the natural result of the perfect upbringing that she had given me. For most of my life I kept a civil tongue in my head and never argued, but I finally rebelled and said what I thought. On one occasion, when I told her that Johnnie had given my daughter a sum of money to spend on the new house, she rang back to say that they were rather put out about it. She and Reg thought that he should have given money to me if anyone. I was appalled. Keeping as polite as possible I said that, with respect, it was absolutely nothing to do with them and that should mind their own business. She didn't speak to me for days and when I telephoned, pretended not to know who it was. Where had the amusing friendly person gone? Maybe I am also on my way there.

By the year 2000, my mother was taking huge doses of anti-inflammatory medication and painkillers and, one day when I arrived, she was in tears with the pain. I had never seen her cry before, and it was a heartrending moment. Like my father, she had had enough and seemed to be holding on for Reg's sake. She wanted to live until after Christmas so that she could make him a trifle.

In mid-November 2000, I arrived to find her in extreme pain, to the extent that she was unable to get out of bed at all. It was impossible to manage at home, and reluctantly she went into hospital. At first she seemed to rally but then started going downhill. The staff never said that the situation was as bad as it was. All they would say was that we must take it one day at a time. Wake up out there; we nearest-and-dearest would like to know what is going on. She held on for days but eventually she was moved into a side ward. She knew the end was in sight and she said, "This is the day I have been waiting for".

At six o'clock in the morning of Sunday 26th November, she died. She had taken a long time dying, in spite of the huge doses of Diamorphine and her willingness to depart this mortal coil. She was a very tough old bird.

Reg was devastated; Dorothy had been his whole life. He was filled with remorse that he had failed to be the perfect husband and he wallowed in his misery. He never forgave himself for not being good enough, or being selfish and for not giving her more affection. He used to write little 'wish' notes asking for forgiveness, from God, I suppose. I hope I was able to offer a ray of light to him when I told him that she had said to me not long before she died "Where would I be without Reg?".

The thing that David and I always found strange about them was that they used to sit at either end of the sideboard, completely hidden from one another. This totally precluded any companionship or conversation. We always take chairs at right angles so that we are together. Maybe this was her way of excluding him in the same way she did with me when, as a child, I had misbehaved.

I hoped that I would now be freed from my role as char-lady, but apparently Dorothy had given him his orders the night before she died, and insisted that my services were retained. Fortunately, my talents as a cook were now of prime importance, and the house no longer demanded the same attention. I still went twice-weekly and in addition, I was seconded as a chauffeuse/companion every Wednesday. On this day, I drove and we went on little excursions to Hull, Hessle, Cottingham or Pocklington and Reg paid for lunch. I always went in to the pub or café first, to ensure that the prices were not too high, and tried to find bargain meals.

He steadfastly refused to make any effort to join any organisation or club and shut himself away in his burrow. His only hobby was himself and his health, and so it was not too long before he got into alternative therapies. As was his wont, he spent huge sums of money on massage, chiropractics and secretly took a course in Reiki healing. Since being a young man, he had nursed an ambition to play the cinema organ but had never even learned to play the piano. Eventually, I persuaded him to take lessons and to buy himself a keyboard. That totally absorbed him, gave him something to do and someone else to whom he could give Christmas presents. I subsequently discovered that his music teacher's two sons received the same amount of money each year as my grandchildren, plus a huge tin of Quality Street. Each! Both the gardener and my late mother's hairdresser received five times as much and that was more than I received. Never mind, I'm now laughing all the way to the bank. Maybe, because he knew that one day I might be doing just that, he felt that I could wait.

Russell and Sarah had married in Sri Lanka, but the grooms family were not able to attend as it was all arranged at fairly short notice. Our holiday allowances not to say our bank balances did not permit unexpected vacations but a 'Blessing' was later held when everyone could attend. Reg declined naturally.

When Brad married Katharine, the ceremony took place at Sledmere House in the most elegant setting, the weather was glorious, and the food at a convenient local hostelry was excellent. The bride wore a lovely, tasteful, ankle length dress and coat, and cried a good deal. The groom just managed to fight back the tears but was shaking like a leaf. Unfortunately, Reg still was not prepared to bury the hatchet and would not attend if Russell was going to be there, so yet another ostensibly happy family occasion was overshadowed by his absence. I firmly believe that there are certain times when one should put personal grudges aside for the benefit of others. I was totally unable to make Reg see the injustice of his prejudices.

On his birthday, December 3rd 2003, Reg went in to hospital to have a pacemaker fitted because he had been suffering from tachycardia. In addition, the consultant felt that "subtle changes in the lungs" indicated that the patient should come off the medication that he had been taking for a mild heart condition for many years. Reg was a dedicated hypochondriac and spent hours every day counting his pills and taking them, along with enormous quantities of vitamins and herbal remedies. However, the tachycardia persisted and another operation was planned for early the following year, but at least he enjoyed being an invalid for a while.

Christmas 2003 was a jolly time. Reg came for lunch on Christmas Eve and Dani and company visited so that they could see him. We spent the next day with Dani and her family and were very honoured to be invited. The rest of my gang came for pre-lunch drinks and presents were opened. Russell had entered the spirit of things and was garbed in a Father Christmas outfit. Two days later, David and I went to London to spend a week sightseeing and used Russell's house in Fulham as a base. We had a splendid time doing the museums and we managed to meet some former cruise cronies. We also managed to effect a reunion with my old school friend Pat, our first time in about fifty years. She hadn't changed a bit.

On January 17th my seventieth birthday party was celebrated at home. Against the advice of all my children and some of our friends, I did the catering and we managed to seat sixteen people for a simple meal. I am much happier in my own home and was able to invite some neighbours for after-dinner drinks. A good time was had by all, and the tables and chairs, the washing-up, and clearing-away happened without pain. Naturally, Reg was absent.

He, along with most of the population, had been suffering from a cough and had received two lots of antibiotics and three bottles of linctus codeine from his doctor. He did not improve, but I knew so many folk with a bad chest, I made light of it. Obviously, the doctor did too, and he was all too accustomed to his patient running to the surgery with the least little thing.

On the Monday lunchtime when I arrived to make lunch, Reg was still in bed so I got on with what I could and prepared the meal. It was not unusual for me to arrive at midday and find him still unwashed and in his pyjamas, so I presumed he'd had a poor night's sleep. Reg has always had an ability to sleep for England, and almost to the end Dorothy used to get up and take him coffee to bed. He would then lie there and read the papers. He ate a good lunch, although it was only tinned stewing steak and mash with frozen peas, because he had not taken anything out of the freezer for the meal. When David came home from work, he asked if I had heard my horoscope on the radio. Apparently, Capricorns were about to have a substantial windfall on the Thursday of the same week. Maybe some of the sick shares we held were going to rocket in price.

However at 7.45 a.m. the following morning, Reg rang to ask if I could go to collect his new prescription from the surgery. On my arrival, I decided that he needed a visit from the G.P. who reluctantly arranged for the patient to be admitted to Castle Hill Hospital. Reg perked up considerably at the thought of that and walked briskly in to the admittance ward wearing an overcoat over his dressing gown and joked happily with the nurses. It really looked as though all he needed was a little tender loving care, and a sedative, to help him get a good night's sleep. We were expecting a visitor the following day that I did not want to cancel because he had problems of his own, so I arranged to go again the next teatime.

The patient had been moved to the Cardiac Intensive Care Unit and was wired for sound when I arrived. He was not supposed to talk in an effort to save his breath but was waving his arms and gesticulating so much in an effort to communicate with me that they gave in and took off the oxygen mask. All he wanted me to do was take the money from his briefcase and put it in my handbag. "You keep it", he said. I presumed he meant that it would cover my wages and travelling expenses. He lay back on his pillows and said "Thank you". I left, because my presence would only trigger more efforts to communicate.

A nurse followed me off the ward and asked if I wanted them to telephone during the night if there was anything to report. I assumed that she referred to moving him to another ward as they had done the previous night, waking me after an hour's sleep. I lay awake until 7:30 a.m. that time, so I replied "No, please don't. There is little I can do, is there?". She concurred. Suddenly, it registered. "Are you suggesting that he might die?" I asked.

She nodded as though it was a foregone conclusion. "Oh yes", she said. It was the first intimation that his condition was serious. I really thought that he had been moved to the C.I.C.U. because he also had an existing heart condition and not because that in itself was the problem. It transpired that the heart medication had caused a dramatic deterioration in the lungs rather than the "subtle changes" of which the consultant had tactfully spoken. In retrospect, 'sinister changes' would have been closer to the truth. Once again, sleep evaded me and around 7:30 a.m. the sister phoned to say he had passed a disturbed night, and had been given a sedative. I said that I would give him time to sleep it off and go in around lunchtime. Isn't it interesting that at times like this we wear an invisible polythene bag, which protects us from reality?

On my arrival that day, I never got close to the bed but was whipped into a side room where two doctors and a nurse joined me. It was very simple and I had a choice to make. The doctor was blunt; they could keep him on life support and keep him alive for a few more hours, even days, or switch him off and let him take his chances. Once again, they shoot horses, don't they? I made the decision. He died within minutes and a major chapter in my life was over. The day was Thursday. I had indeed come into some money.

I was stunned. I often thought that he could outlive me. After all, he was only fourteen years my senior, and it was on the cards that he would wear me out.

I'm good at covering-up and coping. I become bright and flippant, never more so than on this occasion but, strangely, Reg is the one I have missed the most of my three elderly parent-figures. Both my mother and my father were glad to go, the latter having departed long before his body gave up. Reg was desperate to live even though he was inconsolably lonely without Dorothy.

It was time for some displacement activity so I immediately drove to his house, took all the tea towels from the drawer, and wrapped up the Lladro and Royal Doulton to take back to Kirkburn. I also took the strongbox containing the will and a few hundred pounds, went home, and telephoned both Brad and David leaving them both the same cryptic message "The cat got on the roof", a family password for someone having died.

Within two days, some neighbours asked to have first refusal on the bungalow and subsequently bought it. The task of disposing of all their treasured furniture was enormous; I had trouble even giving it away. The cupboards were full of receipts, some of which dated back to 1947, old utilities bills, income tax returns, and newspaper cuttings. It was a salutary lesson wading through it all and I have tidied my cupboards since then. Brad was a huge help and between us we cleared the lot.

We cremated him, and this time the whole family was there: Reg could hardly get up and walk out because Russell was present. The choice of music was unusual, and entirely mine. When we went together to arrange my mother's departure, Reg had asked if the funeral director had any Victor Sylvester strict tempo dance music, but they were under-supplied in that department. Why he did not suggest taking some of his huge collection, I do not know. When it was his turn to go, I made a selection. My first choice was the bandleader's signature tune but when I remembered the title, 'You're Dancing on my Heart', I gave it some further consideration. I settled for 'Stars in my Eyes'. For his final exit behind the screen, I chose, the Toccata and Fugue by Widor, since that is a stirring piece for the organ. I hope it is what he would have wanted.

We had a slap-up meal on the Inland Revenue, because the funeral expenses are the only allowable expense that can be taken out of one's estate other than debts. He still owed me for a bill from The Nuffield Hospital and the solicitor forgot to pay me but I was not about to complain. The house was spoken for before the funeral, and six months later I became very well-off indeed. I had worked for it, and in spite of my efforts to advise him, he still gave a very large sum to the taxman, which someone else could have put to good use. Reg always knew best. I suppose his hard-up childhood had made him overly cautious and squirrel-like, and he was always afraid that he would not be able to pay for private medicine or a luxury care home. By the time I am dribbling and soiling myself, I don't think I shall care whether I eat steak or sausage. In the meantime, I hope to invest some out of the chancellor's reach and spend the rest, if I live long enough.

It is strange that with a fortune within my reach, I became anxious about my mortality. Driving to Driffield became threatening. I want to travel to far-off lands and feel that this must be undertaken with urgency before I am stricken with some life-threatening ailment. So much to do and so little time left to do it in. I want to be able to give my hard won cash to the folk who I want to have it, and not have any haggling and argument after I've gone. Hey, you out there, you might remember this when you are dividing things up your way. Some of the claimants might have walked over my corpse to get at the pickings. Some may hardly know me. And there are those who have given their love unstintingly. You can decide into which category you fall.

What a jolly chapter this has been. Its original title was to have been 'Two Weddings and Three Funerals', but anyone born after 1985 would miss the point of that one. I hope it has not been sad. The passing of old people is not sad, but it is tragic when the main player is a young person. May the next funeral be mine. But not yet!

It is August 2004 and I am free of my old folks and loaded. Then along came Jake.

CHAPTER 19
AS SHE SINK SLOWLY IN THE WEST

My second eldest grandson was in a state of conflict with his mother and had gone A.W.O.L. I eventually persuaded him to come here and stay overnight. The visit turned into a permanent arrangement and it looked as though my new-found freedom was to be short-lived. However, Jake decided that the country life was not for him so by the time three months had passed, he moved out again and took his chances, sleeping on whatever floor was available. We were free again!

Recently I have been privileged to reinstate myself as a dancing teacher. Several months previously, I had joined a Tap Dancing class that I attended with my young next door neighbour, just for the exercise. I had been unable to join one run for and by the U3A, an organisation set up to try to occupy and continue the wider education of retired veterans of life. This was because it took place on a day that was committed to cooking and caring for my stepfather. Once I was able to do whatever I wished with my time, I went along to the afternoon U3A class with my tap shoes. Unfortunately or fortunately, depending on your point of view, the young teacher became beset by family problems and I volunteered to step into the breech, for a few weeks. It looks as if I have a job for life. Interestingly, I have never actually taught tap-dancing before in spite of taking professional exams when I was sixteen. That first class, I felt as though I had always done it.

We are all ladies of advanced years though I am undoubtedly the most advanced. One day, we were reminiscing about the distant past and this memory came back from the sands of time. Although this to me had already been put to bed, I could not resist re-opening it and trying to find a space for this recollection. It does not belong here but since this final chapter is a trifle undernourished and could use a few laughs, I decided to stick it in. I hope my descriptive powers and your ability to visualise are up to the job.

In the early 1950s, we women wore corsets or roll-ons, which served the dual purpose of keeping our tummies flat and providing an anchoring point for the suspenders, which held up our stockings. A company, still well known today, invented an all rubber and seamless version of this garment known as the Playtex Roll-on. Getting this on to my ample form was not easy but with some wriggling and contortions, it was eventually achieved. The entire garment was perforated in order to allow the skin to 'breathe'. Once on, it was impossible to move it since the skin became damp and the rubber clung like a second skin. Unfortunately, it did not smell like skin and when the temperature rose as the evening got under way, a distinct aroma of warm rubber assailed one's nostrils. I imagine it also reached one's dancing partners olfactory organ as well. On arrival home on a cold winter night, in the days before central heating was the norm, it was pleasant to toast the rear end in front of the fire. Big mistake. The rubbery aroma became overwhelming.

Eventually, it would be time to undress. Remember that there were no zips or openings of any kind in those early models and attempting to divest oneself of that latex support involved gyrations of epic proportions. It was impossible to pull it down and the only reasonable alternative was to roll it into a tough heavy-duty rubber band and then attempt to escape from the confinement of what amounted to a veritable chastity belt. My contortionist aunt would have been proud of me. Eventually, I would become free of all restrictions and the offending item lay solid and grey on the carpet. I needed a bath on order to remove the smell and a bath was a once a week event in those days. What is so amazing, is that in spite of all these privations, I would struggle into the thing the following day and when it finally ripped from end to end, I went out and bought another one. They were not cheap but it was a small price to pay for a flat stomach and a bottom that was squashed into a shapeless mass, totally robbing that body part of any sex appeal. This was the order of the day.

If my flat backside and cast iron tummy did not dampen the ardour of any prospective suitor, one would have assumed that the smell of rubber would have done it, though it did not make any apparent difference to the stronger sex that I encountered. Men were men in those days.

One of my twinkle-toed ladies commented one day that she would love to learn to ballroom dance. "You set it up and I will teach" was my reply. Thanks to a television series which has reawakened the public's interest, and of course, my undeniable charm and expertise, I am pleased to say that about twenty older folk are waltzing around the Church Hall on a regular basis, revving themselves up to tackle the Cha Cha Cha and the Rumba.

At the class last week, for some reason, I was reminded of a couple of dreams I had experienced some years before and David insists that they go into this memoir. I suppose there should be a heading " 'Regrets' I've had a few."

Remember, I did not meet David until long after my first marriage had broken up but occasionally, I dream that there is some conflict in my life between my feelings for my two husbands. I suppose it is a way of expressing my regrets that the first marriage did not work out, if only from the point of view of providing a secure home-life for my children. I must put on record that no doubt as to the success of my second marriage has ever existed or as to the choices I made. In my dreams, I have been unsure who I was married to and I seem to have had both men in my life. During one of these, I awoke and still befuddled by sleep, I was confused as to the identity of the man I felt sleeping by my side. It was dark but the solution came to me in a flash of clarity. I reached out and stroked my companions face. To my relief, the physiognomy encountered by my hand was decidedly hairy. Jimmie was clean-shaven.

The second dream sequence involved my having an illicit romance with one of the two contenders for my hand and I had received a letter written on blue deckle edged writing paper from my swain. I was standing by the telephone when the rightful husband, whichever he was, entered the room and it was necessary to dispose of the letter with some dispatch. In time honoured spy fashion, I decided to eat the evidence. Deckle edge paper is substantially heavier quality than normal paper and masticating these pages became difficult. Bear in mind that I was still asleep.

Eventually, the problem became insurmountable and I felt that I had no alternative but to spit out the indigestible mass and I proceeded to attempt this manoeuvre. I regained full awareness as my real husband stood over me and said "Tea, darling" and removed my upper denture from my lips, from where I had been trying to expel the free floating item.

This is destined to be the final chapter of my book, and it is a little like closing the lid on my own coffin. I am half-afraid that if I stop, my life will come to an end. I am reminded of the first time I wrote out my will. There was an awful acceptance of the reality that ones life span is limited. Maybe this is why so many folk die intestate; they are unable to face the fact of their own mortality. Poor old Reggie was convinced that one's will was set in stone but the truth is, that if all beneficiaries are in agreement, a deed-of-variation can change everything. If the testator is rich enough, and wily with it, there are ways of fixing things a little.

At this moment, I cannot imagine that my final chapter will hold a candle to the others in terms of length. In fact, I have run out of past and cannot foretell the future and there is little profit to be made in going on and on for the sake of length. This strikes me as being a relatively tidy finale. I hope that when I am a goner, someone might quote some lines from 'In the Morning of My Life' and say of me "She was brave, and strong and true". Sing no sad songs for me, and let no one suggest that I was a nice person. I am difficult, demanding, sometimes amusing, entertaining, determined, hardworking and have a vicious sense of humour. Nice? Not me!

If I had always been half as wise as I sound now, life would have been easier and I would have been a nicer person. Tough! It might not have been as interesting. I hope that I may have been a great deal more stimulating than merely nice. I also hope that, although I will grow older, uglier, and even more irascible, those who I love will still find it in their hearts to care for me. I am grateful to the people who have loved me, and to those, who have accepted my love.

I hope to be able to travel the globe in the next few years; China and Japan are on my list. Recently, our friend Rodney asked if foreign travel had always been a priority, and where did it all begin. Reading about far-off lands, and listening to radio programmes at the time when popular radio consisted of more than non-stop music, was the natural breeding ground for a desire to explore the world. In those long past days travelling was a major adventure and beyond the reach of the average mortal. I still remember hearing about the Caves of Drach in Majorca when I was a child, and that was my first port-of-call when I was old enough to venture further than the Channel Islands. Going on a package-deal holiday to Tenerife may give you two weeks' rest and relaxation, but it does little to broaden the mind. I overheard a couple of young girls talking about holidays, and one said that she had been to Benidorm. Her pal asked where was Benidorm. The answer: "I don't know, I flew there".

For several years, it has been a dream of mine that, if ever I could afford to do so, I would like to rent a house in the sun for a number of weeks and have my grown up offspring and my grandchildren to spend a holiday with us, a few at a time. Overall, we prefer to go somewhere with some historical or geographical interest and spend weeks researching the area with a view to doing excursions and adventures. Sitting by the poolside all day no longer appeals to me as it did a number of years ago, unless we are fortunate enough to meet up with some fascinating couple and bore each other with our life histories. If this dream is ever to become a realisable goal, we must all understand that the umbilical cord was severed decades ago, and none of us need babysitting by the others.

If a holiday with any other people is going to work, it needs to be understood from the booking stage that, if everyone agrees on the content and approximate time of meals and who cooks, washes up and sweeps the floor, the remainder of the sojourn is sans frontiéres. I will not sulk if they want to go off on their own and climb a mountain, and I don't want them trying to talk me in to joining them. This must be an entirely recipro-cal arrangement and, as far as my adult children are concerned, it has worked well in the past and I would hope that it would in the future. In the meantime, perhaps those of the younger generation who are of a like mind with us may enjoy a few special trips, while I am still fit enough to go. Their parents can then clear off on their own.

Alternatively, I would like to have them accompany us on a rather more exotic trip than they are accustomed to taking. There are two reasons for this: the first being that we would not get stuck for someone with whom to have a conversation during the vacation; the second being that I firmly believe that travel can add a good deal to a persons outlook. I am not talking Benidorm here. It would seem that, at present, my mob would prefer to do their own thing and if that is what turns them on, good luck to them. Time is running short for me; I do not want to take my holidays with a minder to push the wheelchair. It gives me great pleasure to give the opportunity to enjoy different experiences to the younger generation. They might as well enjoy something of value now, rather than waiting to see if there is anything left to spend after Inheritance Tax. Even if there is, in another five years, they will all have commitments of their own and it will be too late.

I still have a desire to see Alaska, and David has an unquenchable appetite for travel, regardless of the distance. I have lost my enthusiasm for spending any more than four hours at a time on an aeroplane, and that includes boarding and disembarking. Cruising is good, because I do not have to lug a suitcase, hike around an airport, and sit for two hours or more waiting to go. Except on a fly-there-to-meet-the-boat trip. On a cruise, one wakes up in a different place every morning without having to pack the suitcases or haul them on or off a coach. We favour the smaller vessels.

A small boat means that paper trails and maps are not needed in order to relocate the cabin, and does not land one with an impossible number of travelling companions. The super-cruisers may have spectacular facilities, but I travel in order to see new places, not to spend time in the gym or the beauty salon. I have no desire to spend a fortnight with two thousand other people. Even when the passenger manifest amounts to five hundred, you still disembark at the end of the trip saying "I don't remember seeing that face before".

So, what about buying a property abroad? It has been tempting over the past years but at that time we did not really have the resources, though we have looked at some incredibly cheap places in France. Many gullible folk have gone down the timeshare path, often disastrously. We have looked around some of these places and it has all looked very glamorous and tempting. On the other hand I really do not want to commit myself to taking holidays in the same place year in and year out or to having a management company make the decisions about refurbishing and the cost of this being passed on to me. The heyday of timeshare has long been over and I am relieved that we never became involved. If I am going to invest in a property, I want to be totally in control.

To own a house in France, which is accessible by ferry and car and to have the time to spend months there, is a slightly more practical idea. I would still consider the Gallic hideaway if it was to be shared with my family, but who amongst them wants the responsibility? If we were to go for a month at a time, what about our dogs? No, I do not fancy driving all that way with two smelly, panting, animals in the car. It is quite bad enough with the two that are in the front seats and, since the dogs weigh many kilos, think of how much more booze we can carry without them.

I have reached the age where I go upstairs for something and, halfway up, I ask myself what I am going for. Sometimes I bend down to pick up an item and then wonder if there is anything else I can achieve while I am down there. Of course, I have always been economical with my time and for years have saved it by cleansing my face while sitting on the toilet emptying my bladder. I feel that I must point out that an entirely separate cleansing fluid is used and the two functions are not inextricably linked. This operation is not performed on every visit to that small room, you must understand: only the last one of the day. I can also eat breakfast standing-up, while simultaneously putting on my cosmetics such as they are, and occasionally also washing-up before the cereal is finished.

Unfortunately, while my ability to juggle these functions remains intact, I do suffer from dreadful lapses of memory. As recently as today, I was asking someone to give my husband a message and I had difficulty recalling his name. I gave in, in the interest of speed, and said it was the chap who was tiling the bathroom. It wasn't that given time, I could not have recalled it. Two or three seconds would have done but just at that moment, the window in my mind was fast-closed. Maybe it is due to my enthusiastic consumption of alcohol rather than age.

The worst nightmares, which actually I have been experiencing for years, are the ones involving me hiding items of value or actual cash in places where the casual housebreaker will not think to look. Over some twenty-five years, this habit has resulted in frantic searches for the missing items, the lifting of carpet edges, and feeling the hemlines of curtains in an attempt to locate the elusive treasures. On one such occasion, my gold chain bracelet had been missing for months, though I had a strange sense that it was somewhere in the bathroom. I usually pick the right room and sometimes which side of that room. I clearly remembered being in that area when I hid it before a holiday, but no amount of searching revealed the hiding place. I became convinced that I had rolled it up in toilet tissue and left it in the waste bin, but had failed to remember this before the bin was emptied.

I decided to make an insurance claim and got a valuation and a claim form. Immediately before leaving the house en-route to post this off to the claims department, I decided to have one final search. I just seemed to receive significant vibrations in the bathroom, where I was taking the precaution of spending a penny before leaving the house, so I took out my holiday sponge bag and removed every item, one by one. I had previously looked in there on at least three occasions without success. A large gold chain could hardly go unnoticed. We must have been away several times since the bracelet had been last seen, and the items in the bag generally lie undisturbed until the following trip. I did wonder why I had been carrying a small plastic pill tub containing what I knew to be only two or three sleeping pills. I never used them unless I knew I had hours in which to sleep off the effects. I picked up the small plastic drum and it was unexpectedly heavy. Hardly surprising really, a double gold Albert chain weighs quite a bit.

Unfortunately, I never learn and keep doing similar things. Once, on our return from holiday, I had to report that all my bank and credit cards were missing: I discovered them a week later in the bottom of a Corn Flake packet. I have started to adopt a policy of telling someone the whereabouts of these items. Unfortunately, I forget who it was that I told, and have to telephone the whole family to ask if they know. I try to inform the younger generation, Robin and Katie, in the hope that their brains are still in first-class working order. It would be a waste of time telling Jake: he remembers even less than I do.

I learn a fresh trick on the computer, then the next day I have not a clue how to start. However, I can quote you a list of the kings of England, spit out times-tables, and conjugate French verbs. (Many people think that conjugation is some way of exerting their marital rights.) I can clearly remember clothes that I wore for special events when I was four years old. I recall riding in a pushchair, even sitting in a pram. I remember waking up one summer night in my cot, I know it was summer because it was still daylight in the bedroom. In an effort to block out the light, a blue and white blanket had been draped over the top of my cot. The first things I saw on waking were the dripping fangs of the Big Bad Wolf leering at me. I know which wolf it was, too. It was the one Huffing and Puffing rather than the one who devoured Grandmothers. Not that this was important, I would have been equally terrified whichever wolf was looming above my head. No wonder I have always had sleeping problems.

Where have I put that jar of peanut butter I bought yesterday? Even more vital, where is the "?" on the keyboard? If I do not use it for an hour, I have to examine every key individually. My nearest and dearest have learned to live with my shortcomings, but I know I try them sorely sometimes.

Initially, I intended that this work of literary genius was to be solely for my nearest and dearest but so many others have expressed an interest that I have come to modestly believe that I would be like Emily Bronte and hide my light under a bushel if it were to be kept from a wider audience. I have tried not to give offence to the living, although, I may well have failed in that duty.

My eldest son advised me that the number one selling point in a book title is SEX. While I never intended that the book should be sold, for fifteen minutes of fame, I can prostitute my talents with the best of them. My former brother in law once told me that I could play the part of a wicked witch without the aid of make-up. When I wanted to play the part of an elderly nun in the local Dramatic Society production, I was informed that my wicked eyes would not suit the role. The producer wanted me to play the bitch part, naturally. However, I won the day and gave a stunning performance of eighty year old Sister Magdalen. It suddenly registered with me that I have conveyed an aura of wicked-ness from an early age and maybe this was the moment to revel in the adjective.

You may well be wondering where were all the demons and sprockets? If you have read with any perception, you will have recognised many of the demons. One of them is in a previous paragraph. There is the bogeyman and the police officer who I was told by one grandmother, would come for me if I was less than well behaved. There was the mythical black man with whom my mother might abscond if I incurred her displeasure. Why he had to be black, I cannot imagine. What about the kidnappers who would steal me, the Yellow Peril and the Savage Hordes, the Russkies who may remove my children and put me in a gulag. More realistically, there all the authority figures who might disapprove of me and then withdraw their approval. We all have our own special examples.

You could be asking exactly what a sprocket is. I will quote one dictionary definition: "a cylindrical wheel, with teeth on either or both rims, for pulling film through a camera or projector". The number of men I have asked, who were unable to give a description, has surprised me. I thought that this was a man-thing. I knew what it was, but thought it was called a cog. The cog is an individual tooth. There have been many cogs and many sprockets. The sprockets are all the people who have made my machinery work and the odd strokes of good fortune, which have greased the wheels.

The road I have taken through my life has not been direct or even straight. It has made many deviations, and has had several twists and turns. I am deeply grateful that the often-rough path I chose to take has enabled me to leave a footprint, I would hate to pass this way only once and not leave a ripple on the sands of time. I do not think I hid my light under a bushel, (I wonder if it is a bushel of anything special?)

One thing remains true. The people we meet and the friends we make along the way, are part of our lives forever. There can be no dismissing the effect they have on us or on the directions the road may take, and as we progress from act to act, new players enter the stage and play their own roles. We can blame our fellow players for the bad times or applaud them for the good but sooner or later we must all learn to take responsibility for ourselves and stop blaming someone else for the fact that we are less than perfect. Life is not fair, and the sooner we accept that, the happier we will be with our particular lot.

I told my lovely daughter many years ago, to change whatever she was able to change, to learn to live with what could not be changed, and to hope that she had the wisdom to know the difference. Sometimes we cannot have what we want, so we have to learn to be contented with what we can have and do the best we can with it. The only problem that I have with this philosophy is, at what point do we give up on the struggle to achieve more and settle for less? If the bluebird of happiness is really in our own backyard, and the yellow brick road only tells us that there's no place like home, what reason is there to look for fulfilment anywhere else. We would still be living in caves and wearing bearskins. Mind you, Londoners still think that, north of Watford Gap, this state of affairs remains true.

I am happy to say that my family helps, supports and tolerates each other without having to live their lives in the other's pockets. We are all well aware of our own failings and of those close to us and still care for one another, warts and all. I know that more than one former member of our magic circle, and possibly their relatives, has said that our family is not normal and they are probably right. 'Dysfunctional' is the word that has been bandied about. This tells how much they know about functionality. In my book, and let's be honest here, this is my book, a functional family allows its members to live their own lives but is on hand when they are needed. I believe that our family relationship is based on reality, and not on some stylised, fictional family pattern. I do not like my family without reservation, any more than they like me. We have all come to accept each other as we are and to be grateful that none of us are any worse than we are.

At this point, I would like to give my thanks to the friends and acquaintances that have enriched my life. All of them. But I shall name only a few.

To drop a famous name, if you are old enough to recognise it, Larry Adler, who encouraged me to dare to be different, may he rest in peace. To the unrelated Smiths, Don and Betty, who told me I could do it and set me on the road to academic success. To Anne Lester, Chris Hemingway, Helen Ezard, little Johnny Heaton and others who listened and believed when I told them the same thing and who went on to prove me right. It is in part due to them that my footprint has remained visible. The fact that others have achieved, because I encouraged them, has given me great satisfaction. I am happy that I may have helped them fulfil their lives. My gratitude to my own family may need putting on record, so thanks a bunch for putting up with me. I have not neglected to express my appreciation to my lovely David in spoken words.

Many others have played a large part in this story. Among these are all the friends past and present, particularly Annie Sanderson, who I thought I would never find again. Thanks to the Yorkshire Post and an observant neighbour, we spent hours on the phone this very day, 43 years after our last meeting. I have been fortunate to re-establish contact with long-standing and long-lost friends: particularly the two Pats. One of these last, disappeared from my life from a practical point of view as our lives changed in 1946 and I re-established contact in 2002 The other one, known to me as Pate Mate, also pursued a different path when her first husband and she parted company in 1958. We managed to meet very infrequently over the intervening years but because she is the sister of my ex-husband's widow, I have managed to re-establish contact with her more recently. Only a very few of those who were around in my childhood have survived: after all, most of them were older than I. The Prince Charming of my make-believe games, Cousin Joy, is still out there, as is the lovely Norah, my mother's friend. She was 92 in September 2004 and is still as pretty as she ever was; I have never heard her say an unkind word about anyone. What a splendid mother and grandmother she would have made.

There you are, my children. Perhaps you can pick the bones out of this and use some for my eulogy. (Maybe Helen will read a bit in my absence.) Well, I shall be there but I expect to remain very quiet on my final appearance in public. I used to think that I wanted a quiet family only funeral, now I have decided on the contrary that a huge gathering of people reminding each other how fantastic I was in my heyday would be nice. I really do not care if they are only there to say "Well, you got yours, you old witch." I would like to have a huge collection and send the money to The British Epilepsy Association because they are a low profile organisation and desperately underfunded. I would like any potentially lachrymose member of the congregation to do it elsewhere so that they do not set the rest off. They will all be laughing anyway. They certainly will if I have my wishes respected and am brought in to the strains of "The Frog Chorus". In a bright yellow box with cartoon frogs all round it..

Do you recall that I said that this chapter was going to be very short? The elderly have a tendency to drivel on and I am no exception to that rule.

There you are. As the Bard said "All our yesterdays have lighted fools the way to dusty death".